SCANTY PARTICULARS

SCANTY
PARTICULARS

The Scandalous Life and

Astonishing Secret of

Queen Victoria's Most Eminent

Military Doctor

RACHEL HOLMES

RANDOM HOUSE / NEW YORK

Library of Congress Cataloging-in-Publication Data
Holmes, Rachel Scott Russell.
Scanty particulars : the scandalous life and astonishing secret of Queen Victoria's
most eminent military doctor / Rachel Holmes.
p.   cm.
Includes bibliographical references and index.
ISBN 0-375-50556-3 (hardcover)
1. Barry, James, 1795–1865. 2. Surgeons—Great Britain—Biography. 3. Medicine,
Military—Great Britain—History. I. Barry, James, 1795–1865. II. Title.

RD27.35.B368 H65   2002   610'.92—dc21
[B]   2002023698

Random House website address: www.atrandom.com
Printed in the United States of America on acid-free paper
24689753
First U.S. Edition

Book design by J. K. Lambert

FOR JACK, ZACKIE, AND JERRY

There are no pronouns in the English language as complex as I am.

Leslie Feinberg

PREFACE

When I was a boy, I was told that when I began a story, to begin at the beginning and continue to the end.

James Barry

JULY 1865. LONDON SWEATS BENEATH A HEAT WAVE. THE CENTRAL streets of the city are a den of infection. Dr. James Miranda Barry, Inspector General of Hospitals and one of the most senior medical officers in the British military, lies dying at Margaret Street. There are no known relatives to be informed. The doctor is accompanied at death—as in life—by a black manservant of uncertain name and by a dog named Psyche. Owing to a peculiar wit understood only by their owner, all James Barry's dogs were called Psyche.

James Barry was one of the nineteenth century's most exceptional doctors, and one of its great unsung heroes. Famed for opening up the vistas of modern medicine, Britain's most indefatigable colonial doctor specialized in surgery, tropical disease, obstetrics, leprosy, and venereal diseases. Barry campaigned for the humanitarian rights of the patient. A champion of the socially marginalized and economically dispossessed, Barry prioritized the treatment of women, prostitutes, slaves, the insane, lepers, and children. On three continents, Barry implemented new methods of hygiene, sanitation, quarantine, diet, and effective treatment of some of the most virulent diseases known to the age. Barry's medical reforms saved the lives of thousands of people.

Barry's methods influenced the birth of modern medical practice in places as far apart as South Africa, Jamaica, Malta, and Canada. Twenty-one years before the introduction of effective anesthetics for radical invasive surgery, James Barry performed one of the first successful cesarean sections known to Western medicine.

Barry's confidence and ambition as a surgeon went together with a flamboyant lifestyle. A noted dandy, Barry combined extravagant dress with a love of entertainment and social ritual. The charismatic, peripatetic, and irredeemably flirtatious doctor charmed women and men alike. A child of the eighteenth century's dreams of radical democracy and the scientific enlightenment, Barry grew up uneasily into the more austere venture of Victorianism. Barry's grudging but valiant attempts at self-reinvention to accommodate the values of the later nineteenth century failed. Deeply influenced by patrons, teachers, and mentors who were all dissident radical progressives, Barry's heretical roots always showed through.

The exotic trajectories of Barry's career collided with some of the great figures of the day. Francisco de Miranda, the outré ladykilling liberator of Venezuela, was patron to two outstanding achievers: Simón Bolívar and James Barry. Lord Buchan, the progressive champion of women's rights, gave Barry the run of his extensive library and a home during university vacations when the young doctor was a student at Edinburgh. Sir Astley Cooper, the greatest surgeon of the age, was Barry's teacher at Guy's and St. Thomas's in London. At the Cape of Good Hope, Barry met Ngqika, the chief of the Xhosa, at a crucial political summit between the black leaders of southern Africa and the white colonial settler administration. In a strange twist of ancestral history that the emancipationist doctor would have found most displeasing, Barry's name was inherited by the prime minister of the first Nationalist government of the Union of South Africa, General James Barry Munnik Hertzog.

Fitzroy Somerset, Lord Raglan, became Barry's champion and protector following the death of his brother, Lord Charles Somerset, to whom Barry was intimately connected and utterly devoted. Sir Josias Cloete and Lord Lowther were among those who counted Barry as a personal friend. Barry appears in the memoirs of many nineteenth-century naval and army officers whose names were prominent in their time, such as George Thomas, the earl of Albemarle, and Sir William Henry Dillon. Napoleon's closest ally, assistant, and friend, Count de Las Casas, described the youthful doctor as "an absolute phenomenon," and the Hapsburg emperor Maximilian was so impressed with Barry's skill as a surgeon that he sent a fabulous diamond ring as a gift of thanks.

Barry also had many detractors, whose fear and envy of the ostentatious, sparkling doctor was expressed in tones ranging from patronizing disdain to venomous hatred. Many of these occupied themselves in conspiring against Barry—resulting in more than one court-martial and, most famously, a sexual smear campaign. Barry infuriated Florence Nightingale, but none of Barry's other detractors remain significant enough to be recognizable in our own day.

Edward Lear doodled a caricature of Barry. Charles Dickens published a heavily embellished version of the life of the "Inspector General" in his bestselling magazine *All the Year Round.* Sybil Thorndike reveled in playing the breeches role of James Barry on the London stage.

A great surgeon and scientist, James Barry was remembered also as a rake whose famed relationship with one of the British empire's most roguish and imperious governors scandalized the government and societies of two nations. The intimate, ambiguous affair between Lord Charles Somerset and his personal physician, Dr. James Barry, was whispered around the British colonies. The sodomy libel regarding Barry and Somerset was tried in a notorious court case at the Cape of Good Hope and became a matter of public debate among parliamentarians at Westminster.

James Barry never married. Moving through the most important locations on the map of Britain's colonial empire, Barry's retinue was made up of the familiar companions of the black manservant and the ubiquitous Psyche, in her several incarnations. Barry loved parties, balls, christenings, weddings, clubhouses, and horseback riding—and had many friends. But after the death of Charles Somerset, Barry remained a resolute loner in affairs of the heart. The inner dramas of Barry's life were concealed by a life of unceasing travel and tireless activity.

By the 1880s, Barry's story had become the stuff of popular fiction. Colonel Edward Rogers wrote a three-volume potboiler entitled *The Modern Sphinx,* loosely based on Barry's life. None other than Mary Elizabeth Braddon, the first feminist thriller writer, whose bestselling novels at times outsold those of Charles Dickens, edited this novel down to a more elegant single volume. Havelock Ellis in his ground-breaking book *Sexual Inversion* declared Barry's life a "distinguished instance" of dissident sexual psychology.

Laid to rest in a simple grave in Kensal Green cemetery, London, with an incorrectly recorded date of death on the headstone, James Barry left behind a lifetime of official correspondence and professional reports that cram the shelves of archives on three continents. A prolific and exacting writer, Dr. Barry was known for penning copious and detailed correspondence. Devoid of flummery, concise in their recommendations, Barry's reports and official letters are also filled characteristically with knowledgeable allusion, irony, tragic touches, and considerable wit. But only six personal letters survive. Barry left also two scientific papers of considerable significance: a contribution to the materia medica on the *Arctopus echinatus,* a treatment for syphilis and gonorrhea, and a university thesis on femoral hernia, "De merocele vel hernia crurali." Despite the importance of these essays, accounts of Barry's life have barely mentioned them. Yet in different ways, each provides significant clues to the inner world of James Barry.

These are the bare bones around which the flesh and blood of Barry's life must be painstakingly re-created. What follows is James Barry's story as I have uncovered it, beginning at its unconventional beginning and filling in many previously missing pieces, until we come once more to its uniquely peculiar end.

CONTENTS

SCANTY PARTICULARS

Chapter 1

BETWIXT-AND-BETWEEN

"Then I shan't be exactly a human?" Peter asked.
"No."
"Nor exactly a bird?"
"No."
"What shall I be?"
"You will be a Betwixt-and-Between," Solomon
said, and certainly he was a wise old fellow, for
that is exactly how it turned out.

Sir James Matthew Barrie,
Peter Pan in Kensington Gardens

*I*N THE FROZEN HEART OF WINTER, A SLIGHT FIGURE VEERED along the pavements of Edinburgh Old Town. With hands thrust deep into the pockets of a man's greatcoat, the body of the young medical student was concealed completely. Only his head was visible. The night was cold and still. Streetlamps lit his way between the grand monumental portals and pillars of the University of Edinburgh. As if drunk, he lurched with an unsteady gait toward his lodgings in Lothian Street. Self-conscious about staggering on a public street, he tried to regain the more confident composure of his usual strut.

It was the winter of 1810 and James Barry, medical and literary student of the University of Edinburgh, had just attended his first lecture in anatomical dissection with his tutor, the famously "horrid" Mr. Fyfe. His sickened body hastened through the streets away from Fyfe's dissection room as if pursued by death and her grotesque procession. Yet his mind raced back to the scene he had just left, drawn by an intoxicating concoction of horror and curiosity.

He recalled the scene like a demonic dream. A room of instruments and shadows, the temperature of a meat locker, somewhere between an artist's studio and a butcher's shop. The air clammy with malodorous condensation. Mr. Fyfe's three greenhorn students huddled in a group, uncertain of the etiquette for approaching the dissecting table, on which a body was laid out beneath greasy sheeting. Fyfe ushered them forward, stationing each with a clear view—and smell—of the cadaver. This uncomfortably intimate proximity to a corpse not yet three days old and of uncertain origin was the privilege the students paid for in signing up with Fyfe as private pupils. A select audience of young gentlemen, with the best view in an exclusive house, were suddenly and horribly fearful of seeing what their money had paid for.

The terrifying experience was optional. Practical dissection was not a compulsory part of the medical degree for which Barry had registered. While required to be proficient in written and spoken Latin, classics, and philosophy, he did not have to do applied dissection. He could have qualified by learning his anatomy from lavishly printed textbooks. But James Barry had a particular fascination with the study of anatomy, with the folds and secrets of the flesh. He breathed hard through his mouth, fighting back panic as Fyfe lifted the sheet, revealing a loose architecture of bones held together with a worn tarpaulin of skin, like an old, patched sail clinging respectfully to the mainmast in memory of prouder times. Age and the shrunken size of the body in death composed Barry's first impressions. He struggled to translate the clean and figuratively precise lines of his anatomical textbooks into the irregular landscape of the purplish swollen body laid out before him. These and his childhood imaginings, swathed in Catholicism, had left him vaguely expecting that a dissection corpse would be luminous and sepulchral, modest even. In reality, the raw material for the surgeon's knives and saws was gray, graceless, and lumpen.

Heart thumping, temperature rising with the bile in his throat, in this claustrophobic space the only heat he could feel was his own. Yet in Fyfe's chilly, candlelit rooms, James Barry's cold sweat of dread turned to the heated flush of fascination. The lamplit faces of the students began to shine with curiosity, bravado, and fear as Fyfe cauterized the body. He spoke in a clear, neutral tone aimed at reassurance as he made his first incision, along the clavicum and sternum, in order to demonstrate the anatomy of the neck and throat. As he made another incision from the top of the sternum to the chin, Barry's startled attention was drawn to the face of the corpse. Stripped of the animation of everyday life, it was a face unsexed.

The blade sank into the flesh, and blood seeped up against the knife. Fyfe drew up the tough fascia with his forceps and began to describe the anatomical map of muscle and glands within. Barry's fascination deepened as the body was opened and splayed out into a three-dimensional space under his gaze. Fyfe lifted skin and fascia. Inky blood welled over the slashed binding of heavy skin; the body disclosed its interior. The external body disappeared. It was confusing to Barry. Without the boundary of the skin to navigate by, the eye lost its bearings. A chaotic topography reigned within. Barry wondered how he would ever learn to distinguish the fibers, membranes, tendons, tissues, arteries, nerves, and vessels sketched by Fyfe's knife. The organs that make so much difference to life were gray and indistinguishable in death.

The flint slish of his tutor's knife was hypnotic. Barry could not take his eyes from the complicated, messy, and stinking body stretched before him. The foul stench saturated the air. As Fyfe wiped fluids from his hand and reached for a saw, Barry became conscious of a curious new emotion—the absence of any appropriate feeling of horror. This, then, was the state of "necessary inhumanity" required to attain this knowledge.

Keen to make the fullest use of the body, Fyfe offered a dissection of the lower torso and pelvis. He decided to leave the legs for another session, since the night was drawing on. Fyfe eviscerated the pelvis, revealing the shadowed cavity of the cervix and the muscular coat of the uterus, grayish in color. Superfluous membrane slipped back to reveal the subcutaneous folds of the groin. He pointed to the anomaly of some thick flesh-colored tubercles.

Fyfe's knife made shapes out of the gray matter of the anonymous body like a painter picking out an invisible line with a fine sable brush.

Barry was looking at the inverted mirror of a woman's body. A life anatomized. The scalpel cut a swath through the history of the corpse, revealing its physiological secrets to the students. Barry discovered things unknown to the woman during her recently ended life. Yet for all this revelation of the messy flesh, the body was stubborn in its silence. A female body devoid of inhibition in front of an uninvited group of closely observing male strangers.

Mr. Fyfe concluded his demonstration by asking the students if they would like to take a little commemorative souvenir before he covered the leavings. John Jobson, Barry's friend, gamely chose an ear. Barry demurred. He already had everything he needed to take away from the experience. He was determined to become an anatomical explorer, adept at navigating the body through the secrets of surgery.

The young student approached the lodgings where he stayed with his guardian, Mrs. Mary Anne Bulkley. He was relieved that the ordeal was over, yet scintillated and invigorated. He wanted to experience it again. He paused briefly, inhaling a final sharp intake of air to clear away the miasma. Then, turning his back to the street, he disappeared through the door of 6 Lothian Street, closing it behind him with a firmness that echoed into the night.

Narrow and crowded, the tall old tenement houses of Edinburgh Old Town where Barry lodged were subdivided and sublet to writers, intellectuals, artists, and students, who lived and worked beside the cobbled streets thronging with the city's swiftly expanding urban populace. The city Tobias Smollett described as "a hotbed of genius" had been the home of the key thinkers of the Scottish Enlightenment in the eighteenth century, including Adam Smith and David Hume. Robert Burns first came to Edinburgh in 1786 in search of a printer who would produce another edition of his poems. He discovered William Smellie, who had produced the first *Encyclopaedia Britannica* in 1768. The unfortunately named Smellie was not related to William Smellie, M.D., the great surgeon-anatomist who had worked in London alongside Cheselden and the Hunters. Described by Roy Porter as "a great horse godmother of a he-midwife," this Smellie was regarded as the founding father of modern male obstetrical surgery. He had printed a famous obstetrical atlas in 1754: *A Sett of Anatomical Tables, with Explanations, and an Abridgement of the Practice of Midwifery.* It was a practical guide to midwifery that quickly became a standard textbook of its time, a bible of creation consulted by medical students, fellow practitioners, and artists. Lavishly printed, Smellie's obstetrical atlas was highly collectible, a coveted acquisition for the private libraries of noblemen and gentlemen. There is no doubt that Barry encountered this textbook in the private libraries of Lord Buchan and General Francisco de Miranda.

The University of Edinburgh was at the zenith of its reputation between 1760 and 1820. Founded in 1726, the medical school in particular had immense prestige and an international reputation by the time Barry enrolled. It was a place where a person reticent about his true origins might reinvent himself. Some were the sons of squires, some of prosperous merchants. All were intent upon proving themselves to be gentlemen of learning. As documented by the university register, Barry's classmates included students from England, Scotland, Ireland, the United States, Canada, India, and the West Indies.

Students from outside the city either took lodgings—preferably at the homes of professors—or found accommodation with their parents in a house. So there was nothing unusual about Mrs. Bulkley accompanying James Barry when he went from London up to Edinburgh. It may be significant that, unlike at Oxford and Cambridge, the Test

Act—which stipulated that students had to be practicing members of the Church of England—did not apply to the University of Edinburgh. Mrs. Bulkley was an Irish Catholic, so the young Barry's religion could have been a factor that made Edinburgh a suitable choice.

The medical degree for which James Barry enrolled was a three-year course comprising anatomy, surgery, chemistry, botany, materia medica, theory and practice of medicine, and lectures in clinical medicine at the Royal Infirmary. The Edinburgh teaching system was regarded as exemplary for offering a combination of practical and theoretical study. At the end of three years the students undertook an oral examination in Latin, conducted by a panel of professors, in which they were asked how they would treat two specimen cases, and to submit a thesis in Latin.

Of the utmost importance to the ambitious young Barry was the fact that the Edinburgh medical school offered exceptional opportunities for those who wanted to develop their skills in the arts of anatomy and surgery combined with clinical practice. The flourishing state of the medical school was largely due to this combined clinical training. Barry duly signed up for all the regular compulsory courses. The medical school allowed its most prominent faculty members to teach at bedside, in the surgical amphitheater, and in the clinical lecture room, an arrangement that conferred importance and prestige on the value of empirical observation and practical activities.

It was not an age of donnish decorum. Gentility and gore combined not only in the dissection room and operating theater, but in the politicking that took place in institutional corridors. Many of these medics were flamboyant, argumentative men. The traditionalists pitched themselves against the intellectual renegades, and the students watched their squabbles with glee. All were regarded with suspicion by the general public.

The names of Barry's tutors were a roll call of the greatest teachers of the age, men who combined practice with extensive publication. He studied physic with Dr. James Gregory, who wore a cocked hat when he lectured. A rigorous skeptic and a challenging lecturer, Gregory had a notorious temper. He famously struck his colleague James Hamilton—also one of Barry's tutors—with his walking stick in a public argument. When forced to pay damages of £100* to Hamilton for the insult, Gregory declared that the pleasure of beating his rival was worth every penny. Dr. Andrew Duncan taught Barry the theory of medicine and medical jurisprudence. An author and private teacher, Duncan founded several Edinburgh medical clubs and was a great champion of the mentally ill. His work in this field led ultimately to the opening of the Edinburgh Lunatic Asylum in 1813. Barry's compassion for the mentally ill—who in this period were still treated more like criminals and entertainers than patients—became a hallmark of his subsequent career, and Duncan clearly helped shape this understanding.

Barry studied chemistry with Dr. Thomas Hope, described as one of the most popular science teachers in Britain, and pharmacy with Dr. Francis Home. Originally an army surgeon, Home held the first chair in materia medica and was a pioneer in the study of drugs. Dr. Daniel Rutherford taught Barry botany, and he took his clinical surgical lectures with Mr. James Russell. A course on military surgery with Dr. Thompson was to be of great use to the young medic in his future career.

The opportunity to study human anatomy was central to the appeal of the Edinburgh medical school. Until 1846, three Alexander Monros in succession occupied the chair of anatomy, in a line of decreasing ability. Barry landed with the third, hapless Monro, with whom he took five courses: three on anatomy, two on morbid anatomy. This was the same Professor Monro who was to deliver a lecture on the brain of the infamous body snatcher Burke—the top of the cranium having been sawn off—after his conviction, confession, and hanging in 1829. Monro was an uninspiring teacher, apathetically delivering lectures from his grandfather's unrevised notes. His incompetence was a cause for hilarity and frustration among the students, who would jeer at him in lectures and on one occasion accompanied their rowdy protests with a hail of peas.

*The equivalent value today would be $5,422.48 (U.S.).

Unlike the better-organized private tutors, Monro also experienced acute problems finding sufficient bodies for dissection to enliven the students' studies.

The shortcomings of Monro, and his increasing difficulties in supplying fresh bodies for freshman students to practice on, led to a rapid development of extramural teaching during this period. Hungry for anatomical knowledge, Barry and his more intrepid peers took courses in dissection with private tutors in order to expand and consolidate their knowledge. Barry's record of his professional education refers rather coyly to his having attended "Barclay and Murray's private lectures in 1810, 1811 and 1812." Dr. John Barclay ran an independent school in Surgeon's Square, adjacent to the College of Surgeons, where he employed six teachers. Barclay's "private lectures" were so popular he had to lecture twice daily, as his classroom was not large enough. Barclay made his own clandestine arrangements to deal with the problem of finding corpses for dissection. The fees paid by the students often found their way into the hands of the Edinburgh "resurrection men," who provided a supply of bodies that the students could practice on without soiling their own hands with grave-robbing.

In addition to his practical work in Barclay's dissection rooms, Barry was also enrolled as a private student with Mr. Fyfe, with whom he took three courses in dissection. For the students with stomachs strong enough and pockets deep enough to afford the additional fees, Fyfe was an invaluable guide around the mysteries of the human body. The pursuit of anatomical knowledge was in its infancy. Even in the context of this growing scientific fashion, Barry's preoccupation with the subject was distinctive.

Barry also took three courses in midwifery with Dr. James Hamilton. Hamilton, professor of midwifery since inheriting the chair from his father in 1800, was well known not only for his pioneering knowledge of his field, but also for his controversial views on the medical education of women. Many of his profession, Hamilton wrote in 1817, did not think that women should be midwives. This view he vehemently contested, and between 1780 and 1817 Hamilton taught mid-wifery to more than a thousand women. Unrecognized by any medical authority or institution, this was the action of a bold pioneer. A lifelong campaigner for the improvement of support and services for pregnant mothers and the process of childbirth, Hamilton also supported the Edinburgh Lying-In Hospital out of his own pocket. Established by his father, Dr. Alexander Hamilton, in 1791 for the purpose of "affording relief to the wives of indigent tradesmen," this hospital with childbirth facilities for women from the lower and working classes was radical for its times. The rich regarded childbirth assistance for the poor as a matter of charity or social work at best, entirely unnecessary at worst. The iconoclastic Hamilton believed passionately that midwifery should be a compulsory component of the medical degree, but colleagues persistently thwarted his efforts. He finally won the battle in 1830, but only after quarrels with his fellow faculty members that ended up in the law courts.

Barry's aggressive pursuit of knowledge of both anatomical dissection and midwifery placed him at the cutting edge of contemporary medical learning. To choose to study one could be seen as scientific curiosity, to choose both was extremely curious.

Encompassing the arts of life and death, midwifery and dissection were ancient practices, stretching back across time and cultures. When Barry entered his training both were still fledgling disciplines, and neither was yet regarded as an entirely proper object of mainstream medicine. From the Renaissance, practical dissection had been seen as primarily the domain of artists and sculptors, not doctors and surgeons. Anatomical knowledge was central to the critical eye of the artist, who needed to understand how the human body was put together, but was regarded as superfluous to the sawbones, whose job was merely to take it apart. The eighteenth century was the great age of anatomy, and innovative surgeons like John Hunter, William Smellie, and Thomas Chevalier were its pioneers. This was an age in which there were no perceived boundaries between art and science, and the relationship between art and surgery was a practical fact. Chevalier, championing the parliamentary bill seeking to establish a royal college of surgeons, argued that practitioners "ought to bear every part of this complicated machine, and all the relative situations of each, as accurately in his mind, as the painter or the sculptor should its outline, and general proportions."

Yet anatomy continued to be regarded with deep public suspicion, and widespread fears of body-snatching often erupted into outbursts of public hysteria. Surgeons were popularly represented as sinister men of the night, to be avoided at all costs. In a religious society, cutting into the body was regarded as an invasion of the sanctity of a once-living form: a deeply irreligious practice. People feared their souls would be snatched along with their bodies. This wildfire of fear and revulsion was fed by the draconian restrictions the state imposed upon the provision of bodies for medical science. In 1752, King George II passed the Murder Act, which allowed surgeons and anatomists legal access to the bodies of executed murderers for the purposes of dissection. Until 1832 this was the only legitimate source of corpses allowed to the surgical fraternity, and—despite the relatively healthy state of murderous criminality in the period—there were never enough corpses for the surgeons' knives. Moreover, the Murder Act linked dissection with ignominy and punishment in the popular imagination, a sentiment encouraged by the theatrical sensationalism surrounding the spectacle of public dissections. Dissection appeared to be a posthumous punishment for murder.

While an image of morbid brutality accompanied the pursuit of practical anatomical knowledge, the territory of gynecology, obstetrics, and—most particularly—midwifery was highly contested. William Hunter, older brother to John, was among the first to point out that knowledge of the origins of life remained uncertain:

Few, or none of the anatomists, had met with a sufficient number of subjects, either for investigating, or for demonstrating the principal circumstances of utero-gestation in the human species.

Roy Porter reminds us that until the eighteenth century, "Birthing had essentially been a women-only event." The ground of ownership for the birthing process shifted in the middle eighteenth century, when it became fashionable for a "man-midwife," or *accoucheur,* to attend on wealthier women. Claiming more advanced knowledge, these male medical practitioners pushed aside the traditional knowledge of "granny midwives," characterizing them in the process as ignorant and meddlesome. A struggle for social responsibility for pregnancy, childbirth, and lying-in ensued, and this fight for territorial rights over the reproductive female anatomy became one of the longest-running medical conflicts in history.

Until the man-midwives usurped female authority, midwifery and care for the pregnant and birthing mother had been shunted to the sidings of charity and social work. Midwives attended to the poor, and were equally poorly paid. There was no official state licensing of midwifery in the eighteenth century, and so disdainful was the Royal College of Physicians of this manual, feminine art that it banned male licensees from its practice. Childbirth was securely the domain of women. The only involvement the male medical profession had in the process was to assist with difficult labor. The use of surgical tools being restricted to surgeons, male practitioners would be called in to extract, piecemeal, stillborn children. This dreaded practice, known as craniotomy, was undertaken with hooks. Contemporary female midwives argued forcefully that men were interested in childbirth only when it enabled them to wield new surgical instruments, especially the new *tire-tête:* the forceps. This was no tender art. Trained on wooden "birthing dolls" and dead bodies, the instrument-wielding surgeons were violent and brutal in their interventions in the woman's body. It is no surprise that female midwives so vehemently opposed the expansion of their influence.

Anatomy and midwifery were the apotheoses of difference between masculine and feminine pursuits. Dissection: a masculine practice claimed by clinical, confident men eager to assert the professional authority of modern medicine. Midwifery: a traditionally feminine art, circumscribed by the tenderness and fear of female secrets and the mysteries of the woman's body. Yet as physical arts they shared a deep practical similarity. Theirs was the terrain of the slick viscosity of the human body—a slimy, sticky subject delved into by inquisitive hands in search of the secrets of creation. Invasive and analytical, cautious and dextrous by turns, what was it that so fascinated the young Barry about these slippery subjects?

Barry was born in an age when sensitivity in gentlemen of intellect and learning had not yet become regarded as unmasculine. It was the qualities of masculine sympathy characterizing the age of the early Romantics that made it look so suspicious to the macho philistines of the gathering Victorian age. Barry was born on the cusp of modern masculinity in transition, betwixt and between a now-forgotten time when real men were effeminate, and women, inspired by thinkers like Mary Wollstonecraft and Lord Buchan, aspired to be gentlemen of learning.

Earnest, expectant, and studious, the young James Barry found himself at the apex of Edinburgh life, which was centered on the twin passions of art and science. His lodgings were situated at the hub of university life. Older students frequented the taverns and theaters, played golf, went bowling and skating, and attended dances and concerts at the Assembly Rooms and St. Cecilia's Hall. The gentleman students were known in the city as great pranksters. Henry Brougham, later the lord chancellor, recalled spending evenings as an Edinburgh student wrenching the shiny brass knockers off the doors of New Town houses. Student societies, like the Royal Medical Society, abounded. Reticent and eccentric, Barry was an intellectual and emotional loner. His vigorous pursuit of his studies, evident talent, and stubbornly individual sense of antifashion made him a visible figure. Many students passed through the doors of the University of Edinburgh, but only the successful few are remembered. That people in Edinburgh still wished to gossip about Barry fifty years after his death is testimony to his oddity.

In contrast to the wildfire persona that was to define Barry's adult career, at Edinburgh he was remembered as a quiet, hesitant, and cautious figure. Barry was recalled as an isolated figure who avoided the "roaring beer parties" that were "the key sport of his fellows." For the first year of his degree, he went about pursuing his studies with a singleminded composure and determination that belied his apparently youthful years. He did, however, develop a friendship with a fellow medical student named John Jobson. The pupil register at St. Thomas's shows that the two studied alongside each other in London after Edinburgh, and both resolved to become military surgeons. They achieved their ambition, but having joined different regiments they never met again.

In 1895, a Janet Carphin, still living in Edinburgh, wrote a letter to the *Lancet* recalling with fascination the stories her friend Dr. Jobson had told her about his university friend Dr. Barry. Carphin expressed the hope that "these scanty particulars might interest your readers." Jobson, who died in 1880, recalled that the young Barry "was remarkable by the persistency with which he avoided his fellow students, and was also laughed at because, in contradiction to the shooting-coats which all the other students wore, he invariably appeared in a long surtout." Jobson was as short as Barry, but more athletic. He remembered his disappointment at not being able to teach his friend to box. "He never would strike out, but kept his arms over his chest, to protect it from blows."

Janet Carphin's correspondence also recounts the occasion on which Barry invited Jobson to his lodgings and "introduced him to his mother, with whom he lived." Jobson's recollection that Barry introduced Mary Anne Bulkley as his mother is in startling contradiction to Barry's own insistence that Mary Anne Bulkley was his aunt. The certain simple truth of James Barry's early life is that it was grounded in uncertainty.

James Barry had influential and powerful mentors who helped him at university and at the outset of his career. All these associations led back to his namesake, the famous history painter James Barry, R.A. This talented, notoriously irascible artist was the brother of Mary Anne Bulkley.

James Barry, R.A., was born in Cork on October 11, 1741, to John Barry, a coasting trader, and Juliana Reardon Barry, a pious Catholic. The eldest of five siblings, the aspirant artist left for Dublin, where he met Edmund Burke. The philosopher took a liking to the feisty, ambitious young artist and encouraged him to travel to London in search of better opportunities. In the spring of 1764, Barry set out for London with Burke's brother, William, and the following year the two left for Paris and Rome. This association was one of many that the artist developed with the thinkers and artists at the forefront of the Romantic revolution.

Barry set up a studio in London in 1771, and by 1773 he was a full member of the Royal Academy. His output during these years was prolific, but his critical acclaim was never quite matched by financial support. It was in 1782, when he was elected professor of painting to the Royal Academy, that Barry's quarrelsome nature came to the fore. He used his six annual lectures to lambaste the painter Joshua Reynolds, a former friend. His relations with his colleagues soured further when he blamed them for a burglary of his house in 1794 in which he lost his hoarded savings of £300. In his lectures he articulated his passionate views on the value of artistic education. He blamed the indifferent talent of the academicians as "the cause of students' want of ability," and argued that the study of painting would improve the general good taste of English women. In 1799, following an inquiry, Barry became the first and only artist to be expelled from the Royal Academy. His endlessly contumacious behavior was given as the cause of the inquiry, but his politically radical views no doubt equally fueled hostility against him.

One of the reasons Barry was always desperate for money was that he "found the idea of private patrons distasteful" and instead sought public commissions for grand-scale projects. Believing that the artist had a responsibility to society, Barry was an outspoken advocate of social reforms. While many of his contemporaries believed that good art was a basis for a good society, Barry believed that a good society would be the basis for good art. He supported the French Revolution and American independence. A noted printmaker, Barry used prints to comment on current affairs. One of his favorite subjects was America liberating herself from Britain, and he dedicated his *Conversion of Polemon* to the radical politician Charles James Fox. Barry was a member of the Dissenters Club at St. Paul's coffeehouse, and here rubbed shoulders with Joseph Priestley, Richard Price, and Benjamin Franklin.

James Barry, R.A., received commissions for individual portraits from politicians and aristocrats. In June 1789, the Prince of Wales sat for him. The artist, however, preferred the company of radicals to royalty. Mary Wollstonecraft's husband, William Godwin, also numbered among Barry's acquaintances—it was to Godwin that he grumbled when he was expelled from the Royal Academy. Barry held true to his beliefs into a cantankerous old age. He never stopped lamenting England's failure to provide a proper system of state patronage for artists. For Barry, art and politics were ever bound together. The young medic who took his name believed with equal vehemence that medicine and politics were intertwined. When James Barry, M.D., embroiled himself in a lifetime of disputes, his behavior mirrored the tactics and radical eccentricity of his namesake.

James Barry, R.A., lived with an obsessive austerity among his paints and was always regarded with suspicion by his neighbors. Toward the end of his life he lived in Great Castle Street, in London, near the lawyer Henry Curran. Curran reported that Barry's home was the target of frequent attacks and that the locals whispered that his house "was occupied by an old wizard, or a necromancer." Quick to take offense, Barry argued with and alienated most of the friends he ever made. Only those who could match his vision or eccentricity survived, particularly Lord Buchan and the endlessly patient Dr. Edward Fryer. Yet when he died, in February 1806, he was honored with a grand funeral and burial in St. Paul's Cathedral. He was interred alongside Joshua Reynolds, with whom he had been reconciled in later years.

The studies of the young James Barry at Edinburgh were not just made up of medicine and morbidity. He was a literary student as well. His studies of the classics introduced him to the world of myth, populated by tales of transformation and discovery, of origins, heroic journeys, of adversity overcome, and magical transmutations. His own progress through adolescence was a process of transformation from an unknown youth of imprecise origin to a dashing and learned young gentleman at the forefront of his profession. His spectacular self-presentation and love of the high life are keynotes in the recollections of all who encountered him. Three mentors guided James Barry onto the stage of his adult life: one a high-ranking aristocrat, one an extraordinary revolutionary, and one a writer and thinker revered by his peers.

This heavyweight trio—and fine living made all of them weighty—linger in the wings of Barry's life, their influence prompting the progression of his early career. Much has been written about the lives of Lord Buchan, the romantic revolutionary General Francisco de Miranda, and the scholar Dr. Edward Fryer, but the parts they played in fostering the fortunes of Britain's most peculiar and brilliant doctor are not mentioned. These men had three things in common. They were all friends of the infuriating but inspiring James Barry, R.A. They all took continuing interest in the preservation of his estate and name after his death. And they were all revolutionaries in their time.

A particular project centered around their friendship with the elder Barry bound Lord Buchan, General Miranda, and Dr. Fryer together. Following the artist's death they collaborated on editing *The Works of James Barry*. Published in 1809, this collection contained drawings, reprints of Barry's essays on art and culture, and a biography constructed largely around his own correspondence. An 1806 issue of the *Gentleman's Magazine* carried a report that Lord Buchan was gathering these materials "with an intention to publish them for the advantage of some indigent relatives of the departed artist." Barry died with £40 in his pocket, and possibly about £2,400 in stocks and savings in the bank, although the disarray of his financial affairs made the true value of his estate uncertain. Whatever the case, it seems that Mrs. Bulkley and her daughters were the "indigent relatives" intended to benefit from the proceeds of the book. This was not the only fund-raising effort. There was a public sale of Barry's effects after his death in which his *Pandora* received a bid of 230 guineas. But the records of sale show that the painting went unclaimed and was returned to Mrs. Bulkley.

A young man must have models upon which to mold his masculinity. In the self-conscious fashioning of his gentlemanly persona, James Barry was not so very different from any young man emulating his romantic, heretical heroes. He was in awe of the painter's three friends, who equipped him with a lot more than essential money and financial security. From Miranda and Buchan in particular, Barry learned the kind of man he wanted to be. He drew into his own personality a self-conscious collage of their temperaments, ideas, and ideals.

If imitation is the most sincere form of flattery, then Barry's regard for Francisco de Miranda must have exceeded all others. Napoleon Bonaparte astutely described the Venezuelan Miranda as "a Don Quixote with the difference that he is not mad . . . General Miranda has the sacred fire burning in his soul." Quixotic in the extreme, the colorful, contradictory Miranda, born in March 1750, led a life of travel, adventure, politics, love, and intrigue that spanned two continents, three revolutions, and more women than he could keep count of. Above all, Miranda had a dream of a liberated Venezuela. The sacred fire to which Napoleon referred was Miranda's passion for republicanism.

As a young man, Miranda traveled to Madrid, where he studied mathematics and the mantillas of the local señoritas with equal dedication. It was here that he began to collect books. Miranda's library became legendary. It became also an essential part of the education of the book-hungry James Barry, who was honored to be allowed to study in Miranda's library in his house in St. James's Street.

Alongside his books, Miranda also collected women. He was as committed a rake as he was a republican, and some of the most fascinating women of the day numbered among his conquests. Described by Robert Harvey as "an indefatigable sexual tourist," Miranda gained an international reputation for his inexhaustible sexual appetites. In France, he was the lover of Madame de Staël. In Russia he attracted the love-struck attentions of none other than Catherine the Great. So intense and abiding was Catherine's passion for Miranda that he was perceived as a potential threat by her advisers, who tried to pay him off when his short visit turned into an apparently open-ended stay. Catherine ignored the political cautions and went to great lengths to keep Miranda in Russia as her paramour. She set him up in a palatial residence and tried to persuade him to regard the arrangement as permanent. Miranda, however, rejected the proffered role of royal consort and left, claiming that as much as he enjoyed the warmth of Catherine's bed, he couldn't abide the cold of the freezing Russian winters.

Miranda visited North America as well, where the War of Independence augmented his belief in the iniquities of colonial rule and the pressing need for republican revolution. In New York he became acquainted with Alexander Hamilton and Thomas Paine; in London he claimed among his friends philosophers, politicians, and military men, including Jeremy Bentham, Lord Howe, Lord Shelburne, and Lord Fitzherbert. And, of course, James Barry, R.A. Miranda loved England, and spent time indulging his compulsion for the arts and culture that London had to offer. He bought the house in St. James's Street, where he lived with his lover Sarah Andrews and their children, Leandro and Francisco. Free-spirited and modish in all things, Miranda regarded this arrangement as a progressive open relationship untrammeled by the constraints of marriage. Spurred by his Anglophilia, rumors that he had been recruited by the British secret service followed him throughout his life.

The French Revolution was a magnet to the firebrand Miranda, but he refused to curb his criticisms and, despite being acquainted with Robespierre, found himself imprisoned and sentenced to the guillotine not just once but twice. It is testimony to Miranda's capricious nature and ridiculous good fortune that he escaped both times, and was each time wholly unrepentant. Explaining his anxieties about what was happening in France he said, "I love freedom, but not a freedom based on blood or pitiless towards sex or age."

Miranda's personality was a constellation of contradictions. It is conspicuous how, temperamentally, the adult Barry resembled Miranda. Described as "conceited," "overbearing," and "apparently unconcerned about making enemies," Miranda was also intensely generous and compassionate. He was a republican idealist who was also "a howling snob," and an intellectual aesthete who expended vast sums on an exquisitely pretentious wardrobe. Miranda defended his independence of mind in a manner that "verged on insubordination," and his superiors regarded him as "prickly" and "rude." An exhibitionist and magpie in his energetic pursuit of all things artistic and cultural, he nevertheless built up his library as a means to an end—a laboratory of modern thought where freethinkers could study for action, not just contemplation. Significantly, this library included "treatises such as might be considered to form a tolerably complete Medical Library for a private gentleman." It was a particular mark of favor to be allowed access to Miranda's private library, famed for its extensiveness and value. The young James Barry was careful to write and thank Miranda effusively for being allowed to use it.

Miranda's sexual avarice was combined with a genuine interest in and support for the ideas of female education and emancipation that were circulating in his social world. Although a great dancer and partygoer, he drank little, and as both guest and host was known for his temperance. Above all, he had the pragmatic idealist's ability to be unshakable and imaginative in his convictions. Despite entrenched opposition, disapprobation, skepticism, and ridicule, Miranda never faltered from following his star. Whatever the exact circumstances of the contact between them, Barry was clearly awed and inspired by Miranda, and fascinated by the version of liberal progressive masculinity his mentor incarnated. No doubt the awakening youth was also dazzled and seduced by Miranda's showy and challenging self-presentation, and his copious manifestation of sexual charm. The fact that he should choose to emulate so complex and strong-minded a figure provides an insight into Barry's youthful desires and ambitions. Here was a young person who had no intention of occupying the sidelines of life. Significantly, Miranda was also a role model of how to fight and follow a cause based on a gut belief in social justice. In later life, Barry put into action in his own career some of Miranda's vociferously defended ideas, most particularly his belief in prison and hospital reform.

In London, Miranda built up a group of protorevolutionaries, students, and thinkers, who gathered at his house to discuss Venezuela's future. Miranda used his influence and ingenuity to petition senior members of the British government to persuade them to support the cause of South American independence. His eventful, energetic life was but a prelude to his desired destiny: in October 1810 he set off for his homeland once again in a renewed attempt to lead the revolution that was the apex of his dreams.

Before leaving, Miranda made arrangements for Barry to follow him when he had completed his medical degree, plans he communicated to Lord Buchan and Dr. Fryer but which never came to fruition. If Barry had gone to Caracas he would have been a member of the inner political circle of the first ruler of an independent Venezuela, where Miranda is still revered as a popular hero. He is remembered today in South America as El Precursor—John the Baptist—the man who paved the way for the Liberator himself, Simón Bolívar.

It is a strange pleat in history that James Barry shared a mentor with one of the most famous Latin American revolutionaries. When Miranda agreed to support Bolívar and his men, he legitimated their cause with the gloss of political authority and revolutionary heroism. Miranda had plucked Bolívar from the ranks and promoted and protected him. Tragically, he had made his own monster. In 1812 Bolívar cruelly betrayed him into captivity. Miranda languished in prison for four years, and died on July 14, 1816. Popular Venezuelan history is reticent about Bolívar's involvement in El Precursor's betrayal, but accords Mi-

randa heroic status. He is remembered as having influenced a generation of Latin American revolutionaries and "through sheer force of personality and intellect" having pushed the cause of Latin American
independence to the forefront of the political agenda.

It is unclear exactly what Miranda knew about his protégé's background and situation, but the Miranda archive contains two letters
from the children in the care of Mrs. Bulkley. Firstly, a set of verses sent
to Miranda by a "Miss Bulkley," one of Mary Anne's daughters, on the
occasion of the death of James Barry, R.A., in 1806. And four years later,
from Edinburgh, a letter from James Barry, medical student. This is the
only known letter in the entirety of the Barry archive in which James
Barry ever alludes directly to his relationship with James Barry, R.A.,
and Mrs. Bulkley.

To General Miranda
Edinburgh
7th January, 1810

Dear Sir

In a letter I had the honour of receiving from my inestimable
friend Dr Fryer, he says that in consequence of your kind en-
quiries about my pursuits, etc, he did not conceal from so particular a friend of my late uncle's any circumstances relative to my
successore; I am truly grateful for the communication, and I think
I may congratulate myself on being thought of by so very eminent
a Man. The last day of the year I dined at the Earl Buchan's, who
said General Miranda was known to him only by Fame but that he
had been introduced to him on his arrival in this Country; I could
not help telling his Lordship what a Treasure you possess in London, and how often you permitted me (Barry's nephew) to par-
take it, it is needless to say I mean your very extensive and elegant
library—of my part—I am studying and attending the Greek,
Natural Philosophy, Chemistry and Anatomy Classes, and am

honoured by the notice of the above mention'd earl and Dr
Monro the celebrated professor of Anatomy, the Doctor speaks of
you whom he knows by Fame and of Dr Fryer whose correspondence with Lord B—his particular friend, he has read with Enthusiasm. — Excuse my troubling you with this letter, but I could
not deny myself the pleasure of wishing you many happy returns
of the new year in which Mrs Bulkley (my Aunt) joins with me. I
must beg the favour when you see Dr Fryer to tell him that Lord
Buchan desires me to say that we drank his health at his house in
George Street this day week.

> I am, Dear Sir, With Respect and Esteem,
> Yours grateful and obedient humble servant
> James Barry

If you should favour me with a line please to direct to James
Barry Student at the University, Edinburgh.

Ostensibly this is a letter from a young, grateful protégé to his sophisti-
cated patron. Through his references to Lord Buchan and Dr. Fryer,
Barry cements his relationship to a circle of powerful patrons. He seeks
to ensure his continued friendship with Miranda, and access to his extensive library. However, the most curious dimension of this letter is
the revealing awkwardness with which Barry refers to both himself and
his family background. He is at pains to highlight and define his relationship to James Barry, R.A., "my late uncle," and Mary Anne Bulkley,
"my Aunt," and even includes a strange reminding prompt of his own
identity, "me (Barry's nephew)."

The letter concludes with this mysterious and peculiar postscript:

> As Lord B— nor anyone here knows anything about Mrs Bulk-
> ley's Daughter, I trust my dear General that neither you nor the
> Doctor will mention in any of your correspondence anything
> about my Cousin's friendship and care for me.

Barry alludes to something about "Mrs Bulkley's Daughter" of which even his patron Lord Buchan is unaware. And then the strange request not to mention his cousin's friendship and care for him. The meaning of these veiled secrets crossed over into silence in the cramped, unwholesome prison cell where Miranda died in 1816, the same year that Barry set out for his first foreign posting—not to Venezuela, as he had expected, but to the Cape of Good Hope.

As Barry's letter to Miranda indicates, he spent New Year's Eve dining with the eccentric and immensely wealthy Scottish nobleman Lord Buchan, probably at his town house at St. Andrew Square. David Steuart Erskine, eleventh earl of Buchan, was one of the elder Barry's closest friends and his most unflagging benefactor. An enthusiastic patron of the arts and literature, Buchan regarded himself as an arbiter of artistic taste. The high society he moved in was less certain of this, and gossiped about what they regarded as his outlandish preferences. A vain, snobbish name-dropper who called both the king and George Washington "my dear cousin," the otherwise erratic Buchan nevertheless had a consistently passionate interest in the progressive ideas of early Romantic society. His most particular interest was in the value of female education, an issue to which he devoted much energy and on which he published extensively.

Buchan's patronage was enormously liberating to Barry. His aristocratic name opened doors. It facilitated Barry's metamorphosis into a young gentleman of good connection and intellectual reputation. It was essential in getting Barry the references and credentials he was otherwise so strangely lacking. Buchan had an honorary degree from Edinburgh, where he exerted considerable influence to pave Barry's way into the university. A note beside Barry's name in a university class register illustrates the vital collateral Buchan's favor gave him: "Known by Lord Buchan, nephew of Mr B."

Buchan flirted with decadence while Miranda lived it. If Miranda was the inspirational idealist whom Barry sought to emulate, Buchan was a benign and considerate—if peripatetic—benefactor who paid close attention to the practical requirements of Barry's professional development toward self-sufficiency. The now-elderly Buchan, such a longtime friend of the irredeemable James Barry, R.A., probably also had an eye toward ensuring that James Barry the younger was more competently equipped to handle his own affairs and take care of himself than his uncle had been.

Despite his reputation for skittishness, Buchan kept a regular check on Barry's academic progress and welfare. In the summer of 1810, he wrote to Dr. Robert Anderson from Dryburgh Abbey to express his gratitude to him for offering the young Barry accommodation:

My dear Sir

I have just now the pleasure of your letter of the 29th, which I cannot but greatly approve in the expression of your kindness to poor Barry, and your willingness to take him under your care as a Boarder when Mrs Bulkley leaves Scotland. Considering the friendship which subsisted between Barry's uncle and myself and other circumstances, I have taken the liberty of recommending him more particularly to your attention as you will see by the two Billets which I send inclosed to your care.

The amiable Robert Anderson, M.D., was a famous editor, biographer, and scholar whose house was for many years one of the literary centres of Edinburgh. Like all Barry's benefactors, Anderson was something of an innovator. Commissioned by a Scottish publisher to edit a selection of English poetry based on the poets Samuel Johnson had included in his *Lives,* Anderson suggested a more ambitious and—by the standards of the times—radical project, including both pre-Shakespearean and Scottish poets. His initially hesitant publishers agreed, and the fourteen-volume project was published as *A Complete Edition of the Poets of Great Britain.* The publication was met with enthusiasm and wide critical acclaim, and Anderson was remembered long after for being the editor who for the first time made many of the Elizabethan poets broadly accessible. As editor of the *Edinburgh Magazine,*

Anderson encouraged and supported new writers, many of whom he also entertained in his home. Barry mingled with a diverse range of lively, talented, and intelligent young men living in Anderson's literary honey pot, a far cry from the quieter life he had led with Mary Anne Bulkley when starting out on his studies.

With the silent departure of Mrs. Bulkley, Barry was finally cut loose from all present reminders of his seemingly shallow past, and free to develop further into a young gentleman of fashion. The context of Anderson's home not only broadened his social sphere, it allowed him to inspect young men at close quarters and to study their mannerisms, behavior, and opinions.

During his holidays, Barry was the guest of Buchan at Dryburgh Abbey. Like Miranda, Buchan allowed Barry free access to study in his private library. In October 1811, Buchan wrote to Robert Anderson again, demonstrating his continuing interest in the progress of Barry's studies and his concern that he should receive every encouragement:

Dear Sir

James Barry . . . has been here for 5 weeks past and has employed himself in my Library very busily in usefull reading of Books connected with his professional views. He is a well disposed young man, and worthy of your notice and advice in his studies.

It will be kind in you and Dr Irving to look to the Latinity of his Thesis which he tells me he is about to prepare this winter, and tho' he is much younger than is usual to take his Degree in Medicine and Surgery yet from what I have observed likely to entitle himself to them by his attainments.

He means to go by invitation of General Miranda to The Caracas.

I am, Dear Sir, Yours with esteem,
Buchan

How flattering and gratifying for the gifted James Barry, in the process of developing his alter ego, to be referred to as "a well disposed young man." Better still, the earl had clearly formed a favorable impression of his protégé's intellectual development. Buchan's comment on Barry's apparent youthfulness was prescient. It was not long before Buchan would have to intervene on his protégé's behalf in a dispute on just this issue.

Fostered by a romantic painter, a progressive aristocrat, and a revolutionary, James Barry was cultivated into a radical tradition. These heretical roots were to be manifest throughout his career. James Barry, R.A., had turned to the blank canvas to fulfill his ambition, filling it with brilliantly executed figures, classical and contemporary. His figurative art earned him friends, patrons, and financial favor. Born to a mercantile family with no care for and much suspicion of art, he became one of the most prominent and notorious artists of the day, moving in circles of enormous social and political influence. He was a self-made man. His "nephew" inherited a name that was a passport for recognition among influential mentors. But there was more to it than this. What the younger generation inherited from the older generation was the spirit of the age; the intimacy between art and science reflected in the common inheritance of artist and medical scientist.

James Barry, M.D., as in all things, went a little bit further to the edge of the known world. Like his uncle, he was a self-made man. Unlike his uncle, the blank canvas he turned to for his invention was himself.

Chapter 2

"AN EAGLE'S EYE, A LADY'S HAND, AND A LION'S HEART"

Actors and surgeons . . . are all heroes of the moment.

Honoré de Balzac, *The Atheist's Mass*

Until an actor is at home in his dress, he is not at home in his part.

Oscar Wilde, *The Truth of Masks*

JAMES BARRY SAT WRITING, HIS BACK ROUNDED OVER HIS DESK like a question mark. With a steady concentration he filled the pages before him with his forward-sloping hand. The plush cuffs of his jacket darted between page and inkwell as he dipped his nib and shuffled through his notes, from which he transcribed with deliberate care. A Latin grammar lay open at his elbow. He wore a briskly cut emerald-striped jacket over a square vest of embroidered maroon silk, the whole finished with a starched yellow muslin cravat. His cuffs were decorated with buttons, and the shoulders of his jacket stiffly padded after the latest fashion. Absorbed in his thoughts, Barry was unaware of the figure framed by the full-length cheval mirror standing in the corner of his room; but if he had paused for self-reflection, he would have seen the very picture of a young nineteenth-century gentleman at study. It was May 1812, and Barry was at work on the thesis on which depended his qualification for his medical degree.

Barry had begun research on this project, "De merocele vel hernia crurali" (An Inaugural Medical Dissertation on Merocele or Femoral Hernia), at Dryburgh Abbey during the autumn of 1811 while the guest of Lord Buchan. The sprucely presented student attended parties, picnics, recitals, and readings hosted by his gregarious benefactor. He learned to affect the manners and passions of Buchan's eclectic guests, among whom were artists, writers, progressives, politicians, reformers, aristocrats, and professional decadents. Whatever the temptations of Buchan's salon, Barry spent most of his days in his host's private library, and after evening entertainments always returned to his studies—a diligence noted approvingly by his host. In particular, Barry labored to improve his written and spoken Latin, the language in which he had to both write and defend his thesis. Barry never stinted on his studies. The vulnerability of his circumstances must have been a prime motivation. Without a family or secure prospects to fall back on, he had little choice but to succeed. The completion and defense of his thesis were essential for him to gain his M.D., the qualification that was his passport to a professional future.

Providing himself with a means to earn his own living was essential to Barry, as was the continued support and goodwill of the benefactors on whom his professional development depended. Yet for all this, Barry's preoccupation with the subject of his thesis went beyond pragmatism and patronage. He applied himself to his chosen subject with an unwavering and obsessive zeal.

The successful diagnosis and treatment of hernia was one of the most significant innovations in early-nineteenth-century surgery, and the man who was almost single-handedly responsible for these advances was Sir Astley Paston Cooper, universally praised—and grudgingly envied—as the greatest surgeon and teacher of the day. Cooper's motto that the surgeon should have "an eagle's eye, a lady's hand, and a lion's heart" described his own exacting standards.

Hernia was a research specialty of the Edinburgh medical faculty. Several of Barry's own tutors had published extensively on the subject, and it made sense that he would choose this topic to complete his academic studies. All these men based their research on the innovative work of Astley Cooper, who had recently pioneered a new operation that cured the complaint and saved the lives of acute cases. "There is not . . . any disease presented to surgeons, which requires so minute and accurate a knowledge of anatomy for the administration of the appropriate means of relief," wrote Cooper in his *Treatise on Hernia* in 1804. The minute and accurate understanding required was no less than intimate knowledge of the seat of sexual differentiation itself—the genitals. The inner thigh, the groin, the scrotum, the testes, the penis, the anal passage, the lower abdomen, the uterus, and vagina: the complex network of interconnecting parts that made up the sexed body of man and woman. And these were cultural genitals as well as physical. In studying hernia, Barry was probing the anatomical parts most closely associated with ideas about sex and reproduction.

Cooper was insistent that anyone studying this subject had to throw away reliance on received wisdom and medical precedent. In the preface to his *Treatise on Hernia* he bluntly stated that he had "uniformly . . . avoided quoting the opinions of authors on this part of surgery." Instead, he insisted on the primacy of relentless case study and practical observation.

ALTHOUGH COOPER HAD PROVED THE CONDITION WAS OPERABLE, his radical surgery was regarded as complicated and risky. The medical profession was still arguing over his method a century later. "It is a disorder . . . which seldom allows the surgeon much time or consideration as to his proceedings," Cooper wrote. His process depended upon instant decision-making and lightning-speed use of the knife. While Cooper was legendary for excelling at both, his methods' detractors tended to be less able colleagues not confident of their quick-cutting and quick-thinking abilities. Cooper knew that the decisive mind was as important as the certain hand. As one awed observer remarked of his skill with the instruments of cutting, "It is of no consequence what Mr Cooper uses; they are all alike to him, and I verily believe he could operate as easily with an oyster knife as the best bit of cutlery in Laundy's shop." Laundy, London's leading maker of surgical instruments, prided himself on supplying Cooper's surgical equipment. Like all other aspirant surgeons, James Barry went to Laundy's to get his cutting kit when he arrived in London.

Enraptured by Cooper's groundbreaking work, Barry researched the medical history of the hernia, explored the sources from classical to contemporary times, and turned his research to the purpose of substantiating his own radical position on the subject. Cooper, the source of his intellectual inspiration, was sternly insistent about the need for practical observation: "Sir, to learn your profession,—look to yourself,—never mind what other people may say, no opinion or theories can interfere with information acquired from dissection." Taking Cooper at his word, Barry questioned his own opinions on the disorder presented in the *Treatise.* Measured against the medical standards of the day, Barry's argument was unconventional. He sought to expand medical knowledge and treatment on a vastly understudied subject: hernia in women.

In his argument Barry drew heavily on the things he learned from dissection. From his time at Edinburgh he had a lively enthusiasm for the grave arts of dissection and morbid anatomy. But his study of hernia and its related conditions required him to speculate on prevention, maintenance, and cure in living subjects too. Who or what were Barry's living examples for the speculative argument of his thesis? The intellectual sources are assiduously cited, but the identities of the living subjects on whom he based his observations are more vague. This puzzle was to remain encoded for nearly two centuries in his Latin prose.

Finally it was finished, and Barry was ready to submit himself for examination. The procedure was daunting, and many students failed on their first attempt, including Barry's friend John Jobson. The largest part of the exam had to be conducted as an oral defense in Latin, and candidates had to prove they were proficient in the language before they were allowed to proceed. (Buchan had showed foresight in his anxious request to Anderson, "Look to the Latinity" of Barry's thesis.) Members of the medical faculty would assemble at a colleague's house and students would be put through their paces. Faced by a phalanx of interrogative tutors, the student would first be required to answer questions on his thesis. Next he had to account for and exemplify two aphorisms by Hippocrates, and then round up the oral defense by analyzing two unseen case studies. The fact that the examination process was a public performance made it an unnerving experience. For James Barry it was a potentially hazardous ordeal. Not only did he need to show himself to be well versed in his medical knowledge and Latin (lately learned), but he needed to be confident of defending a contentious thesis that challenged the learning and opinions of the people who had taught him. And this was not all. He had to give a performance that proved he was every inch the young gentleman, worthy to become a graduate of the Edinburgh school and embark upon what was a skilled and highly privileged profession. Surgeons were expected to convince and persuade in the face of often extreme human anxiety or skepticism, so the requirement to perform was an essential part of their professional training. Rehearsals were over. Theater and audience were to become the center of Barry's professional operations. Thoroughly prepared, full of hopeful optimism, buoyed by the bold confidence of his youth, Barry was ready to face the examination. But precisely at this moment, a crisis erupted.

Along with his fellow students, Barry had applied to the University Senate for permission to enter for the degree examination. Unthinkably, his application was refused. Barry had never given a moment's thought to the possibility that his application might be blocked. His experience of the institution up to this point had been benign. The university was a new and exciting sphere that he trusted as a secure place in which to experiment with rhetoric and writing and the exchange of ideas within a learned community. Suddenly he was confronted by the possibility of exclusion.

The reason given by the senate for refusing his application was his "extreme youth." Lord Buchan had already commented to Barry's landlord, Dr. Anderson, on his apparent youthfulness the year before. Swept along by the excitement of his environment and the possibilities it held out to him, Barry had made little concerted attempt to offset the cheekily youthful appearance of his body with a pronounced show of the gravitas of his maturing mind.

His hopes plummeting, Barry appealed to Lord Buchan. The aristocratic Buchan occupied the high ground of influence at Edinburgh, and he intervened with a personal deposition to the senate in which he pointed out that there was no absolute rule in the university regulations stating the minimum age for degree candidates. The senate accepted Buchan's argument, and disaster was averted. With characteristic impudence, Barry made reference to the dispute in the cheeky epigraph to his thesis, archly appealing to the examiners by citing a quotation from the Greek dramatist Menander: "Do not consider whether what I say is a young man speaking, but whether my discussion with you is that of a man of understanding."

By the summer of 1812, the path was cleared for Barry to present himself for examination. He passed with notable excellence, and received the coveted diploma of Doctor of Medicine. His performance consummated the self-creation of James Barry as a scholar and man of medicine. "I received a Diploma dated in 1812 as Doctor of Medicine from the University of Edinburgh," Barry states in his *Return of the Services and Professional Education of James Barry MD*. Although no one noticed it at the time, he had made history. Not until after his death would the true significance of this achievement be understood.

The newly minted Dr. James Barry wasted no time, and proceeded directly to London. He had reason to make haste. Sanctioned by his formal qualification and invigorated by the confidence of his recent success, he saw that the opportunity to continue his professional training with one of his heroes was within his grasp. Each year, Guy's and St. Thomas's, the preeminent teaching hospitals in England, offered a limited number of places for pupil dressers—that is, trainee surgeons.

Barry wanted one of these dresserships. A letter of advice written to a contemporary student by Dr. Cline the elder, whose son was to become one of Barry's tutors, outlined the cost and requirements of being a pupil dresser:

> I have to observe that being a dresser for one year is an expence of fifty pounds. The number of dressers for each Surgeon is limited to four. My lectures and the privilege of dissecting is fifteen guineas for a winter. There are also other lectures, on chymistry, the practice of physic, and on midwifery; all of which are subscribed to separately.

There were only twenty-four dresserships in the United Hospitals. The places were highly competitive, and the young medics who got them were a fast-track elite. These privileged positions were highly sought after, and regarded as being open only to gentlemen. Like every other hopeful student who applied, Barry also wanted to work with Astley Cooper, who had so inspired his research. By far the most popular surgeon in the United Hospitals, Cooper was able to cherry-pick the students who showed the most exceptional talents. Barry's application for one of these places was a measure of the breadth of his ambition. Fortunately for Barry, Edinburgh medical school held a place of special favor in Cooper's estimation. He had studied there for seven months in the winter of 1787, and during this period had worked with Dr. Gregory, Dr. Hamilton, Dr. Rutherford, Dr. Black, Dr. Hope, Old Monro—whom he likened to a grunting pig—and Mr. Fyfe, whom he "used to mimic very admirably." (Despite the teasing, Cooper set a high value on Fyfe's knowledge and teaching of practical anatomy, and as a teacher always recommended Fyfe's anatomical drawings to his own students.) All of these men had of course trained James Barry. Aside from the familiar names Barry could offer as the pedigree for his training, he had a further asset that probably assisted him in attracting Cooper's attention—his uncle's name.

James Barry, R.A., and Astley Cooper had been close friends. The artist's reference to "My long esteemed and ingenious friend Mr Cooper" in one of his last letters to Buchan is testimony to the endurance of a friendship that prevailed until the end of his life, a rarity in the life of the rambunctious and perenially difficult Barry. Cooper would have noticed shared characteristics between his dead friend and his slightly built nephew. Both had a boundless enthusiasm for "voluminous studies," and although drawn to company shared a focused intensity that leaned sometimes toward impatience with social small talk. Both uncle and nephew sought to "raise admiration" by their remarks, and were easily prompted to become "animated and eloquent on any subject" where they "felt the least interest." The friendship between James Barry, R.A., and Astley Cooper formed another strand in the complex web that bound together the network of people who facilitated James Barry's progress to professional adulthood.

Bolstered by the combined forces of his intellectual achievements and his social connections, James Barry aimed high, and hit his mark. On October 17, 1812, he registered at Guy's and St. Thomas's as a pupil dresser, assigned to Astley Cooper. The Pupils and Dressers Cash Book shows that he paid his enrollment fees of six shillings and twenty pence promptly. Barry could not have done better: he was enrolled at the premier teaching hospital in the country, apprenticed to Britain's leading surgeon. His friend John Jobson was less fortunate. It took him a further year to pass his exams and obtain his M.D. By the time he enrolled in July 1813, Barry had moved on.

BARRY HAD RETURNED TO A GRANDIOSE CITY OF A MILLION INhabitants—the biggest metropolis in the western world. Regency London was a vortex of pleasure and bustling activity. Pitt's war against France was still in full swing. The outcome of the Napoleonic Wars was to prove decisive for Barry's future career. Energized by culture and commerce, London was also pestilential, sprawling, and beset by poverty, vice, and disease. Crucially, it offered the delights of anonymity in a city of strangers, a larger but also more cluttered stage upon which the increasingly confident young Barry would have to learn to excel.

Barry was now a young gentleman, graduate, doctor of medicine. With a profession to pursue in a fashionable, highly visible field, Barry was taking to the center stage of London life. Maximizing such opportunity required endeavor, endurance, and imagination. The test he faced was in orienting himself to a new existence. While at Edinburgh, Barry had a finite part to play—the completion of a medical degree and the fashioning of a gentleman. The world of early-nineteenth-century London provided the protean Barry with an ever-changing script of increasing complexity. His challenge was to make himself at home in a new life without any fixed means of support.

Barry must have seemed odd to his new colleagues and friends. There was no one, apparently, who could vouch for his childhood. Bereft of family, he was, it seemed, an orphan, yet he had proven connections that placed him beyond question in high and, at that time, resolutely impolite society. In order to maintain the security of his claim to these connections, he had to constantly show himself worthy of the confidence invested in him by his mentors. The sharpness of his intellect and the distinction of his academic achievements were not mere embellishments to his gentility—they were essential also to his economic survival.

His choice of hernia as the subject for his thesis was astute. Cooper was, it seems, predisposed to take a professional and intellectual interest in an ambitious youngster who claimed inspiration from his work. Yet Barry was no slavish follower of Cooper's opinions on this topic. Although his project concluded that Cooper was quite clearly the leader in the field, it started by precociously challenging his knowledge of the intellectual history of hernia. Barry had a probably unconscious knack for sharing the ideas of his mentors and idols, but questioning and disputing them in a way that gave him something to bring to an otherwise unequal relationship.

Amid the ferment of early-nineteenth-century London sat Guy's and St. Thomas's Hospitals. Guy's had been established in 1725 by Thomas Guy, a Lombard Street bookseller who made his fortune by printing Bibles and by unusually astute investment in South Sea stock. St. Thomas's had a longer pedigree, dating from the early twelfth century. Surgery and instruction by lecture and demonstration were already being offered at St. Thomas's in the Elizabethan age. It also boasted the first regular teacher of anatomy in London, the pioneering ophthalmologist and anatomist William Cheselden, described by Alexander Pope as "the most noted and most deserving man in the whole profession of chirurgery." Situated in convenient proximity, Guy's and St. Thomas's actively cooperated, especially in surgical teaching, and became known as the United Hospitals—although this unification was not without its periodic political rifts and disputes.

The register of pupil dressers originated in 1750 at St. Thomas's. Dressers were stationed by the operating table in the well of the theater, a perfect vantage point from which to observe skilled surgeons at work. Their role was to pass the surgeon instruments and dressings. By Barry's time the responsibilities of the pupil dressers had expanded and they had become surgeon's assistants. The dressers worked long hours and were frequently thrown responsibility for problems beyond their experience and years.

Though the work was arduous, there were definite advantages to being in the capital. London gave the dressers the opportunity to see the latest and most up-to-date treatment of the more serious accidents and diseases. The anatomy lectures and dissecting-room instruction were regarded as the best in the country, despite the ghastly institutional facilities. Also on the positive side was the fact that the dressers were given real responsibility, as one student explained: "The Dressers possess the advantages of not only assisting the Surgeons in the performance of operations, but of having patients and important accidents confined to their care in the absence of their superiors." Once he had passed his exams, a pupil dresser could present himself for membership in the Royal College of Surgeons. The RCS was a newly invented professional body that had replaced the Company of Surgeons in 1800. Membership, open only to men, was a prerequisite to professional advancement. For the young medic wishing to become a surgeon, his time as a pupil dresser was effectively an apprenticeship. None of James Barry's correspondence survives from this time, but a letter written by one of his contemporaries to a friend describes the responsibilities of the role:

> He has the absolute execution of everything but the great operations, the smaller and most frequent ones he is allowed to perform when he has been long enough in train to lose the trembling hand, in short, before the end of his year he becomes, as it were, an Assistant Surgeon, for all the accidents are submitted to his care and judgment, he takes up the vessels after operations, puts on the bandages, and acts a foremost character in the presence of numerous spectators, by which he must acquire confidence and courage.

Frequently asked to step out of the wings as understudy, the dresser was required to provide a convincing performance in front of a critical, often learned audience. Acting in the bear pit of the anatomy theater, confidence, showmanship, and theatricality were as crucial to the development of a successful medical career as the ability to wield a knife. The idea of the surgeon as actor, performing his skills theatrically and inspiring confidence in an anxious public, is one that goes back to the birth of surgery. An invasive technician who may at any time reach inside of us and rectify secrets of bodies that we little understand, the surgeon is a figure who has always inspired both terror and fascination. He is the stranger to whom we entrust our lives.

The surgeon's job was to map the unfamiliar structures of the body, and improvise the boundary between death and life. To be a surgeon was to live a life of performance under daily public scrutiny. In order to reassure, surgeons needed to delight, amaze, or scandalize. All the great surgeons of Barry's age were consummate actors and, like their thespian counterparts, not a little vain and conceited. Surgeons had an aura of glamour, risk, special knowledge, and the glint of the parvenu about them. Their dissecting arts were arcane and novel, and the occasion of public spectacle contributed to their celebrity. Astley Cooper famously dissected an elephant that had died in the Tower of London menagerie in 1801. Londoners crowded the streets to watch the passage of the dead elephant, wheeled on an open-sided float on its way to the temporary open-air dissecting theater that Cooper had erected outside his house in order to deal with his unusually large subject. So many curious people thronged around this postmortem pageant that Cooper ordered his assistants to hang large rugs in the scaffolding to obscure the carcass from prying eyes while the ringmaster went about the business of his deathly show. More ordinary, but no less popular, were the public dissections of murderers, where the morbidly curious could purchase tickets to watch proceedings from the gallery.

It was the age of Romanticism and revolution. God had lost his position as key protagonist and heroism had come down to earth. This was the epoch of the rising masses and bourgeois liberal republicanism, and in its midst enlightened professionals became heroes of the age. The surgeon took center stage as the all-knowing subject who cared for a physical body that now belonged to man, not God.

All this glamour had to be worked at. There were many hopefuls in the medical world, but only a few made it to the top. The training was hard. Barry did not keep a record of his daily activities at this time—in this regard he was much like his mentors. Cooper taught his students that practice was their daily account, and dissection the record of what they had learned about the body. This was physical, dynamic work, and the combination of the practical with the theoretical elements of the dressership meant that the young medics were practicing, studying, or partying. It was a life that lacked much time for reflection, and thus was perfect for Barry. One of Barry's contemporaries wrote to his brother to tell him of the daily rush of his activities as a pupil dresser:

> You are anxious to know what I do every hour, that to satisfy your enquiries, I must begin with the day, before I am out of my slippers. Well then, as soon as I am out of bed, and almost before I am awake, I go to the Midwifery Lecture; next I break my fast, and put on my boots, then to a lecture on Chemistry or Physic, till eleven, at this hour the business of the hospital commences and I go round with the dressers and assist them in holding the fractures, applying some bandages, and when any of them is absent I take his box and attend his patients . . . about one o'clock the business of the Hospital is finished, and soon after the Anatomical Lectures begin, this lasts till three, when our labours cease, and our appetites begin to crave for dinner, after which some little respite from business is proper, and pleasant conversation lulls until evening, when I look over some books, write down cases and observations, or employ myself agreeably, as I am now doing, in corresponding with a friend. I forgot to mention that on Saturday evening there is an assembly in the theatre at Guy's, to read and debate on a Medical paper; this a very agreeable amusement, and gives an opportunity for those who have confidence enough to display their abilities.

The anatomical lectures were delivered by Henry Cline, Jr., and Astley Cooper, who divided the course between them. The styles of the two teachers were radically divergent, but they shared a common purpose: to persuade their students of the need to develop a scientific outlook on surgery. Dissection stood at the heart of this scientific approach. Cooper had an ambition for notoriety, but he was a fearless surgeon and, "what was rarer in those days, a man who really knew all that was then known of the anatomy of the human body." He gave much time to comparative anatomy, and his preparations in St. Thomas's Anatomical Museum were still being used by students and surgeons long into the twentieth century.

Anatomy was the subject that most keenly interested practitioners and pupils. There were lectures on physic (medicine), chemistry, and midwifery at Guy's, and anatomy was taught at St. Thomas's. During Barry's time at Guy's, these were extramural lectures conducted by the surgeons, and they could be attended by pupils from other hospitals. Anatomical and surgical lectures were delivered in a narrow, cramped theater that was part of the dissecting room. The foul air and confined space made the theater a potentially fatal learning environment. Indeed, so hazardous was it that no one was allowed to use the theater without the direct permission of the hospital grand committee or treasurer. Such were the dangers of the dissection room, observes one commentator, "that many pupils were obliged to neglect that most essential part of professional instruction, practical dissection, lest they should thereby endanger their health and perhaps their existence." The young Barry, however, was not deterred by these fatal dangers. While fellow students sickened or avoided the dissection theater, their resistance to disease depleting as each session progressed, Barry's resilience was huge. He forged ahead, and here, as elsewhere in his career, remained remarkably healthy for someone exposed daily to the inferno of infection and contamination emanating from suppurating live patients and dead cadavers.

While Barry kept no personal diary of his time in London at Guy's and St. Thomas's, there was another young surgeon who trod the same path and maintained a record of his time as a pupil dresser. In October 1815, exactly three years after Barry signed the pupil register, a young medic named John Keats enrolled as a pupil dresser assigned to senior surgeon William Lucas. The diminutive Keats, like Barry, was a student of Astley Cooper—of whose inspiring lectures he kept copious notes—and Henry Cline, Jr., of whose dull lectures he did not. Cline's lectures lasted for an hour and a half and were delivered in what the weary student described as a "dreary monotone." Cooper's theatrical presentation held the student's attention, whether at his lectures on anatomy in the afternoon or his lectures on surgery in the evening.

Keats enrolled at Guy's and St. Thomas's with the serious intention of completing his training and embarking upon a medical career. But unlike Barry, who got to work with Cooper, Keats was less fortunate in being assigned to Dr. William Lucas. "Billy" Lucas had inherited his post from his father. Described as "a poor anatomist and not a very good diagnoser," he was a reasonable theoretician, but terrifyingly incompetent when it came to the practical requirements of wielding a knife. And wield it he did. His bungled operations always took longer than similar procedures conducted by any other surgeons. On one occasion his students begged him to desist from trying to complete an operation he had been laboring over for more than two and a half hours, fearing for the life of the patient. He was known to have mixed up limbs during amputation in several instances. One pupil dresser was aghast at the fact that Lucas, having turned away from the operating table to receive an instrument, was in a state of confusion when he turned back. Unable to remember on which limb he had intended to operate he walked around the table, inviting advice from any onlooker who might have a better recollection. His students were revolted, and he maintained the highest student drop-out rate among all the teaching surgeons. Those who lasted to the end generally failed their exams. When Keats sat in the window of his cramped rooms in Southwark and wrote "A thing of beauty is a joy forever," he was not referring to the skill and inspiration of his terrifyingly incapable tutor. The supreme ineptitude of Dr. Lucas probably played a part in Keats's decision to take up the pen rather than the knife.

Keats died of pulmonary tuberculosis in 1821 at the age of twenty-five. At the time of his death there was speculation that he had contracted the disease while a medical student. James Barry proved more resilient. It was while studying in London that Barry began to practice a code of self-care that kept him healthy throughout an ebulliently long life. The notion of gentlemanly behavior appropriate to a hard-working, hard-living trainee medic included rowdy after-hours relaxation. Drinking, smoking, drug-taking, whoring, and incessant profanity were central to the social self-development of the medical student. While Barry cursed along with the rest of them, he was a cautious drinker and apparently reticent about sex. Later in life he became well known as a virtual teetotaler—a form of abstinence rarely found in a medic. Barry was also vegetarian. Half a century before Florence Nightingale, he argued for the nutritious benefits of milk over meat. Stranger still by contemporary standards was his preoccupation with cleanliness and disinfection. What now seems common sense was then a set of principles that appeared willfully idiosyncratic. Barry's personal laws of health set him apart from his fellows far more, probably, than the way he looked.

Although there were students with lofty ideals, the all-male medical schools were boisterous playgrounds for exuberant and exhibitionist students who hung around in rowdy groups. Dickens famously described medical students as "young gentlemen who smoke in the streets by day, shout and scream in the same by night, call waiters by their Christian names, and do various other acts and deeds of a facetious description."

Barry's moderation when it came to drink, drugs, and heavy eating were in inverse proportion to his excessive addiction to clothes and fashionable society. As Dickens later wrote of Barry in his journal *All the Year Round,* he was "unique in appearance, and eccentric in manner." It was in London that Barry developed his eye for flamboyant dress and fine living. London was gripped by a "rage for fashion" during George IV's regency, according to William Hazlitt. A dizzying array of fops constituted their own sects, all competing to set new and increasingly outrageous fashions: bucks, bloods, blues, coxcombs, ruffians "on their mounts" vied with exquisites, fashionables, dashers, butterflies, and exclusives. Two main classes emerged to claim preeminence, "Hercules" and "Adonis." The intent of the Herculean was to "appear more manly than he was," while followers of Adonis desired to appear extremely effeminate. Influenced by the Napoleonic Wars, both sects were enslaved by military or semimilitary fashion. The contemporary French commentator Eusebe Arcieu claimed the unthinkable—that London had replaced Paris as the headquarters of fashion.

Summarizing the Adonis type, Arcieu described how many men "went to bed wearing oiled gloves to keep their hands white and soft . . . took baths of hot milk . . . [and] wore corsets and lorgnettes." Both Herculean and Adonis types "padded their coats at the sleeves and shoulders" and "adored cossack pantaloons that thickened their hips and legs." The Herculeans were particularly fond of endowing themselves with phony musculature. A man was judged as to how well he was endowed according to the shape of his calf. Hosiery shops did a roaring trade in prominently displayed devices for stocking padding and strap-on false calves, much to the annoyance of one gentleman's magazine: "How foolish of them to hang their padded stockings on their doors and windows, letting everyone in on the secret. A young man could hardly enter a drawing room without everyone looking at his legs to see if they were natural or false."

Whatever sect a man of fashion belonged to, the term *dandy* covered them all. By a strange quirk of history, James Barry and dandyism arrived in London simultaneously. When Barry signed the pupil register in 1813, *dandy* was beginning to insinuate itself into the English lexicon—or rather, to announce itself loudly with impenitent ill-taste and brash self-consciousness. By the end of the nineteenth century the word was to conjure images of sartorial elegance, modern flair, and urban sophistication. Yet as every Wildean knew, the origins of authentic dandyism lay in an intentional and monstrous affront to good taste. And in this visible affront was symbolized resistance to accepted moral values and the conventional upholstery of all well-fashioned polite society. "What a strange body a dandy has!" observed Lady Morgan, struck by the distinctive disfiguration of the body to which dandies aspired. As George Cruikshank illustrated in his caricatures of fashionable *Monstrosities,* early dandies presented a mode of flagrant irreverence and cockeyed stylishness. A visit to observe the dandies parading in packs in Hyde Park was on the itinerary of every tourist to London. One visitor marveled at the excessive starching of the dandies' "horse collars" as well as their jacket skirts and tails, describing them as "stiff as though lined with a sheet of iron." Dandies were the punks of Regency London. They called their tailors "man-makers," and in their eclectic view, clothes entirely made the man.

James Barry was captivated by the possibilities of this new fashion. But he was not alone. The medical students at Guy's and St. Thomas's were energetically style-conscious and competitive. Hampton Weekes advised a younger brother following his footsteps to St. Thomas's to pay attention to investing in the right wardrobe, and to make sure that his coat, waistcoat, and pantaloons were of the right style. Careful attention was to be paid to colors and cuts: "If the Dr orders a blue or black coat, and a pair of blue pantaloons, also a winter waistcoat or two that will wash well such as yellow kersemere with black stripe or orange ground instead of yellow, made shortish and not so long as he has had, it will do very well." Weekes warned his brother to "let Hessian boots alone" until he got to St. Thomas's Street, where he should "have a pair made directly he arrives" to ensure they would be of the most fashionable style. Knitted breeches, a suit, a hat, and laced ruffles were essential wear for the young pupil dressers. It was regulation to remove the hat "with the courtesy of a gentleman" when walking the wards. This was a theatrically pronounced formality of gesture that Barry—a great lover of hats—relished.

Beneath their hats the students wore daringly dyed and powdered hair. Wigs, like jackets without built-up shoulder pads, were increasingly regarded as stuffy and old-fashioned. Barry took assiduous care of his hair, which at this time he dyed red. His style was "short, brushed forward at the sides and falling in scattered waves" above his "high forehead." This flame of hair falling over "large, tender blue eyes" must have given Barry the look of a truly dandified Adonis. Powder for the hair was a current craze when Barry was at the United Hospitals, and students purchased "Bagg, Puff, Powder & Pomatum" in order to be appropriately coiffured to walk the wards. Striking a pose was equally studied by the dandies, who believed that presentation was all. After Barry's death it was recalled that "what struck most people" who knew him as remarkable was the manner in which he carried his arms, "with elbows *in* instead of outward." The poetics of this personal gesture were an essential element of the self-conscious Adonis repertoire.

Dandies indulged in an orgy of accessorizing, which fashion-conscious students aped with their own sartorial code. Students carried snuff-boxes and wore signet rings, lorgnettes, collar buckles, and breech buckles. They were also fastidious about shaving; to appear unshaven "would have been regarded as the act of an intolerable coxcomb, and resented as such." A smoothly shaven face was prized above all other signifiers of dandified, effete masculinity. A professional acquaintance, Colonel Wilson, recalled that Barry "had not a hair" on his face, "and never had."

Standing in a league of dandified professionalism all his own was Astley Cooper, one of the best-dressed men in London. London's most famous surgeon was also its greatest lover of silk stockings, kid breeches, and finely cut jackets. The students adored his seamless elegance, and never tired of telling how he would lift his shapely stockinged leg on to the lecture table in order to demonstrate the course of an artery during his classes.

Dandyism was the style of the parvenu. It suited the modern professional who wanted to demonstrate his indifference to convention. His was a new urbanity in the republican spirit of a postaristocratic age. While what Balzac dubbed the new "elegantology" challenged prerevolutionary hierarchies of social class and privilege, dandyism above all its offshoots played with conventions of gender.

This self-conscious reshaping of the body inverted the conventions dividing masculine from feminine dress. As women became more straightforward in their dress, young men became increasingly clothes-conscious. Arrayed in wasp-waisted padded frock coats reinforced with built-in stays, dandies increasingly resembled "featherbrained women." Contemporary journals were much preoccupied with this phenomenon of monstrous gender inversion:

Even as our ladies have usurped trousers, the sex that should remain masculine in everything has borrowed the feminine toilet, by wearing corsets, quilted stomachers, trousers as wide as petticoats and even trousers that are so similar to skirts that it is difficult to tell the difference.

Although the dandies delighted in the confusion produced by their high artifice, this problem with telling the difference reflects an undercurrent of anxiety in the society at large about the gender inversions sported by the dandies.

The chest and upper sleeves of Barry's dress and frock coats were stuffed with malleable wadding that reshaped the upper body. His day boots and evening shoes were worn with stacked heels, and his favorites were "dandified top boots with red heels," dyed to match his hair. Stays held up his sharply tailored jackets, and like every self-respecting dandy he employed the services of a stay-maker to shape his corsetry. He strove to realign the shape of his body through the artifice of his clothes. And in doing so he was conforming to the most avant-garde male fashion. He was an unusual, feminized "monstrosity"—and thus typical of the very apotheosis of male fashion of the time.

James Barry was examined and passed as a Regimental Surgeon on January 15, 1813, by the Royal College of Surgeons in London. In June 1813 he passed the army medical board examination, and on July 5 received his first commission as a hospital assistant, posted to the Plymouth garrison. The expense of being a pupil dresser at Guy's and St. Thomas's had forced Barry to complete his studies and gain the qualifications necessary to becoming a regimental surgeon as quickly as possible. It was a good career move. In the second decade of the nineteenth century, joining the military as a surgeon offered the almost certain opportunity of going to the colonies. Military medics got plenty of practice and—an important factor for the self-reliant Barry—quickly earned good money. It was also easier to penetrate high society in the smaller social worlds of the colonies.

There were other considerations as well. Barry's plan to join his beloved benefactor General Miranda could not be realized. Miranda

was still a political prisoner languishing in a cell in Cádiz. Ever the op-
timist, Miranda continued to plot his escape, and smuggled letters out
to England by bribing his jailers. Possibly one of these letters instructed
Barry that under the circumstances it was not possible for him to join
Miranda at this time. Barry continued to nurture his expectations that
he would ultimately be able to join Miranda as arranged, but in the interim he had to make other plans. A second related factor was the con-
tinuation of the Napoleonic Wars. Demand was high and supply short
for surgeons and doctors to serve the needs of the war. Years later, when
Napoleon was on St. Helena, Barry was recommended by the military
authorities to attend him. Napoleon died before Barry arrived, but although they were destined never to meet, the general's war had played
a key part in furthering Barry's professional career.

Barry's arrival at Plymouth was not without controversy. The staff
medical officer objected to receiving him on account of his curiously
"childish appearance." Luck—or some more mundane power—was
on Barry's side. When the medical officer raised the matter of Barry's
strange appearance with the authorities he was flatly advised that "it
was not desirable to agitate the question." It is possible that Buchan
had a hand in smoothing Barry's passage into this new appointment.
Dr. Skey, who was in charge of Plymouth General Hospital, had received a letter from Buchan recommending his protégé's abilities and
qualifications. In return, Buchan received a complimentary report on
Barry's performance from Skey in November. Buchan forwarded this
report to Dr. Anderson, Barry's former Edinburghian landlord, in a
letter that demonstrated his continuing interest and care for the young
medic:

> I send you a letter relating to poor James Barry which came to my
> hand a few days ago from Dr Skey of the General Hospital, Ply-
> mouth, to whom I had recommended him. Dr Skey's handwrit-
> ing is almost illegible but I make it out after a good deal of
> decyphering, and find that he found favour with his principal,

whom I intend to thank for his attentions and request the continuance of them.

"Poor" James Barry was in fact doing extremely well. As long as he held his course as a hospital assistant, he could expect to be promoted in two years. Most of his time during this period was spent in Plymouth, interrupted by a brief sojourn at the Chelsea barracks about which little is known. Always a lover of towns and cities, Barry would have welcomed the return to London, and especially the opportunity to attend regimental dinners at Chelsea. A portrait of Barry at this time was displayed in the barracks for a century after his death. In the picture he wears an elegantly tailored military jacket with a stiffly starched and intricately embroidered collar, so high it reaches over his earlobes. Barry looks out over the top of this face-framing collar, down the plane of his famously "long Ciceronian nose," fully resplendent in military dress. His hair is curly and full, swept back on top and forward at the sides. A single stray curl lies hooked on his forehead. Both of his eyes fix on the viewer with a direct, almost expressionless stare. Above one of them his eyebrow is, almost imperceptibly, arched.

Chapter 3

AN ABSOLUTE PHENOMENON

*The whole affair is opera bouffe—personally I always figured
to myself Barry springing up from the world, born of swords
and dragons' teeth and nothing more human.*

Réné Juta, *Cape Currey*

*The rarest qualities of Esculapian Talent . . . the most mischie-
vous propensities of a Monkey, and all the subtle wiles of the
Serpent.*

Josias Cloete on James Barry, personal papers

THE CAPE OF GOOD HOPE. EVEN ITS NAME SUGGESTS IT IS AS
mythical and fantastic as it is real and historical. Early European callers
at the Cape gave it this name in the "hope" of reaching the more lucrative markets of India and the Spice Islands. But the Cape of Good Hope
also had a darker, more foreboding aspect in the European imagination.
It was a liberating but also disturbing turning point for early voyagers, a
point where the limits of the old world of classical geography ended and
where a new world of modern seaborne travel and colonization began.
Treacherous to navigate, the Cape was also topped by the towering Table
Mountain, visible from miles out to sea. It is little wonder that Luís Vaz
de Camões immortalized the Cape in *The Lusiads,* his epic poem of the

rise of the Portuguese seaborne empire, first published in 1572. For Camões the Cape was transformed into the mythic figure Adamostor, one of the giants who for desperate love of the sea nymph Thetis unsuccessfully rebelled against the gods. Horrified by Adamostor's advances, Thetis tricked the unfortunate giant into embracing a rocky cliff. In a moment of terrifying Ovidian metamorphosis, Adamostor was transformed into the Cape itself, doomed to helplessly watch Thetis frolic in the sea, just beyond his reach. Tormented with frustration and anger, Adamostor became the Cape of Storms, a sign of hope but also a symbol of danger. This was the place of anticipation and danger at which James Barry arrived in August 1816.

The Cape is subject to natural as well as mythical forces. The Cape Doctor, the southeast wind, blows in the summer with a fierce intensity. But like the promontory itself, the Cape Doctor is a double-edged phenomenon. It dashes ships against the rocky coastline, but also brings fresh, cleansing winds that sweep the peninsula, a bracing inoculation against the potentially unhealthy aspects of the Cape climate. It is hot and sometimes devastating, an impish wind, slapping ankles, rising up swiftly and dying down with equal speed. The Cape Doctor is imperious, insistent, unflagging—or it blows gentle, sympathetic gusts, cooling the city and easing its inhabitants. Barry's legacy on the Cape has been likened to this wind. The letters he fired off with alarming frequency in his unrelenting campaign for medical reform were described as blowing like "icy blasts down the staid corridors of the Colonial Secretary's office." Barry was the first and most influential colonial doctor of his kind at the Cape. His twelve years there were a tempest—personally, politically, and professionally.

The Cape—the Halfway House of the World, the Tavern of the Oceans, the Cape of Storms—was a place of momentous rites of passage for James Barry. He fell truly in love for the first time. He became the leading civil and military doctor at the Cape and a radical, tireless social and medical reformer whose influence is remembered to this day. He experienced slavery, racism, and colonization, all of which deeply fashioned his views on social justice and humanitarianism. This was his first taste of Africa, his first encounter with different people, different cultures, and exotic wildlife. It was a place both strange in its difference and recognizably familiar in the Europeanness of its colonial culture.

Barry was about twenty-five when he arrived, in August 1816. His name first appears in Cape records as a hospital assistant. As a military officer, he was entitled to accommodation at the adamantine Cape Castle built by the original Dutch settlers. It was in this hexagonal fortress that the Cape colony had been handed over to General David Baird in January 1806. This formalized British possession of the Cape, which would last until January 1910, when, in the same place, the castle keys changed hands for the last time and the British imperial authorities handed them over to the Union of South Africa. When Barry arrived, Cape Town was bustling with a diversity of peoples whose cultural mix bore rich testimony to the pathways of nations who had found their ways to these shores. The colony had changed hands among the Portuguese, the French, the Dutch, and—twice—the British, to whom the French had finally handed over the colony in January 1806. By the time Barry arrived, many of the colony's Cape Malay inhabitants, transported as slaves from Malaysia, had been given or bought their freedom, and a honeycomb of mosques and brightly painted houses formed geometric patterns on the foothills of Table Mountain.

When Barry arrived at the Cape, it was not the lush, verdant place it is today but a tough, wild frontier settlement on the periphery of the British empire. It seems that Barry was eager to move out of his barracks quarters at the castle, as he soon relocated himself in more comfortable lodgings at 12 Heerengracht, where he was a tenant of the Widow Hercules Sandenberg. The Heerengracht was the hub of the colonial quarter of Cape Town, the main thoroughfare, through which ran open sewers. Small bridges crossed the "Gracht." Each side was lined with fashionable lodging houses, coffeehouses, apothecaries, and official buildings.

Barry's first priority was to establish the perimeters of responsibility for his new appointment, but he was equally anxious to ensure an early audience with the governor. Lord Charles Somerset, who had assumed the governorship of the Cape in May 1814, was the only governor of the colony who originated from the aristocracy rather than the gentry. The second son of the fifth duke of Beaufort, he came from a royal, and limitlessly wealthy, family. Through favor and purchase he had risen through the ranks of the military, and finally, favored by George III, he was promoted to major-general. In 1796, Lord Charles went to Parliament to represent Scarborough. He was made comptroller of the king's household and a member of the Privy Chamber. He also held office at court, and as Gentleman of the Bedchamber to the Prince of Wales had shared his passion for "horses and turf" with his royal employer. Somerset's name was put forward for the Cape in 1813 when Sir John Cradock asked to be relieved of his appointment. Mounting gambling debts meant that Somerset needed desperately the considerable salary of ten thousand pounds per year. The Prince Regent announced his appointment and he embarked for the Cape in December 1813. Lord Charles was a complex character:

> He was an eighteenth-century viceroy in a nineteenth-century governorship. He too showed, along with the traditional arrogance of his class, an outlook softened by the ideals of the Enlightenment. He did more than any previous Governor to ameliorate the condition of the slaves at the Cape and to prepare for emancipation, which came six years after his governorship ended.

Yet Somerset's benevolence was circumscribed by his autocratic, undemocratic approach to leadership and his ignorance of the territories over which he held political sway: "It was . . . the time when the distant and unknown interior of South Africa experienced some of the most momentous events in all African history, events which barely penetrated the consciousness of Lord Charles Somerset."

Barry arrived at the Cape with a letter of introduction from Lord Buchan to Somerset. He had carried this letter with sedulous care on the passage from England. Cut adrift from the anchors of blood, family, and entitlement, Barry set great store by documents of recommendation, certificates, registrations, letters of appointment, and professional awards. He regarded as talismans the pieces of paper that confirmed his qualifications and institutional status. They were his collateral in a world where he lacked the sanction of blood ties.

No doubt Buchan had counseled Barry on the wisdom of securing his connections as soon as possible. The letter is missing from Somerset's official correspondence, but Buchan's recommendation must have struck the right note, for Barry soon found himself invited to Government House to be introduced to the governor. It was an auspicious start for someone who was a relatively junior appointment. It was Buchan's enthusiastic endorsement and Barry's reputation in London as something of a prodigy that secured him Somerset's attention, not his status as a military hospital assistant.

There is no record of the first meeting between James Barry and Lord Charles Somerset, but they were to become the most infamous couple at the Cape. What did the aristocrat and the young officer see in each other that so galvanized their rapid intimacy and their apparent disregard for local gossip and murmurs in political corridors regarding the impropriety of their relationship? Lord Charles, the florid, energetic, but laconic aristocrat and career politician, Barry, the dandified, effete, intellectual doctor. Barry blew into town full of knowledge useful to a young colony. He was coquettish, opinionated, and full of acerbic wit. He exuded certainty and a bias for action. His idiosyncracies would have appealed to Lord Charles. Like Somerset, Barry enjoyed horseback riding and parties. In political matters the governor was an inflexible autocrat, but he indulged his family and friends, and was passionate about his animals. Very quickly, he was drawn to the unconventional, intelligent, and outré Barry.

Somerset was to Barry a remote and romantic figure. A commission had been purchased for him and two more secured by the time he was twenty. The Beauforts claimed direct descent from the Plantagenets, and combined enormous wealth with social and political power. Somerset was a contentious politician and ostentatious aristocrat. He was no stranger to controversy. In his youth, he had scandalized the aristocracy with his recklessness in affairs of the heart. Ignoring the forceful opposition of his father, Charles Henry had courted the honorable Elizabeth Courtenay, the beautiful but financially insecure daughter of viscount Courtenay of Powderham Castle. In line with three brothers and nine other sisters, Elizabeth had no fortune. In May 1788 the *Caledonian Mercury* gleefully reported a court scandal:

> Lord Charles Somerset, youngest son of the Duke of Beaufort, from Lord Hopetown's masquerade, eloped with the third daughter of Lord Courtenay, and on Wednesday evening they passed through Newcastle on their route to Scotland. His Lordship has yet not attained his twentieth year, and the Lady is scarcely turned of sixteen.

Still in their party attire, Charles and Elizabeth sped away from the masquerade in a post chaise bound for Gretna Green, where they immediately married. The *London Morning Post* reported that the "elopement with Miss Courtenay has occasioned much noise in the fashionable world and mutual discontent in both families."

The love match stood the test of time. Somerset was deeply affected when Elizabeth died at the Cape in 1815, having never properly recovered from an illness contracted on their voyage out the previous year. Writing to his brother he described his distress at the loss:

> Thank God she died without the slightest pain, and went off in a sort of stupor in which she had been upwards of two days. My mind is as yet scarcely composed enough to view the Magnitude of the Calamity that has befallen me—the more I think the more

weighty it appears, and if I look back to the Happiness which her
attachment and affection for me have afforded me I am in a state
almost of Destruction and Despair.

When Barry arrived in the Cape in 1816, Somerset was a bitterly grieving widower. He simmered with barely repressed anger at his household doctor, the head physician of the colony, who had disastrously
misdiagnosed Lady Somerset's symptoms and only a few days prior to
her death assured her anxious husband that "there was not the slightest
cause for apprehension." Not only had Somerset lost the love of his
life, he was also on the lookout for a more competent replacement for
his failed physician.

Although Somerset carried the assumption of his birthright, status,
and class with an inflexible hauteur, he could be genial and humorous,
and, as one historian recently observed, "Autocrat though he was, he
nevertheless was gifted with a strong sense of grace and kindness." Lord
Charles was confident in his sexuality, and brimful of physical energy
and exertion. Ruddy, energetic, and boyish with family and friends, he
loved all forms of hunting, dancing, and theater. Arch and expansive, he
enjoyed teasing his daughters and their many suitors, as well as his employees and servants. He was in short an aristocrat of the pre-Victorian
age; a louche Romantic, maintaining a precarious balance between dis-
solution and dedication. He was also the most powerful person in the
colony, commanding respect from his immediate employees, even
among the younger members of his entourage who disagreed with his
conservative stand on political issues. Barry was irresistibly drawn to
the forty-nine-year-old Lord Charles. He offered entertainment, social
advancement, political protection, and—crucially—adventure and fun.
Somerset was an outdoor type, while Barry had spent his youth and
student years in gray northern cities; in Cape Town he was out in the
open, and this was his first opportunity to stretch his legs and engage in
physical pursuits. Somerset shared key characteristics with Barry's
mentors. Miranda, Buchan, and Astley Cooper were all larger-than-

life personalities who enjoyed great freedom of movement and physical and intellectual expression of their passions.

The failure of Somerset's physician was to Barry's advantage, fueling the governor's impatient curiosity to meet and appraise the skills of the young doctor who came with such glowing recommendations from the educated and worldly-wise Lord Buchan. Somerset seems to have taken an instant liking to Barry. His rakish insouciance was effervescent and appealing. There he was fresh out of medical school, witty, amusing, intelligent, inquisitive, charming, and evidently eager to please. James Barry must have seemed one of the more curious creatures to arrive at the Cape. Crisp in his new military uniform, full of energy and eager to prove himself in his new role, he also had an air of missionary zeal about him. He was proud of his Edinburgh education and training, and keen to show off his knowledge. His outward showiness and flamboyant dress were consolidated by a sharp and uncompromising wit and by quickly discernible professional abilities. Barry had learned sound professional skills from Cooper, but—ever the watcher—he had also learned much from observation of how Cooper operated and seen that part of his success lay in his appearance of unhesitating decisiveness. Even in life-and-death situations Cooper exuded certainty. Barry understood and mimicked Cooper's strategy, and found his confidence inspired certainty in others—most particularly in his patients.

Barry's dress was exaggerated, but it needs to be remembered that all military dress for officers was calculated to distinguish and set its wearer apart. After the fashions of the time, Barry took the conventions of military dress and overstated them with a dandy's embellishment. Barry's boots were thigh height; his breeches were worn uncompromisingly tight on the thighs; his jackets were long bodied, high collared, and finely structured to encourage a striking deportment; and his dress sword was worn long enough to trip over. Nevertheless, as a member of a military elite Barry stood out at the Cape with his metropolitan air. Beneath this finery Barry was lithe and agile, and his quick, decisive movements gave him the elemental aura of quickfire and fast-moving water. He was a chimera. Conventional and insistent on propriety in social manners, he was wildly insubordinate and argumentative in matters of principle and political difference.

Reports of Barry's voice are contradictory: some posthumous memorialists insist on its unmistakably high, thin pitch, but others remark on its resonance and flat, uninflected masculine certainty. Nonetheless, Barry's voice was the vehicle of his physical presence. Its projection and penetration compensated for his medium height, making him seem bigger than he actually was.

The gossip about Barry's appearance is always full of redness—his hair, his uniform coat, his "top-boots with red heels." These crimson codes owe more to the fact that Barry made many people see red than to the assertion that it was a color he wore. They recall a Barry who was fiery-tempered, quick with argument and wounding wit. In fact, Barry's favorite colors during this period were on the spectrum of blues, greens, and yellows. The pea-green satin dress breeches he wore to balls and dances were much in keeping with his image as a supple young blade, and his kinked hair, which he was ever pushing back from his forehead, crowned the whole. Barry's curly hair stood high on his forehead, bristling with light and his own animation. His hair was now a sandy blond. It seems that the myth that Barry still dyed his hair red derives from the fact that his dress wig was a showy, fiery red. (Wigs were still in fashion and required for official functions and social celebrations.)

Somerset was thus presented with the unexpected when he first met the new hospital assistant who was preceded by such august written recommendations. Buchan's letter was an advance messenger of Barry's intellectual brilliance and professional potential. It is likely that Somerset had not expected these talents to be embodied in the person of the appealing dandy who presented himself at the governor's residence. Barry was one of a new breed of ambitious, professional modern medics who were redefining the role of the doctor in society. Men like William and John Hunter and Astley Cooper inspired their students to, quite literally, dig deeper into the bowels of human anatomy while presenting themselves in the mold of the romantic, progressive gentleman scientist.

Since 1815, Somerset's two daughters had acted as the hostesses of Government House. Whether or not they were present at the formal introduction of Barry to Somerset we cannot know, but it is certain that it was not long before they met. Barry's early popularity at Government House may have owed something to the curiosity of these two young women. Barry was a bright new star in the rather dusty constellation of beaux and state functionaries who passed through the Cape. There has been some speculation about a romantic relationship between Barry and the governor's eldest daughter, Georgina Somerset, but there is no evidence to support this idea.

The colonial bourgeoisie must have looked on perplexed as Barry swiftly become Somerset's pet. Within a few short months, the governor had taken command of Barry's heart and admiration. Did Barry know that he loved Somerset? In these years he was mesmerized, ardent, unstintingly loyal. In return, Somerset made sure that no door was closed to Barry, and not only appointed him an official member of his household retinue but made him a resident of his home too.

Having received Somerset's sanction and blessing, Barry found himself quickly absorbed into the upper echelons of the city. In addition to his responsibilities at military occasions, he was placed on the invitation list of the notables of Cape Town society. Barry was seen in the governor's party at civil dinners, balls, masquerades, hunting parties, and—most particularly—at Cape Town's English theater. An avid theatergoer, Somerset kept a box at this theater, where Shakespeare, farces, comedies, and tragedies were performed, "as long as the army was numerous enough to furnish officer actors." Just as in other areas of Cape colonial society there was an acute shortage of women, so were there few women in the colony willing to put themselves forward as actresses, for fear of the accusations of sexual impropriety that inevitably surrounded the assumption of such a role. Occasionally, a couple of actresses on their way to Calcutta would stop and perform for a season, but more often the

English-speaking audiences of Cape Town were dependent on the rudimentary services of cross-dressed military volunteers. During a particularly thin season, the colonial secretary, Colonel Bird, despaired of the fact that there were only army volunteers available to play the petticoat parts:

> Of late there has been no performance; for although many actors remain, who can endure a raw-boned fellow of six feet high performing the part of Juliet or Lady Teazle? And there are here at present no English females who have confidence enough to tread the boards. Nothing is so disgusting as the public exhibition of a man in petticoats, acting a female part in a love scene. It is not so with the other sex. When an actress assumes the character of Sir Harry Wildair, although at the first entrance the fan sticks may be raised before the face, they are soon dropt. Curiosity, accompanied by admiration, is gratified at seeing a female of elegant symmetry and form, act with spirit and effect, the part of one of the lords of the creation.

As Somerset's patronage opened the most salubrious doors of colonial society to Barry, he became an avid socializer. Barry particularly loved social rituals and the opportunity they provided to dress up. There were dances at private houses, "subscription assemblies" at the Society House during winter, and the regimental balls. Barry attended them all. His dress at such events was studiedly ostentatious. His favorite outfit was "a coat of the latest pea-green Hayne, a satin waistcoat, and a pair of tight-fitting 'inexpressibles.'" Gossip followed Barry's flamboyant appearance at these dances: "It was also noted that Dr Barry flirted with all the best looking women in the room." Barry's popularity with women earned him the enmity of many of the less socially adroit men on the social circuit, who muttered with irritation, claiming they were unable to see what their wives and daughters saw in this fey peacock. Barry made an impression on all who met him. A woman who met Barry at a military ball during this period described him to her granddaughter as "a perfect dancer who won his way to many a heart with impeccable bedroom manners. In fact he was a flirt—I expect this was one of the many affectations designed to avert suspicion. He had a winning way with women . . . and his beautiful small white hands were the envy of many a lady of that date." Lord Albemarle recollected sitting next to Barry at a regimental dinner at the Cape in 1819. He described him as "in appearance a beardless lad with an unmistakable Scotch type of countenance, with reddish hair and high cheekbones. There was a certain effeminacy in his manner which he was always striving to overcome. . . . His style of conversation was greatly superior to that usually heard at a mess-table." Albermarle concluded that he was the "most skilful of physicians and most wayward of men."

ASIDE FROM THE HIGH-SOCIETY FUNCTIONS, THERE WERE ALSO the hugely popular and often controversial dances known as the "rainbow balls." Colonel Bird explained the name:

> Whilst the public and private balls of the upper classes are going on there are continual dances amongst the other orders, denominated rainbow balls, composed of each different hue in this many coloured town. The females are chiefly slave girls of the first class, and girls who have acquired their freedom; and amongst the men are seen officers, merchants and young Dutchmen. It cannot be pretended that these meetings add to the morals of the town.

It seems that it was at one of these rowdy rainbow balls that Barry met Sanna, one of the Cape slaves whose freedom he is said to have purchased. Barry must have cut a curious figure in his green britches and yellow-lined coat. Sanna's identity, though, was even more likely to draw curious looks: strikingly attired at the ball in the brightly colored skirts of a "slave girl," Sanna was well known to be a hermaphrodite.

Barry's impact on Cape society was not only felt in its social circles. Lord Charles clearly recognized Barry's professional potential as well. He did not just promote him to bedsides and banquets, but precipitated his involvement in the very heart of colonial politics. From the very outset, Barry was entrusted with politically sensitive missions. In January 1817 Somerset allowed him an influential role in handling a tricky political prisoner, Count Emmanuel de Las Casas.

Las Casas had been appointed Napoleon's chamberlain in 1809, and then became a member of the French state council. Napoleon's most favored and loyal companion, he had accompanied him into exile on the windswept rock of St. Helena. Napoleon was supported and cared for by four key attendants on the lonely granite island, each of whom produced his own gospel of the emperor's life, composed during his captivity on St. Helena. Las Casas's obsequious loyalty to Napoleon had earned him the nicknames of "Ecstasy," "The Cockroach," and—for his ability in justifying Napoleon's behavior—"The Jesuit." "Ecstasy" shared rooms adjacent to the emperor's damp chambers at Longwood with his teenage son, also called Emmanuel. The young Emmanuel acted as his father's secretary, laboriously transcribing his father's interviews with Napoleon recording his life and career. Caught trying to smuggle letters to Napoleon's supporters in England in his clothing on a return trip to France, Las Casas, along with his son, was detained as a prisoner at the castle in Cape Town.

The seventeen-year-old Emmanuel was ill, and on January 20, 1817, a captain from the station at St. Helena brought Barry to the castle to examine him. Barry found that the teenager was suffering from lack of proper air, food, and exercise, and nervous exhaustion, no doubt engendered by the burden of poring over Napoleon's endless stream of consciousness (the Las Casas *Mémorial* of the conversations ran to some eight volumes when published). Having confirmed that there was no disease, Barry prescribed hot baths and salts. This, however, was not all. Barry seemed particularly concerned for the plight of the motherless and overburdened Emmanuel, and he left the castle after his first visit formulating a plan to better assist the health of the languishing youth and his distressed father.

Las Casas was intrigued by the encounter, which he recorded in his Napoleonic gospel, *Mémorial de Sainte Hélène: Journal of the Private Life and Conversations of the Emperor Napoleon at Saint Helena:*

> Knowing the state of my son's health, he [the captain from the station at St. Helena] brought a medical gentleman along with him. This was a mark of attention on his part, but the introduction occasioned for some moments a curious misunderstanding—I mistook the Captain's Medical friend for his son or nephew. The poor Dr who was presented to me was a boy of 18—with the form—the manners and the voice of a woman—But Mr Barry (such was his name) was described to be an absolute phenomenon!
>
> I was informed that he had obtained his diploma at the age of 13 after the most rigid examination—that he had performed extraordinary cures at the Cape and had saved the life of one of the Governor's daughters after she had been given up which rendered him a sort of favourite in the family. I profited by this latter circumstance to obtain some information which might serve as a guide for my conduct with respect to the new Governor—to whom that day I addressed a letter.

Las Casas's *Mémorial* was published shortly afterward, in 1823. Its significance cannot be overestimated. Following Barry's death, endless memoirs were published in which people remarked on Barry's strangely androgynous or effeminate appearance. Yet these were all published with the benefit of hindsight, after his death in 1865. Each account borrowed from another, until it was clear that people's "memoirs" were a compound of what they had read about Barry, not what they actually remembered.

Las Casas's *Mémorial* is the only account expressing suspicion about

Barry's appearance to have been published during his lifetime. In his reference to Barry saving the life of one of the governor's daughters, Las Casas reveals that his diary was written up some time after his imprisonment at the Cape, as it refers to an episode that was not to take place until later in 1820. Nevertheless, the fact that Las Casas took the trouble to update Barry's activities indicates the continued interest he took in his career.

Whatever Las Casas suspected about Barry's unusual appearance, he kept his conclusions to himself. This was the first of several meetings between the two, and Las Casas seems to have considered the confusion his own error. A mutual interest between the Bonapartist and the doctor developed, Las Casas confessing to his journal that "The only stranger I saw was Dr Barry, who frequently visited me. I found his company very agreeable." In a very short space of time, he was depending on Barry for amelioration of his circumstances, and even encouraging him to exert his evident positive influence over Emmanuel. He clearly understood Barry's abilities and political influence with Somerset. Given Barry's progressive republican background, it is possible that he harbored Bonapartist sympathies. Certainly there were indications that he may have been sailing closer to the wind than Somerset realized. J. M. Howell, a contemporary journalist, recalled having met at Barry's own lodgings "the celebrated Dr O'Meara, author of *Napoleon in Exile*, and two French noblemen belonging to the suite of Buonaparte—if I remember right one was Count Bertrand." Howell's letter throws light on the fact that Barry's interests may have been political as well as medical.

General Miranda had admired Bonaparte, and this alone would have earned Barry's empathy and support for Las Casas's plight. In turn, the ever-sensitive Barry must have been persuaded by Las Casas's courtesy and recovery of composure from his initial bewilderment on meeting him. We must imagine that Barry had to face down this kind of hesitation, the look of confusion or suspicion in people's eyes, throughout his life. During his time at the Cape he was learning how to grapple with this; most often, he gave offense or parried with wit to block and obscure further curiosity. His quick temper and deliberately flamboyant behavior were ruses, to deflect the eye and attention of the beholder, to subtly focus their attention on something other than his own physical person.

There is a further, elegiac reason why Barry may have taken such a solicitous interest in the count and his son. It was less than a year since his adored Miranda had died in prison. This had been a deep shock to Barry, who had expected to be standing by the side of the first leader of free Venezuela.

Emmanuel was offered safe passage back to England but refused, insisting on standing firm by his father. Las Casas asked Barry to persuade the boy to depart, for his own good. Barry, however, took the boy's part, as Las Casas records in his journal: "But instead of listening to me, he hastened to Emmanuel's chamber, and embracing him, expressed his approval of his conduct, observing that he should not have respected him had he acted otherwise." Barry then did something both playful and considerate of the needs of a young teenager starved of the company of his peers. He took Emmanuel to the window of his cell and called down to two glamorous young society women seated in the coach below:

> Conducting him to the window he introduced him to two ladies whom he had left in their carriage and mutual salutations passed between them. These ladies were the daughters of Lord C Somerset, who had this morning themselves brought the Dr as far as the court-yard fronting our prison.

It was a generous gesture, designed to improve the spirits of the sequestered Emmanuel. Barry clearly felt that most of the teenage boy's ailments were the result of the circumscribed conditions he lived under. On St. Helena he had shared damp, unwholesome apartments with his father, and the castle too was designed to be damp and inhospitable. It was also a clever move calculated to secure the curiosity and pity of the Somerset daughters, whose opinions on social matters and propriety held much sway in their father's household. Barry wanted to persuade Somerset to allow the count and Emmanuel to be transferred to house arrest at Newlands, the governor's airy Palladian villa outside Cape Town. The apartments were spacious, the landscaped gardens shaded by oaks and bright with English-style flowerbeds, and there was a bountiful vegetable garden. Barry was successful in his petition, and Somerset agreed to Las Casas and his son being moved to Newlands. The small wave at the window was a passing act of kindness, but Barry demonstrated also a politician's knack of understanding how social etiquette could be turned to strategic advantage.

Las Casas owned that Barry had been politically helpful to him in making his advances to the Governor. It is highly likely that Somerset sent Barry as his deputy to mediate with the French prisoner—it was a delicate and potentially embarrassing situation. That Somerset was fully aware of Barry's activities is shown in his reassurance to Earl Bathurst that Las Casas was being properly looked after: "I furnish him [Las Casas] with the best medical attention. Dr Barry (who attends my own family) has constantly prescribed for him." This letter clearly indicates the speed with which Barry had found favor with Somerset, and that although the post would not be formalized until December 1817, Barry was already acting as the Somerset household doctor. A mere four months after his arrival, Barry had become a preferred member of the Somerset entourage.

When Napoleon fell ill in February 1821, it was suggested by the governors of St. Helena and the Cape that Barry should attend him. Doubtless Las Casas supported these recommendations. It may also have been around this time that Las Casas heard the story of Barry's success in restoring Georgina Somerset to health. Preliminary plans were made for Barry's departure for St. Helena, but Napoleon died before Barry could leave. Napoleon's death had a negative impact on the Cape economy, which had benefited from the additional demand for livestock, foodstuffs, and, most particularly, the large volumes of Cape claret created by Napoleon's incarceration on the island. Had Napoleon and Barry met, they would have had in common their mutual connection with and admiration for Francisco Miranda, whom Napoleon had described as the "Don Quixote with the difference" and the general with "the sacred fire burning in his soul."

At the beginning of 1817, Barry was invited to join the governor's party on a sensitive mission to the eastern frontier. The Somerset administration was anxious about the instability of the eastern border of the Cape Colony, whose frontier was the Great Fish River. Despite the string of armed forts placed along its western bank, bands of Xhosa had been regularly crossing the Fish and carrying out cattle raids on settler stock. Due to deepening drought, there was an alarming increase in the number of these raids, which frightened the sparse population of settler farmers. Somerset was also concerned about the military deserters and Khoikhoi farm laborers and slaves fleeing into Xhosa territories, where in exchange for guns, ammunition, or military expertise they were given wives and cattle and welcomed into the community. The Xhosa chief Ngqika had already formed an alliance with the colonial government, but in the view of the crown was failing to enforce his commitments. Most suspected he was the chief beneficiary of most of the cattle thieving. The object of Somerset's bush summit with Ngqika was to make him "fully responsible for all these problems." As well as securing the political will of Ngqika to prevent further incursions, the British also planned to make a show of military strength to intimidate the Xhosa and bolster the morale of the weary, ill-equipped, and besieged settlers who were packing up and leaving the hostile eastern frontier in steadily increasing numbers.

The party departed from Cape Town on January 27, 1817. It included Somerset, Colonial Secretary Colonel Bird, Colonial Paymaster Captain Tom Sheridan (the eldest son of the dramatist), Somerset's daughters, Georgina and Charlotte, and Barry. Somerset's daughters had acted as hostesses at Government House and for official functions, and they accompanied the party to perform this function at Knysna, where they were to be entertained by the legendary landowner George Rex. It was "the largest and most impressive British viceregal mission yet to travel inland to the frontier." The party traveled in heavy ox-wagons and on horseback, and were supported by a large retinue of guides, servants, and trackers. These servants were overloaded with the comforts that Somerset insisted on for the journey, as well as his hunting equipment. "Lord Charles Somerset's two vices were horseracing and swearing, in which he was aped by younger men of the colony," declared Senator Munnik, a merchant and politician. Somerset was indeed an avid huntsman. He had imported a pack of hounds from England and hunted on the sandy Cape Flats, with "the Cape jackal doing service as the little red fox." His favorite run on the Eerste River was known for many years as the Fox and the Hounds. He retreated from affairs of state to the Round House, his hunting lodge, to shoot lion and leopard in the foothills of Table Mountain.

The journey to the eastern frontier followed a magnificent route along the southern coast of Africa, passing through lush vegetation, dramatic canyons, and lagoons trimmed with white sand. Elephants, rhinos, buck, exotic birds, and vultures were encountered by day; jackals prowled at night. Four months after his arrival in Africa, Barry was on a trek. It was utterly unlike anything he had previously experienced. The splendor of the landscapes and unfamiliarity of the large wildlife and game must have been overawing. Hitherto, the only examples of these animals that he had seen had been in William Hunter's specimen jars at the Royal College of Surgeons. Knowing his later interest in botany, we can surmise that Barry was also fascinated by the abundance of unfamiliar flora he encountered.

Despite the thrill of the wildlife and dramatic landscape, this journey was an unimaginably hard undertaking. The trip lasted for three months, and covered more than five hundred miles of rough tracks that were more rock than road. The circuitous route required passing through mountain barriers and crossing swift-flowing rivers. Wagons frequently slipped backward down riverbanks, and axles shattered on the steep slopes of the rocky mountains. All of this was undertaken at the height of the summer in the punishing January heat.

The party must have been relieved to arrive at the flamingo-filled lagoons of Knysna, a British coastal settlement three hundred miles from Cape Town where they were the guests of George Rex. Rumored to be the illegitimate son of George III and Hannah Lightfoot, Rex lived like a contemporary Virginia planter, on a rolling twenty-five-thousand-acre estate on which toiled over a hundred slaves. He entertained the governor and his party with sumptuous grand dinners in his fine manor house, Melkhout Kraal, arranging hunting parties, fishing, and shooting for Somerset. Colonial Knysna was a shimmering oasis of faux Englishness transplanted to the Cape, in that exaggerated colonial style that was more English than England. George Rex had eight children at this time, the older of whom later recalled that Barry gave them lessons on various subjects during his stay. He also followed up on their progress before he left the Cape. As in the case of Emmanuel Las Casas, Barry paid particular attention to the needs of the children.

Leaving behind Knysna, and Somerset's daughters, the group embarked on the more serious work of its mission. As they passed through to the frontier, the viceregal party were joined by "100 dragoons, detachments from British infantry regiments as well as the Khoikhoi manned Cape Regiment, field artillery and an armed commando of 350 Boers." The two key frontier officials were present: Andries Stockenstrom, the landdrost (magistrate) from Graaff Reinet (whose wife would later become Barry's patient), and the commander at Grahamstown, Major George Fraser. The agreed meeting place was on the Kat River. The governor encamped in an imposing marquee and the troops were deployed around it. Bird describes in his journals how the "troops and burghers were drawn up and formed 3 sides of a square, with two small cannons placed on the right and left. In the centre was the Governor's marquee." Ngqika was intimidated and displeased by the show of strength. Fearing that the meeting was a trap set to capture them, the Xhosa chiefs were reluctant to meet with Somerset and his deputations. It took a fortnight of persuasion to induce Ngqika and his government to come. Finally, on April 2, 1817, Ngqika arrived with his uncle, a group of other chiefs, and a guard of about three hundred warriors armed with assegais:

> Cuyler and Stockenstrom then took Ngqika and Ndlambe by the arm each and, supporting them, brought them forward to the large white marquee where Somerset sat between two pieces of field artillery. Somerset, Bird and Dr Barry rose and advanced to meet the chiefs, and escorted them back to the marquee, where mats had been spread.

The ceremonial formalities complete, Somerset moved swiftly to political bargaining; a system for protection for the colonists' cattle was agreed on, as was a plan for establishing a series of military posts to police the frontier. Somerset insisted that Ngqika take responsibility for stopping the cattle raids. Exchange and barter took place involving all parties. Somerset's gifts included a gray horse for Ngqika and a sack of tawdry presents for the other chiefs: shoes, handkerchiefs, shawls, buttons, knives, beads, mirrors, and tinder boxes. The proceedings were carried out in a multilingual dialogue of Xhosa, Dutch, and English. Only the Xhosa Dyani Tshatshu, assistant to the missionary Joseph Williams, was able to speak all three languages, and thus was the only participant who fully understood the outcome of the proceedings. Somerset believed he had established a binding treaty. However, as Ngqika— already an unpopular leader with his own people—tried to explain, he was not empowered to represent the Xhosa nation:

> We do not do things as you do them; you have but one chief, but with us it is not so. . . . Although I am a great man and king of the other Xhosa, still every chief rules and governs his own people.

The outcome of Somerset's mission was of enormous significance to the future repression of the Xhosa and colonial justification for stealing their land and cattle. Somerset announced that the English would establish patrols to track livestock losses, creating an excuse for strengthening the British military presence along the eastern frontier. Most ominously, the patrol system became a notorious strategy for legitimating colonial surveillance, disruption, and reprisals against the Xhosa people. When Somerset and Ngqika met again a few years later, it was as enemies in outright war. This meeting was a part of a much longer process that led ultimately to the Xhosa being dispossessed of the land that was rightfully theirs.

The party arrived back in Cape Town on April 21, 1817. For three months, Lord Charles and James Barry had been daily in each other's company in the unknown African wilderness. They had not been thrown together merely by chance. Barry served a practical role on the trip, but it was Somerset's decision to bring him into the absolute center of the operations along with the other dignitaries. At times they had bivouacked under the lustrous constellations of the southern skies, and sat together by campfires stacked against the unfamiliarity of the African night. For all its discomfort and danger, the trip held out an inescapable element of romance for Barry. Thomas Pringle, the poet later to become one of Somerset's most articulate political critics, described the landscape of the eastern frontier from the perspective of a new arrival thus:

> We continued gazing at the scene long after sunset, till . . . the constellation of the southern hemisphere, revolving in cloudless brilliancy above, reminded us that nearly half the globe's expanse intervened between us and our native land . . . and that here, in this farthest nook of southern Africa, we were now about to receive the portion of our inheritance, and to draw an irrevocable lot for ourselves, and for our children's children . . . and we now waited with anxiety for the curtain to draw up and unfold . . . the

scenes of novelty and adventure to which we had so long looked forward.

The distance of "half the globe's expanse" intervening between southern Africa and England was also the distance of convention and social constraint. Even the physical practicalities of Somerset's and Barry's lives on this expedition stripped back some of the conventions of their more mannered existence at Cape Town. They returned to the city with a renewed intimacy that, although frequently challenged, remained unbroken for nine years.

Following their return, Somerset was assiduous in his recommendations of Barry. To the ailing Andries Stockenstrom of Graaf Reinet, he wrote, "to entreat that you will not trifle with yourself but that you will repair to Cape Town without delay to have the advantage of Dr Barry's very extraordinary skill." To Sir Hudson Lowe, the governor of St. Helena, whose wife was ill, Somerset wrote to encourage him to send her to the Cape, where she would benefit from the climate and, he went on, "I have besides here, quite a prodigy as a physician, a Doctor Barry, whose skill has attested wonders since he has been here. Indeed it would be well worthwhile for an invalid to come here solely for the purpose of obtaining his advice." Given the circumstances of the demise of his beloved Elizabeth, Somerset's recommendation of Barry to a husband concerned about the health of his wife was great confidence indeed. Barry was also recommended to passing senior officers requiring medical treatment. On his way back from China at the end of 1816, Captain William Henry Dillon of HMS *Horatio,* anchored in Simon's Bay, wrote:

> The ship had not been long at anchor when I was attacked by a violent inflammation in both eyes. . . . As I suffered so much I applied to the family physician of the Governor, Lord Charles Somerset. This gentleman was in the army and considered extremely clever . . . [he was] extremely assiduous but did not ap-

prove the remedies resorted to, plainly telling me a milder treatment would have sufficed. Having written down his instructions and explained fully the system I was to follow, he took his leave and demanded only his travelling expenses to the ship and back.

In September 1818, Somerset began to complain of feeling unwell. Barry requested that he reduce his official and social engagements, and to desist from hunting and theater visits. Somerset stubbornly ignored him, as a consequence of which he quickly found himself confined to bed in "a state of great debility." The business of government was suspended while the small colony awaited the determination of the fate of Somerset. Barry's diagnosis was "typhus with dysentery." Barry realized he must share his anxieties with Colonel Bird. The extent of Barry's concern is shown in a letter Bird wrote to Earl Bathurst on September 29, through which rings the unmistakable tone of Barry's voice.

> There appears to have been a return of disease for the last three or four nights at about 10 o'clock, and last night his Lordship was delirious. Lord Charles's habits of great temperance are probably much in his favour, but Dr Barry nonetheless expresses so much apprehension that I cannot delay making your Lordship acquainted with the state in which he now is. Should an unfavourable turn take place I shall forthwith despatch the Colonial Schooner to England with the tidings. . . . I shall, however, entertain hopes that it will not be necessary.

The ordinary business of the small Cape Town colony hung in an uneasy state of suspended animation while the town awaited the outcome of Somerset's illness. To add to the tension, a dispute appears to have developed between Barry and his superiors regarding the proper handling of Somerset's case. Tempers were wearing thin, and an argument broke out between Barry on the one hand and the inspector general of hospitals and three consultants on the other. These medics appeared to regard the outcome as a foregone conclusion and wanted Bird to send his dispatches warning the government to expect the worst even before Somerset's condition was clearer. Conversely, Barry believed there was still hope. He later described this event in his official correspondence:

> When I was young, very young, I took on myself the heavy re-sponsibility of differing in opinion from the Inspector-General and three eminent professional men in the case of the Governor, Lord Charles Somerset. At my request, the Colonial Secretary [Bird] stopped the dispatches for forty-eight hours and I was left in sole possession of the case.

It was a critical test of Barry's professional competence. He had to prove that the confidence Lord Charles had invested in him was justi-fied. And he had to control his anxiety that his own errors could kill the person he admired and cared for above all others. He stayed at Somer-set's bedside, supervising all his treatments and personal needs. Later in his career Barry was to become an expert on the treatment of both ty-phus and dysentery, but in 1818 he had little experience of these dis-eases, and in this crisis with Somerset combined a small amount of personal experience with a large amount of textbook knowledge.

The morning of October 1 dawned with an air of greater certainty than the colony had experienced for the previous fortnight—Somerset had "rallied a little and was last night without fever." Thanks to the ministrations of Barry, it was not necessary for Bird to dispatch HMS *The Mary* to England bearing news of Somerset's demise. Instead, Bird sent his dispatches with the good news of Somerset's return to health, and credited his recovery to the skill of Dr. Barry. Writing up the event later in life, Barry smugly recalled the soundness of his own judgment: "The event justified the difference of opinion—His Lordship survived for many years."

Three months later, in December 1818, Barry's appointment as personal physician to the governor was formalized. The appointment came with a set of apartments in the governor's residence at Newlands, and more money. He bought himself a buggy and a set of grays, and persuaded Somerset to let him take on a manumitted Malay slave, Dantzen, as his personal servant, outfitting him in a bright livery that included a set of sunshade parasols matching his own outfits.

It was in Cape Town that Barry acquired his first dog, a poodle called Psyche. From this time onwards she became a feature of Barry's retinue. As soon as one Psyche died Barry replaced it with another. Wherever Barry went, Psyche went too.

Perhaps this first Psyche was a gift to Barry from Somerset or his daughters. Somerset had an obsession with animals, keeping extensive stables and domestic and hunting dogs. His daughters were bequeathed kittens, birds, and, occasionally, small exotic animals like tamed monkeys and caged snakes and lizards, with which they playfully taunted their official visitors.

Psyche's name mischievously inspires an unspoken question: exactly who was Cupid? The teasing name drew attention to the idiosyncrasies of Barry's personality. Would he point attention toward himself with this canine joke? On the other hand, naming a white poodle Psyche has the stamp of Somerset's indulgence and love of *entre-nous* wit. Somerset was a great joker with his family and intimates: everyone had a nickname, he was an inveterate tease, and he liked his secretaries and closest reports to keep him amused with gossip—just so long as he was not its object. Lord Charles was a generous giver of apposite gifts, and Barry's Psyche may have been a token to accompany his formal appointment and move into Somerset's residence. If this was the case, was it Somerset's intention to imply a role for himself as Cupid? Or was the playful suggestion that Barry was Cupid—hero of a myth whose theme was to caution against being too curious about the appearance of a lover? To Cape society at this stage it may have looked as if Somerset was tacitly declaring his sanction of Barry as a desirable bachelor who could be respectably courted by the society daughters of colonial families. Somerset was, after all, an aristocrat of a rapidly receding age, and such tokens were transactions indicating favor, patronage, and the stamp of social authority.

At forty-five Somerset was still handsome, energetic, and powerful. He was a bear of a man, twice Barry's stature, and twenty years older. Was the allusion to the myth of Cupid and Psyche a wry admission of something he playfully acknowledged society would regard as "monstrous" yet which he himself knew to be a thing of hidden beauty? The offspring of Cupid and Psyche's coupling was their daughter, called Pleasure. Whatever the provenance of Barry's beloved pet Psyche, the lifelong allusion was maddeningly suggestive.

Psyche is written about as Barry's chief accessory, his most constant companion, his other half. Psyche appears in Edward Lear's cartoon of Barry, limping pathetically in the shadow of a stooped, querulous caricature of Barry at Corfu. Psyche is a prominent subject in the only known photograph of Barry, taken late in his career. Psyche's presence is a constant invocation of the absent, elusive figure of Cupid, a continual reference to the mysterious coupling in darkness whose product was Pleasure.

During these years the compact between Barry and Somerset was at its most intense. The extent to which Barry could count on Somerset's unqualified support is shown by the way he got away with countless acts of insubordination, flagrant disregard for official process, and direct insult to senior members of the colony. In each instance, Somerset protected him. Shielded on the political and professional front, Barry took confidence in his public persona. He courted controversy and took a series of risks for sometimes superficial reasons. Yet to regard him as deliberately provoking is probably to mistake his personality. In fact, during these early years his insouciance was unselfconscious, and his idiosyncrasies the expression of a unique mind. Despite the criticisms of his less able peers and professional colleagues, his challenging behavior was rarely premeditated. He took risks because he enjoyed them. He stacked the odds against himself because it made an ordinary task more interesting. He did not suffer or care overmuch about fools, and as a consequence fools were much preoccupied with undermining him and detracting from his evident abilities. If Barry had been deliberately manipulative in his waywardness, he would have calculated outcomes much more carefully than is testified to by this "most wayward of men" who was always precipitating situations that called for drastic resolutions and grand gestures, or backing himself into a corner. When Barry got into arguments and disputes he constantly left himself exposed, often without a route of retreat from his keenly defended position. This is the method of the impassioned idealist, not of the careful, intentional strategist.

Barry had a reputation for being "plucky and fearless," and popular myth has it that he fought at least three duels. Although formally outlawed, dueling was a welcome opportunity for officers and gentlemen to demonstrate chivalrous behavior. One of Barry's favorite tags during this period was the motto of the order of the garter: "Honi soit qui mal y pense," Evil be to he who thinks evil. He was fond of quoting this in both his personal and professional life. He was also experiencing for the first time the expectations of outward behavior that went along with being a colonial officer: military parades, horsemanship, hunting, physical discipline—and the mating display of highly stylized flirtation and seduction. Dueling provided the opportunity to strike a gentlemanly pose and to demonstrate a savoir faire attitude to prohibition, while also potentially forming a male bond with his opponent, who had to agree to secrecy. In response to a query from Lord Erskine—a younger brother of Buchan's—who was "immensely interested" in the stories of Barry's dueling escapades, William Cattell obliged with the following account in his memoirs:

> [Barry] made love to a handsome Dutch girl of whom another officer (Mannering) was enamoured, and won her affection. They taunted Mannering who flung a tumbler of wine in his face. The duel followed in which Barry allowed himself to be slightly

wounded. The next day he told Mannering he had never really loved the girl; the latter ultimately married.

In truth the only duel that it is certain Barry fought was that with Abraham Josias Cloete, aide-de-camp to Lord Charles Somerset. Josias Cloete was the son of one of the oldest and most influential Dutch settler families at the Cape, owners of Alphen, a large and beautiful estate in the verdant Constantia valley outside Cape Town. As a child Josias was sent to Holland to be educated at Utrecht, and then to the military college at Marlow, where his father's political connections with the English who now ruled the Cape provided him with good introductions. He was, however, swiftly plucked from Marlow by Colonel Grant, the duke of Cumberland, who thought the Dutch boy would do better training in his own regiment, the 15th Hussars. It is likely that Cumberland recommended Cloete to Somerset in England, and that Cloete was invited to join Somerset as his secretary as he prepared his entourage for departure to the Cape. Cloete served Somerset throughout his governorship of the colony. Later, in 1842, he famously became the "red-coated Dutch-speaking British Army Colonel" who annexed the Natal republic to the British Empire. Following his extensive service in South Africa, he was appointed to a range of other colonial posts, most notably as major-general in command of the windward and leeward forces in the Caribbean.

Following Barry's death, Cloete told the story of his duel with the infamous doctor to Sir William MacIntosh, who had met Barry in Corfu during the Crimean War:

When I was ADC to Lord Charles Somerset at the Cape, a buxom lady called to see him on business of a private nature, and of course they were closeted for some time. Dr Barry made some disparaging remarks about this: "Oh, I say, Cloete," he sneered, "that's a nice Dutch filly the Governor has got hold of." "Retract your vile expression you infernal little cad" said I, advancing and pulling his long ugly nose. Barry immediately challenged me, and we fought with pistols, fortunately without effect.

Novelist Réné Juta fictionalizes the episode in her 1920 novel *Cape Currey,* and amusingly portrays Cloete as speaking afterward "of his feeling like an overheavy-weighted cock, matching himself against a young bantam lightweight scarce red on the comb." Cloete recorded the event in his personal papers, following the military convention of referring to himself in the third person singular:

> At this time (1820) there was at the Cape a very remarkable character in Staff Assistant Surgeon, Dr James Barry, MD, who combined in an extraordinary degree, the rarest qualities of Esculapian Talent, with the most mischievous propensities of a Monkey, and all the subtle wiles of the Serpent.
>
> An altercation with this strange little being, having caused the infliction of a personal insult on him, led to the necessity of giving him satisfaction by a hostile meeting in which he had his shot, which he subsequently declared had carried off "The Peak of the Captain's Cap" (Captain Cloete).

The note of humorous indulgence and admiration in Cloete's recollection reflects the friendship that he later developed with Barry. It was a friendship that was to last to the end of Barry's life.

However, when the two hot-blooded gallants met on the grounds of the Alphen estate at the appointed hour of a crystalline Constantia morning, they were indignant foes infuriated by what each saw as the other's effrontery. As he so often did during this time, Barry was daring himself. He was no adept with firearms, while Cloete was a skilled opponent noted for his marksmanship. Barry was an intellectual, a scientist, a distinguished medical professional, and a fop. His fantasy notions of gentility were cultivated in the coffeehouses of London, while Cloete had already logged time in barracks and encampments.

Riding across from Newlands in the chill hours before dawn, Barry may have approached the encounter with justifiable trepidation. Quarrels of a trifling nature were often occasion for dueling between officers of the Cape garrison; it was virtually a gentlemanly sport. The event was typical of Barry's risk-taking style. It was a grandiose challenge, but whose honor was he defending? Challenges were most commonly issued in defense of an insult against a lady, or between rival suitors. Yet here were two gentlemen apparently quarreling over the honour of an aristocratic gentleman whom they both revered and a prostitute whom neither knew.

It seems that Barry had arrived at the governor's rooms expecting an audience with Somerset. He was used to having easy and preferential access to Lord Charles, and would have quickly lost patience when he found his way barred by Cloete, insisting that the Governor was indisposed and unable to see him. An amiable man aware of Barry's preferred status as a member of the governor's household, Cloete probably confided to him that Lord Charles was detained by the charms of a prostitute. Incensed by a sudden sexual jealousy, Barry flung out his insult: "Oh, I say, Cloete, that's a nice Dutch filly the Governor has got hold of." In truth it is more likely that the prostitute was a Malay slave. It was a common though unspoken practice in this prurient society for seemingly respectable landowners to make the sexual services of their female slaves available to their friends and neighbors, and Malay women in particular were prized for their rumoured prowess.

Goading Cloete with the suggestion that Somerset's whore was a Dutchwoman, Barry hit his mark. Cloete, ever sensitive about his Dutch ancestry, took offense at what he interpreted as Barry's needling slur against his own nation. Somerset was famed for his love of horseflesh and expertise at stud farming. The inference was clear.

While Cloete struggled with interpreting the Englishman's meaning, Barry seems to have been thrown off guard by an eruption of fierce sexual jealousy. Somerset's appetites were varied and extensive, and Barry must have known they included the attentions of prostitutes selected to see to the needs of the wifeless governor. It was one thing knowing, but quite another being confronted with the fact, of Somerset in flagrante on the other side of the door. Barry knew very well the true source of his rage and emotion. His fervent sexual jealousy was, however, concealed from the astonished Cloete, who suddenly found himself challenged by the diminutive household physician about whom so many rumors were whispered. Barry had to confront the fact that he had a share of Somerset's affections, not his sole attentions.

The illegal duel took place against the dramatic backdrop of False Bay, the sun rising over the Indian Ocean. Barry was seconded by his manservant and Cloete by a fellow aide-de-camp. Some accounts suggest that Psyche was present, sternly ordered to stay well out of the way of stray gunfire by the apprehensive Barry. What a strange spectacle this must have been, this little group of stiffly attired military officers, a servant hesitant of the unfamiliar proceedings, and the ever-watchful Psyche dwarfed by the prehistoric grandeur of the purple mountains and the crashing expanse of the Indian Ocean. Cloete may have deliberately fired to miss. Each had made his point, and Cloete would have been mindful that as the most eminent surgeon at the colony Barry was too valuable a resource to seriously damage. Cloete's recollection that Barry "subsequently declared his shot had carried off 'The Peak of the Captain's Cap' " is a wry observation on the nature of Barry's narrative embellishments and bragging behavior when it came to proving his daring and honor as a gentleman.

Barry and Cloete became great friends as a result of their encounter. They had in common their admiration and affection for their employer, Somerset. It is possible that this friendship was also based on the fact that both were cultural outsiders working in the English establishment. Cloete was a Cape Afrikaner and Barry an itinerant of uncertain ancestry—both occupied uneasy terrain in the British army. Many years later, Barry was to visit Cloete in Jamaica. By this time the heavyweight cock had become a major-general, and the young bantam an inspector general of hospitals.

In 1819, Somerset applied for a leave of absence from the colony. There seemed to be an official concern that he needed to normalize the arrangements in his household and restore a Lady Somerset as hostess to the governor's official engagements, entertainments, and children. Whether pushed by his advisors or having himself reached this decision, Somerset went to England to find a wife. He did not ask his physician to accompany him. Perhaps Barry had got tied up in his duties attending the cholera outbreak in Mauritius, and it was not logistically possible for him to accompany Somerset. Yet advance notice of Somerset's leave of absence had been given, and his intentions of going to England to bring back a new wife were well known around the colony. This was the most extended period of time Barry and Somerset had been out of each other's company since their viceregal tour to the eastern frontier in 1817.

At least one biographer has hinted at a mystery regarding Barry's sojourn in Mauritius at this time. June Rose maintains that the severe outbreak of cholera at Mauritius in November 1819 was not reported at Cape Town until the end of 1820, when a report arrived on HMS *Hardy* from the governor of the Bourbon Island. Rose questions whether Barry was really, as he claimed, on official business to nurse the cholera stricken. The notion that this was not an official mission is flatly refuted by Barry, who claims strenuously in his Memorandum of Services that "during the lengthened period of my service I obtained leave of absence on private affairs on only one occasion, and then only when I conceived my prospects in the service were seriously compromised for want of a personal appeal at Head Quarters." This is a reference to a leave of absence in 1828, but interestingly it is inaccurate: in fact, Barry went absent *without* leave. His deliberate fudging of this episode throws suspicion on his activities in Mauritius nine years earlier.

Whatever the case, Barry was back in town when Somerset returned to the Cape aboard *Hyperion* with his new wife, Lady Poulett. The local wits, Barry included, doubtless punned on the name of the new wife of the animal-loving governor. Somerset was now fifty, his new wife thirty-five. On November 30, his ship anchored at Table Bay. An official welcoming committee was rowed out into the harbor and went on board *Hyperion* to greet the governor and be introduced to his new wife. The group included Somerset's son, Captain Henry, Major Josias Cloete, and Dr. James Barry.

Chapter 4

SIEKETROOST

Who cares for him who once pastured this spot,
Where his tribe is extinct and their story forgot?

Thomas Pringle, *The Caffer Commando*

In the natural sciences, the truth of principles must be con-
firmed by observations.

James Barry

Sieketroost: medicinal remedy for sickness, gentle balm for
the weary, Dutch; vernacular sieketroos

ON A MORNING IN MARCH 1822, DR. BARRY AND PSYCHE SET OUT
for Mrs. Saunders's Coffee Shop on the Heerengracht. The trip was an
almost daily event. Each day except Sunday, Mrs. Saunders would put
aside a wrapped parcel of sugared buns for Barry. On the days when he
had not been called away to ride out early to attend a patient, visit the
Hemel-en-Aarde leper colony near Caledon, or attend a morning
briefing with the Governor, Barry would visit Mrs. Saunders. There he
would read the *Courant,* the daily government gazette, over a bowl of
Dutch coffee while Psyche preened to the attention of Mrs. Saunders—
or, more exactly, paid due attention to Mrs. Saunders's sugar buns. For,

as the reputable baker proudly informed her curious women customers, the Doctor took only one bun crumbled with his coffee, while
his poodle would eat two or three. Barry and Psyche were among Mrs.
Saunders's most loyal customers, and when scandal later broke over
Barry's head the indefatigable Mrs. Saunders was to be one of Barry's
most steadfast allies and voluble critics of the wagging tongues along
the Heerengracht.

However, there was no whiff of scandal in the air on this gusty, fresh
March morning. Barry and Psyche were surprised to be intercepted on
their way to Mrs. Saunders's by a runner from Government House,
who handed Barry a letter sealed with the stamp of the colonial office.
Standing on a walkway on the Heerengracht with all the bustle of a
busy Cape Town morning flowing past him, Barry cracked the seal.
The letter was from his friend and colleague Bird, secretary at the colonial office, and was dated that very morning, March 18:

> Sir: Dr Robb who is on the eve of returning to England having re-
> signed the Situation of Colonial Medical Inspector, I am directed
> by his Excellency the Governor to acquaint you that he has been
> pleased to appoint you to succeed thereto.

The news was not altogether a surprise, but to have his new appointment officially confirmed delighted him. The substantial annual salary
for this role was 2,400 rixdollars* a year. It was the culmination of
everything Barry had striven for since he had first arrived at the Cape as
a humble hospital assistant. He now held the premier medical appointment in the colony. In the five years since his arrival at the Cape he had
established an almost legendary reputation for his success in private
practice. Since his appointment as the Governor's physician, he had
treated some of the most senior notables in the colony, who had then
employed his services for their wives and children. The whole colony
had known of Somerset's extreme antipathy for physicians following

---

*Current value: $31,200 (U.S.).

the death of his beloved first wife; yet within a year, Barry had become Somerset's most trusted favorite and personal physician to his entire household. Moreover, saving the life of the governor in 1818 was not only a personal victory, it was a public relations coup. The news of this success reached England, where the government noted the name of the Edinburgh graduate who had saved the life of one of the British empire's most prominent public servants.

During his four years as colonial medical inspector, Barry was driven by great determination and a seemingly limitless store of energy, investigating, challenging, reforming, and rebuilding the ground on which medical treatment and the management of public institutions stood. Sweeping through each of the public institutions of the Cape—hospital, leper colony, prisons, asylums, apothecaries, commerce in medicines— he ferreted out venality, criticized bureaucratic corruption, challenged inefficiency, created detailed policies of medical reform, and relieved suffering. For his institutional reforms and his work professionalizing and regulating medical practice and public services, he earned the respect of senior officials. For his public stand against cruelty to slaves and support for the rights of black people, women, and children to humanitarian medical treatment, he earned the trust and admiration of progressives and, particularly, abolitionists. Of the people he cared for, only the literate were able to record their experiences first hand, but Barry tended many prisoners, slaves, prostitutes, lepers, women, and children.

Barry worked tirelessly to create an image of himself as a professional gentleman, reliable physician, scientist, and active campaigner to reform colonial policy on public health. Although the Cape colony was small relative to other settler colonies, the ratio of aspiring doctors to patients was quite high, and the medics had to fiercely compete with each other for patients in the settler community. Barry frequently undertook new official responsibilities on his own initiative, and without additional pay.

It is impossible to understand the transformation Barry made to medicine and its institutions at the Cape without understanding what he rectified. Much of his hard work was designed to create a cleaner, healthier environment for people subjected to squalid conditions, uncaring attitudes, and needless death. Living up to the ideals of his Romantic, progressive mentors, Barry was a committed humanitarian. In his private practice he attended the political and business leaders of the country and took advantage of his access to men of influence to gain their support. Like justice, Barry held the rich and poor in equal balance in the scales of his treatment. His repeated refusal to budge on points of principle earned him a reputation for being difficult to work with. In truth, the criticisms levied against Barry are those traditionally conferred by the conservative on the progressive: he was too outspoken; he had insufficient respect for authority; he was stubborn, vainglorious, and self-promoting; he was embarrassing. Barry's exhaustive work as a medical reformer shows him to have been a compassionate humanitarian and ardent believer in the rights of man, and woman.

However, Barry was no Romantic idealist. In 1827 he published a paper that forever changed medical understanding of treatment for gonorrhea and syphilis. Barry's "Report upon the *Arctopus echinatus* or Plat Doorn of the Cape of Good Hope" provides a unique insight into his professional methods. Despite the success of his experiments, undertaken in a makeshift laboratory in the back of the apothecary owned by his friend Mr. Poleman, over which he toiled for nearly three years, Barry was adamant that until he had measured its success with actual patients, his findings could only be regarded as purely theoretical:

> The Arctopine . . . promises fair to prove a very valuable antisyphilitic; but as I have as yet had no opportunity of making it the subject of experiment in practice, my opinion must be purely hypothetical, and therefore the proof of its virtues must be left to the surer test of time and experience: *In scientia naturalia principia veritatis obervationibus confirmari debent.* [In the natural sciences, the truth of principles must be confirmed by observations.]

This principle of observation was Barry's lodestar throughout his professional life, and it was here at the Cape that he learned the value of its practice. During his years building up his image as a medical professional at the Cape, Barry demonstrated his unswerving belief in privileging what he saw for himself over what he was told. His mentor Astley Cooper had drummed into his students the need for practical observation. "Sir, to learn your profession, look to yourself, never mind what other people may say, no opinion or theories can interfere with information acquired from dissection." Barry took these lessons from the messy, irregular, and visceral business of dissection into his practical work with patients, with institutions, with his study of disease. His dismissiveness of official explanations and justifications had an almost religious fervor. He never believed what he was told about people or places. He insisted on looking at things and experiencing them firsthand.

An inspection of a provincial prison in 1825 is one among many similar episodes that illustrate Barry's style. In September of that year he rode out to the forest of Rondebosch, then a village outside Cape Town, to inspect its prison. Concerned about rumors of maltreatment of the prisoners in the jail he had instigated his own inspection. The landdrost of Rondebosch objected to what he saw as Barry's planned intrusion, for which Barry gave him short shrift. In his official report on the event he made it clear that he believed all public institutions should be subject to scrutiny and accountable to the people who used them: "It is scarcely necessary to add that all Government and Public Institutions ought from time to time to be examined by a Professional man." Barry was eternally distrustful of the obfuscations of bureaucrats and regarded them with open suspicion. As Barry commenced his tour he discovered that the prison official and warders were "most unwilling" to provide him with answers to his questions about "rations, exercise, ventilation, employment of prisoners and medical visitation." As they refused to answer on any of these points, he shrugged them off and addressed his questions directly to the inmates. Incandescent with rage at

Barry's impudence in talking directly to the prisoners, the hitherto taciturn and uncommunicative supervisor turned to Barry and shouted, "Why ask blacks while Christians are present to answer?" We can only imagine the withering contempt in Barry's riposte to the racist and obstructive jailer.

Barry's encounter at the Rondebosch prison stands for literally hundreds of tours of inspection he made of the institutions of the Cape colony during the 1820s. Barry sought out people in their appalling conditions, examined them, spoke with them, prescribed treatments, and wrote reports containing detailed recommendations for the reform and improvement of their environment.

By the early nineteenth century most western doctors were still working with a strange and often dangerous cornucopia of theories of disease. Such theories were often as mystifying to themselves as they were terrifying to the patients, who were usually doubly stricken once a doctor had inflicted an array of purgatives. Still influenced by the classical notion that all disease emanated from an imbalance in the four humors—blood, phlegm, bile, and black bile—these practitioners were usually harbingers of painful and often damaging methods designed to "rebalance" the humors: leeching, bloodletting, inducing vomiting, applying violent purgatives, sweating and extreme cooling of the body. Although a great believer in the practical botanical wisdom of cures on which many folklore remedies were based, Barry was of an entirely different breed. He came from a new generation of doctors heavily influenced by the medical advances of the Enlightenment, the most important of which were the discovery of the circulation of the blood, the invention of forceps, and the explosion of knowledge of anatomical dissection. In short, he was a radical and progressive modernizer in an age of quacks and mountebanks.

Barry's appointment to colonial medical inspector attracted the attention of Earl Bathurst, secretary of state to the British government. Alarmed when they heard about Barry's panoply of new civil appointments, the colonial office requested him to resign his army commission to concentrate on his new duties. Barry took a firm stand against this request and begged permission to retain his military position. A compromise was reached: Barry remained in the army, but in view of the considerable income he was receiving from his new civil appointments, he was placed on half pay. This decision to stay in the military would prove to be one of the wisest he ever made.

Barry was now colonial medical inspector, inspector of the vaccine institution, inspector of medicines, inspector of the leper institution, and inspector of hospitals and prisons. And when Barry and Somerset found another unscrutinized institution or system that needed reform, Barry became inspector of that too. The post of colonial medical inspector required administrative proficiency and a degree of managerial competence. In many cases, Barry had lobbied Somerset directly. It is no coincidence that Somerset's official correspondence from 1817, a year after Barry's arrival at the Cape, suddenly resonates with the clear, ringing tones of new policies on medical reform and investigation of colonial institutions. The power of authorization belonged to Lord Charles, but the ideas and policy initiatives were Barry's.

One of the first demonstrations of Barry's capacity as a persuasive innovator was his intervention in transforming the Somerset Hospital from a private hospital to a municipal one. The Hospital and Lunatic Asylum (later renamed the Somerset Hospital) was the creation of the philanthropic surgeon Samuel Silverthorne Bailey, who established and ran it at his own expense and who became a professional colleague and close personal friend of Barry. Acting on Lord Charles's recommendation that the Cape needed a public hospital, in August 1817 Bailey opened the doors of the first civil hospital in the colony "for the reception of merchant seamen, and the slave population of the Colony . . . feeling very sensible of the great advantages the inhabitants of Cape Town and more particularly those residing in the country must derive from an establishment of this nature." Up until this time the General Hospital, which was exclusively for military use, had been the only hospital provision at the Cape. Merchant seamen, paupers, slaves, and the insane were accepted in the town jail and attended—barely—by the jail-keepers, or "dieners," in squalid and unwholesome conditions. By 1820 Bailey could no longer sustain the financial burden of running the Somerset Hospital, and he asked the colonial government to take over the running of it as a public hospital. Somerset urged the Burgher Senate, the local colonial government of the Cape Colony, to accept Bailey's proposal, which they did, but short-changed the philanthropist on the transfer of the institution. The municipality immediately scaled down the services at the hospital.

By 1825, the Somerset Hospital was run down and could in no way keep up with increased demand or the increasing complexity and range of the diseases it had to treat. Barry undertook an impromptu inspection in 1824 and complained that "the whole establishment appeared void of cleanliness, order or professional care." Prompted by Barry's persistent reports, in February 1825 Somerset appointed a committee to investigate the hospital. Barry chaired the committee. Its report was detailed and damning. There was not a single resident doctor at the hospital. Patients and the insane were crammed together into six wards, while ten of the best wards had been turned into private apartments for two men who worked for the Burgher Senate. Considered of no use by the municipality, the old apothecary's shop had been closed, so there was no longer any form of dispensary in the hospital. There was no organized hospital staff, and everywhere Barry and the committee looked they found the hospital being used as lodgings for menial servants. Barry asked to inspect the books and found they were kept in a "loose and confused manner."

There were more animals kept in the hospital than patients. Cats, dogs, guinea pigs, turkeys, ducks, guinea fowl, and pigeons wandered the filthy wards. The only nurse who worked at the hospital was an unhealthy sixty-six-year-old man who could not lift anything. As witnessed by Barry and the committee on one of their visits, the only medical care this frail nurse was able to offer to a dying patient was to feebly flap the flies away from his face. Based on frequent inspections, all of which were led by Barry, the committee submitted a full report on the appalling state of the Somerset Hospital, along with a detailed set of recommendations for its reform and improvement. Among its key proposals were the immediate reopening of the medicine dispensary, the separation of the insane from other patients, the eviction of all those who had misappropriated the hospital accommodation (including the Burgher civil servants), new regimes of cleanliness, the appointment of a resident surgeon and a permanent hospital staff, and the keeping of regular accounts. Armed with the committee's report, the government tackled the Burgher Senate to insist on improvements in the hospital conditions. The fight that ensued lasted four years, with Barry following up and reporting in detail on the attempts to implement every new reform and improvement for the care of the patients.

European immigration was the chief cause of the overcrowding at Somerset Hospital. The settlers, traders, merchants, missionaries, escaped convicts, government servants, and professional travelers who arrived on the shores of the Cape brought with them a menacing cocktail of diseases to which the indigenous inhabitants had not previously been exposed. These included dysentery, typhus, pneumonia, smallpox, measles, whooping cough, and a seemingly infinite array of sexually transmitted diseases. During 1821 and 1822, before his appointment as colonial medical inspector, Barry had also played a central part in the reform of the quarantine laws, which needed firm strengthening in order to control the alarming increase in the spread of contagious disease. In 1822, he sat on one of the quarantine boards. This board reported that the existing quarantine laws were obsolete and needed to be rewritten to cope with the increase in contagious disease resulting from the 1820 Settlers program. This was an infamous piece of British colonial policy in which, in an attempt to increase the density of settlement on the volatile eastern frontier, the English government established a scheme to encourage people to emigrate to South Africa and resettle as farmers in the Eastern Cape.

This concerted attempt to increase the numbers of British settlers was a policy for colonization by contagion. In order to control the spread of disease, a system was established whereby the settlers' vessels were quarantined, barred from docking at Cape Town, and sent directly round the coast to the deserted Algoa Bay, where the bemused immigrants disembarked and were sent directly to their destinations with a set of start-up rations and directions to their subsidized land. Having sailed across the world, very few of these settlers actually saw Cape Town or the larger towns of the colony. The quarantine boards also acted to ensure that all vessels arriving from India were quarantined without exception—frequently these ships came laden with cholera and dysentery. The position of the Cape meant that it had the potential to be besieged by diseases from east and west, so the role of the quarantine board on which Barry sat in 1822 was to review the existing policies and make recommendations for measures that would limit the spread of contagious diseases around the colony.

During this period, Barry also made a contribution to the intellectual life of medicine at the Cape. During 1821 he presented an array of medical books to the recently established South African Library, and in each a specially prepared presentation bookplate was inserted. The records of the South African Library Committee show that Barry's opinion on medical works was frequently sought, and his advice taken on what books the library should invest in to build its medical collection. Thus by 1823 Barry had established a reputation for himself as a successful practitioner, intellectual authority, and efficient, bold administrator.

Barry set to work immediately in his new role. On March 24 he fired off the first of many letters in his official capacity to the colonial secretary (Bird), stating his concern about the lack of regulation of medicines prescribed or dispensed without the authorization of a medical practitioner. Barry held strong views on the dangers of patent medicines and the unregulated profiteering that allowed unqualified and often unscrupulous individuals to profit from the ignorance of sick and frightened people. As soon as he was appointed colonial medical inspector, he launched a campaign attacking the free trade and profits that relied on patients' fear and lack of information:

To my certain knowledge many Persons have been Poisoned by Patent Medicines, given improperly; and also, that Pedlars and Hawkers of Drugs in the Interior and in Cape Town, do more real injury to the Inhabitants than the most virulent diseases themselves. Moreover, a regularly Educated Man cannot with justice to himself or the community settle in the Interior, when Quacks and Quack Medicines are first resorted to. It would be endless to state the various injuries arising from the Retail of Patent or other Medicines, by any other Persons than regularly Educated Practitioners. I shall therefore content myself by explaining that His Majesty's Letter's Patent are for making and compounding, not vending certain medicines.

Barry was concerned to evaluate the safety and quality of medicines being dispensed in the colony and to implement a system for ensuring that only qualified practitioners prescribed treatments like opium and arsenic. He was also determined to root out the profitable malpractice of quacks and charlatans who regarded selling medicines as a retail business and not a humanitarian help for the sick. Barry strongly recommended that household remedies "such as castor oil and emetics" should be provided by district surgeons who could charge reasonable prices for them, "then all would benefit."

Barry sedulously studied the abundant advertisements for medicines in the government gazette. Slim on European news, full of society gossip, most of the content of the *Courant* was commercial advertisements for the sale of medicines. Bianchi's, a shop in Plein Street, carried frequent advertisements. A patient who had bought medicine at Bianchi's had died and his family complained to the press that it was because he had been sold the wrong remedy. Barry decided to carry out an impromptu inspection of Bianchi's, and found the shop sold an array of medicines and drugs by an unlicensed proprietor. Imported from Europe, the brightly colored bottles with their brazen labels contained concoctions that had spoiled in transport, had broken seals, or had

turned to poison. Barry wrote a report on Bianchi's, and compiled a
dossier of similar examples of abuse taking place in the sale of medicines. He encouraged country physicians to write to him to tell him of
the problems and cases in their regions, and he persisted with carrying
out his own personal inspections of premises. Barry wrote to Somerset
to announce the initiation of his campaign to regulate the sales of medicines:

> It has been some time a subject of serious Injury to the Apothe-
> cary's and Druggists in this Colony that Medicines are sold by al-
> most every description of Shopkeeper without either Professional
> knowledge or Licence. It is a well known fact that the most dele-
> terious drugs are vended and dispensed by various Persons in
> Cape Town under the denomination of Patent Medicines, Halische
> Medicines etc etc, to the personal risk of the Purchasers. Not in-
> frequently fatal consequences have ensued from the unqualified
> in which these Quack or Patent Medicines have been adminis-
> tered by ignorant and mercenary persons. Besides such medicines
> are frequently spoiled during the voyage or adulterated after, but
> as Patent Medicines they are not subject to being inspected as
> other Medicines.

Barry's intentions in persuading Somerset to revise the laws regulating
the sales of medicines were not, however, entirely altruistic. Barry and
the qualified physicians who supported him on this issue regarded the
unregulated sale of unvetted medicines as a direct threat to their own
professional security. Somewhat dramatically, he stated that:

> If no regulations are made or steps taken against the practise of
> shopkeepers selling medicines, I must absolutely continue to ex-
> perience that the time, expense and trouble to learn the art and
> profession has been thrown away not only, but that myself and
> fellow followers in the art of medical Preparations will ere shortly
> go 'a begging and be ruined.

In April 1824, Barry made his first tour of inspection of the Cape Town prison. He made his report to Lord Charles both verbally and in writing. He called particular attention to the plight of two prisoners, Jacob Elliot and Jan Krier, whose conditions he found completely lacking "in point of humane and proper treatment." Barry had discovered Elliot "with his thigh fractured—without clothes, without a bed, or pillows, or blankets, dirty in the extreme, without a single comfort: and in short exhibiting such a state of misery that if he had not been under the special protection of Providence, he could not have survived." In another cell Barry discovered Jan Krier, a prisoner from Robben Island, in a similar predicament. Krier also had a broken leg, "and the other carefully surrounded with a heavy chain." Barry suggested that if Somerset "could afford himself to walk the Tronk, you could satisfy yourself as to the facts and be convinced that I did not in the least exaggerate. . . . I do here, my Lord, declare that I never witnessed any scene more truly appalling than this."

Barry was told by the prison doctors, Dr. F. L. Liesching and his son, Carel, that they had already made a request that the two prisoners be removed to the hospital, but had never heard back from the deputy fiscal, Mr. Ryneveld, from whom they had requested permission to make the transfer. Taking the Lieschings at their word, Barry pursued the issue with Ryneveld, who interpreted Barry's inquiries as a challenge to his competence. A few days later Barry was summoned to a meeting with the acting colonial secretary, Pieter Brink, at Government House. Brink was an admirer of Barry's, and sought to pour oil on troubled waters by showing him a letter of complaint from Ryneveld. If Brink's intention was to enable Barry to settle the matter with diplomacy, he must have been startled to receive a letter from Barry the following day. It is one of the most complete statements of Barry's view of himself as the model of the English gentleman:

Dr J Barry presents his Compliments to Mr Brink, and with respect to Mr Ryneveld's communication which Mr Brink has favoured him with a sight of; Dr J Barry begs to say that he is at a loss to understand its meaning; as every man in a Public Institution must be aware that Official Duties neither ought nor can become the subject of private "altercations"—upon this principle, Dr J Barry considers it his bounden Duty to disclaim anything like personalities in his Official Correspondence; but at the same time he must, and ever will, perform his Public Duties fearlessly and conscientiously: and he again repeats, that he does not, he cannot condescend ever to be personal. "Honi soit qui mal y pense" is the Englishman's Motto.

Fiercely underlining his statement that "he cannot condescend ever to be personal," Barry pointedly ends the letter without any form of farewell or signature. It is a letter oozing indignation, swagger, and bombast, and it is a letter that clearly warns Ryneveld that Dr. Barry is an opponent who will retaliate against anyone who questions his honor as a gentleman. Here as elsewhere Barry is vehemently defensive of his professional identity. He defends it as if it were the substance of his life—and he seems to believe that it is. Barry assumes a distance and refuses the possibility of personal dispute: he identifies totally with the institution. Barry's letter to Brink is a remarkable example of how completely his promotion to colonial medical inspector made a man of him in his own eyes.

At the same time that he was embroiled in probing the distribution, sale, and quality of medicines, Barry was anxious to put in place regulations governing the licensing of medical practitioners themselves. On this matter he was unbending: the standard must be that delivered by study in a European university:

In the Medical Profession, Laws have been passed by colleges and universities after mature deliberation founded upon Principles, the most Honourable as well as useful, to secure not only the respectability of the Professional men themselves, but also to serve the safety and welfare of the community at large, the lives of many must unavoidably be entrusted to the Discretion, Judgment and good faith of perhaps a single individual.

Barry's recommendation was that Somerset promulgate a law ensuring that anyone who wanted to present themselves as a candidate for examination, to be licensed to practice as a "Physician, Surgeon or Apothecary," would first have to obtain and produce "the necessary Professional documents from the Established Universities or Colleges in Europe." Successful candidates found to be suitably qualified would obtain certification. Not surprisingly, power of examination and granting of licenses was to be invested in the role of the colonial medical inspector.

Somerset agreed to all Barry's recommendations. On September 26, 1823, the governor's office issued a proclamation revising the Cape colony's medical law, originally drawn up in 1807. Under the revised law, no one could be licensed who could not first present "a regular Diploma from a University or College, in Europe, or in the case of Surgeons, Apothecaries, etc., of such Certificate as is usually required for these Arts." Examinations for qualification were to be conducted by Dr. Barry, who was empowered to grant or withhold the licenses. The proclamation also contained a clause relating to the control of the traffic in drugs:

> No Merchant, Trader or Dealer is to be allowed to vend by Retail any Drugs, Medicines or Patent Medicines in this Colony, under penalty of 500 Rixdollars,★ nor is to be allowed to vend the same by wholesale, without such Drugs, Medicines or Patent Medicines having been first submitted to the inspection of the Colonial Medical Inspector.

Barry quickly discovered that creating a law was far easier than its enforcement. The new regulations for medical practice and sale of

★Current value: $6,500 (U.S.).

medicines caused an uproar in Cape Town. Fearful of the threat posed by Barry's new regulations to their lucrative trade, the merchants and traders of Cape Town organized a deputation to the governor, protesting against the inspection to which their goods were now to be subjected. Chief among their objections was the fact that they had invested large sums of money in medicines "on the faith of being allowed to sell said medicines sanctioned by His Majesty's Royal Letters Patent and also by immemorial usage and custom." In a direct attack on Barry they objected to

> the placing in the hands of one Individual a power so great as is placed in the hands of our Colonial Medical Inspector ... a power by which the property of the Importers may be destroyed on the ipse dixit of one Individual, and from whose decision there is no appeal, a Power of condemning English Patent and Dutch Medicines, the component parts of which he may be wholly ignorant of.

In the view of the petitioners this was "an authority that may possibly become ... dangerous." The reach of Barry's powers was beginning to worry the senior members of the commercial community. Finally and tellingly, in the form of an afterthought, the merchants and traders asserted that the goods that they sold had "cured many patients after the doctors had despaired of their lives."

Perhaps sensing the magnitude of the forces marshaled against him, Barry responded with considered arguments and marked diplomacy. Restating his position regarding the danger of patent drugs, he also offered a compromise in order to reassure the merchants: all his inspections would be carried out in the presence of the owners of the medicines, and if they disagreed with his findings, they could refer his report to an independent board. The stakes were raised higher against Barry when Chief Justice Sir John Truter was brought in to make a judgment on the issue. He concluded that Barry was overreaching his powers.

Undeterred, Barry persisted in his determination to enforce these measures. He now had the combined forces of commerce and the judiciary arrayed against him. He called a meeting of physicians, surgeons, apothecaries, druggists, and chemists at his lodgings in the Heerengracht. This group issued a countermemorandum, restating the need for the inspection and regulation of imported patent medicines and "also those called Hollishe Medicines." Their memorandum cast doubt on the truth of claims made in advertisements regarding the efficacy of "wonder cures" like "Balsam of Tilley," "Wonderful Essence," and "Red Powder." They recommended a system whereby hawkers and peddlers of medicine in the interior would be required to buy their medicines from certified surgeons or apothecaries, who could then explain to them the proper use for the drugs.

The colonial office reviewed the debate and, on Somerset's recommendation, found in favor of Barry. It was a major victory. Barry had succeeded in changing the law. Barry's personal friendship with Somerset doubtless gave him a political advantage in this dispute, but it was not long before Barry would discover that he could not unreservedly count on Somerset's support.

On October 25, 1822, Barry rode out along a dust track to the undulating vineyards and wheatfields of the Hemel-en-Aarde valley. "Rightly it has got its name because so high are the hills, which closely embrace the valley all around, that they seem to touch the sky and you cannot see anything but Heaven and Earth," wrote a German missionary. Barry was to find the poetic conceit by which this landscape was named "Heaven on Earth" an insuperable irony as he struggled with one of the most arduous challenges of his career at the Cape: his resolution to reform the treatment of leprosy.

Leprosy was first reported in South Africa in 1756. The physical symptoms of leprosy—encrusted flesh; mutilated fingers, toes, noses, and ears; and bone deformity—made the disease "seem a living death" and led to extreme prejudice against its sufferers. For a modern medic, humanitarian, and scientist like Barry, the epidemiology of leprosy provided a prism through which all thinking about disease could be viewed. To work with the treatment of leprosy aligned him with the plight of the outcast.

In February 1817, persuaded by Barry, Somerset had issued a decree regarding new measures to be taken to deal with the increase in cases of leprosy:

> As an impression obtains (which, however, the most learned of the medical profession hold to be erroneous) that the disease is contagious, the distressed sufferers are frequently left in the state of abandonment which it is shocking to humanity to reflect upon. . . . It appears expedient to allot to Hottentots, Bastards, Freeblacks, and slaves labouring under this evil, a healthy and airy spot, where they may retire to and where they shall receive such aid as is necessary to their future subsistence and comfort, but to which solace the safety of the public requires they should be confined. And it appears that the situation of the Hemel & Aarde . . . is sufficient for the purpose required.

The leper institution at Hemel-en-Aarde was the first permanent specialized hospital in the Cape, and there is no doubt that it was created at Barry's instigation. Still unpersuaded of the value of the Cape colony as a colonial acquisition, the British government was anxious that state expenditure be kept as low as possible, so Somerset was under considerable pressure to reduce, not expand, costs in running the colony.

HUTS WERE BUILT, GARDENS AND VEGETABLE PATCHES LANDSCAPED, and a buffer area between the patients and the surrounding community marked out. The patients were promised that food and clothing would be provided for them. However, no administrative structure or treatment supervision was introduced. Despite the heavenliness of its location, the conditions at the institution made the place an earthly hell for the lepers. So degraded were conditions that they began to rebel.

Understanding that only his direct intervention would avert further disaster at the leper colony, Barry was at his own request appointed superintendent of the institution. He took up the position in 1822 at a salary of 600 rixdollars★ a year. Rumors regarding starvation at the institution reached Cape Town when a group of lepers escaped for the purpose of complaining to the authorities about their treatment. At short notice, Barry called a meeting with the officials responsible for running Hemel-en-Aarde. He gathered the lepers at the institution and explained to them that he was sent by the governor to inquire into their grievances and encouraged them to bring forward their complaints. This invitation produced a flood of responses.

Barry submitted his report on November 4, 1822. He was appalled at the conditions he had found, and submitted a detailed account of every aspect of the institution that he found lacking:

> Nothing . . . could exceed the misery of the lepers, whose clothing was dirty and bad, whose food was scanty and ill managed and scarcely sufficient to support life. They were confined in a small space of the really beautiful and ample portion of land allotted to them by the government.

Barry recorded that severely disabled patients were kept on dirty stretchers on the ground. Those still able to do so stood up and showed him their emaciated forms. They complained of hunger and ill-treatment, and told Barry that even in this incapacitated state they were made to labor in the garden and were punished if they failed to execute their tasks. Barry's attention to detail is demonstrated by the minutiae he later documented in his report. He asked for all livestock to be accounted for and insisted on interviewing the contractor who supplied the food: in both cases he uncovered malpractice and further evidence that provisions were not reaching the lepers.

★Current value: $7,800 (U.S.).

Having concluded his inspection, Barry ordered an immediate increase in rations "in the name of His Excellency." Returning to Cape
Town, Barry submitted his report and recommendations for the improvement of the lepers' living conditions:

> The land allotted to the Institution is one of the most fertile and
> beautiful spots in the Colony; well supplied with water and in the
> vicinity of the sea; the air exceedingly pure and most admirably
> calculated for the Health and Comfort of the Inhabitants; there
> also is a good house and a good hospital—and I make no doubt
> but if the labour of such of the unfortunate persons as were capa-
> ble of it was purchased with a little wine, a few skillings, or some
> tobacco or coffee they would cheerfully contribute to cultivate the
> soil to increase their own comforts.

Barry was recommending a radically modern approach. Not confining
himself to treatments and medicines, he reviewed the entire structure
of the institution from top to bottom, seeing this structure to be as essential to the care of the lepers as the prescription of medicines. Barry
returned to Hemel-en-Aarde on March 11, 1823, and was pleased to
find "the whole Establishment much improved—the people looking
better, and cleaner, not having the least disposition to mutiny, nor to escape—and well satisfied with Mr and Mrs Leitner," Moravian missionaries who had been appointed as the new superintendents. Barry's
approval of the Leitners was short-lived. Within three months Leitner
and Barry were at war.

In this instance, and ignoring administrative process, Barry sent his
findings directly to Lord Charles. His reason becomes clear when reading the letter. Barry wanted to raise a very sensitive subject:

> I beg leave to call your Lordship's attention to a circumstance
> which forcibly shocks me, in the course of my professional inves-
> tigations: that the subjects sent to the Institution are all in an ad-
> vanced stage of the Disease:—it also appears that the generality of

lepers are prize-negroes, or Hottentots, under Indenture, thus; not being actual (or valuable) property, their services are used as long as possible; and when they become useless in point of labour, and disgusting to the sight, they are sent to the Institution—the number of slaves are very few indeed. In the early stages of Leprosy much can be done, and instances are not wanting in this Colony of positive cures having been performed: in the last or advanced stages of this disease little can be done.

The leper colony was being used as a dumping ground for exploited black laborers who had been driven into the ground and then parceled off to Hemel-en-Aarde when they were too sick to work anymore. Indentured labor had no resale value for the colonial employers, who therefore had no interest in maintaining their health or prospects. The practice disgusted Barry for the crude way in which it revealed the contempt and disregard with which the white Europeans treated their black laborers. Knowing that leprosy was treatable made Barry all the more aghast at the attitudes of the white employers. Determined to push back against this squandering of human life, Barry wondered:

Perhaps if your Lordship would be pleased to appoint two or three wards in the Somerset Hospital, as a sort of Detachment Hospital for the reception of Incipient (or even doubtful) cases of Leprosy, I am inclined to think that the sufferers might be benefited and the colonial expense eventually diminished. Should this meet with your Excellency's approbation, it will be necessary to point out a few remarks in the Cape Council; to enable persons at a distance from medical aid to ascertain the disease; such instruction would at least prevent Masters from having recourse to the plea of Ignorance, respecting the state of their Servants.

Barry's target was clear: the dehumanizing "Masters" should be left nowhere to hide. Barry got his wards: five rooms at the Somerset Hospital were allocated to the treatment of lepers.

Barry was grittily determined to leave no stone unturned when it came to reforming Hemel-en-Aarde. A week later, ignoring the increasing irritation of Brother Leitner at his frequent visits, Barry wrote to Bird "with respect to the Diet proper for the Lepers." His opinion was that:

Milk, Rice, Coffee, and when practicable Vegetables should constitute the chief part of their foods—under present circumstances I fear Vegetables cannot be procured (as I do not think a few dried Peaches once substituted to be of the least use) but Rice, Sugar, Coffee or Tea and cows might be easily sent to the Institution. I should think a Soldier's Ration sufficient—However as a keen appetite seems almost part of the Disease I should by no means recommend these poor people being deprived of their pound of Mutton or their Bread. Where there are so many women and children as well as Invalids Soup should always be insisted upon. Two or three persons should be appointed to cook, for the whole Establishment and the overseers should serve out the cooked provisions to every person, and by no means allow raw Meat or Flour to be distributed as Rations. Two Persons also might be appointed as Bakers. The Cooks and Bakers being of course paid a small sum per month for their Labour. I should also recommend two persons as Nurses whose Duties it should be to see the Patients who require Medicine to take it—to see that Hospital be kept clean:— these persons should of course be paid.

Barry had a vision for the entire running of the hospital and treatment of the inmates. His recommendations are testimony to the modernity of his vision. This was written thirty-six years before the publication of Florence Nightingale's *Notes on Nursing,* a prescribed text for student nurses to this day. Nightingale is still credited with being the first to develop the ideas of patient care plans, hospital administration, and planning of the entire physical environment of the patient. Yet Barry's work at Hemel-en-Aarde, consistent with his later restructuring of the Cape Town prison, asylum, and hospital, demonstrates clearly the administrative elements of planning, organizing, and delegating that became the modern-day concepts of authority and responsibility in relation to health care.

Although he never wrote of his own personal life, Barry wrote every day, copiously. A substantial portion of his annual expenses went into "fifty quills, a blotting case, four quires of foolscap, two quires of letter paper, one quire blotting paper and two pencils." His letters, memoranda, and reports flew thick and fast to the colonial office, the governor, the Burgher Senate, and his medical friends. He wrote a set of instructions to help people in outlying rural areas nurse their sick at home, and had them printed and circulated around the colony. He drew up a tariff of surgeon's charges and instructed all licensed doctors to stick to the standardized fees. And every day he wrote a new instruction, report, or suggested treatment for the improvement of the leper colony. Dr. Barry wrote and wrote, but when he wrote about himself it was only from the position of the professional surgeon and scientist. It was almost as if he extended the logic of impersonal professionalism into his own life. As he had said in his retaliatory letter to Brink, he considered it his "bounden Duty" to avoid condescending "ever to be personal" in the execution of his official duties.

The degree to which Barry's methods were regarded as challenging and unconventional can be measured by the fury with which Brother Leitner began to complain about Barry's overactive management of the leper hospital. The Moravian missionary had little interest in medical cure, preferring to "treat the unfortunate as possible converts, and to hold services rather than bathing parades."

In June a requisition of medicines arrived at Hemel-en-Aarde addressed to Mr. Leitner. Attached were a set of manuscript directions from Barry entitled "Rules for the General Treatment of the Lepers, Which It Is Requested Mr and Mrs Leitner Attend to":

1st. The strictest attention must be paid to the personal cleanliness of the Lepers; their bedding and clothing must be frequently changed, and they must bathe twice a week at the least. The children should be bathed daily: the whole party would derive much benefit were it practicable to bathe daily.

2nd. The diet is of great consequence, nothing salted, such as fish, meat &c., should be permitted. Milk, rice, vegetables and fruit should be used as much as possible; fresh mutton and soup once daily, unless otherwise ordered.

3rd. The sores must be washed twice daily with Tar water and dressed with Tar plaster; the old plasters must be thrown away.

4th. The state of the bowels must be attended to, and recourse had to the medicines as directed in this book. The venereal cases must be kept apart from the other, and treated as ordered.

5th. The very bad cases of Leprosy must be separated from the others, and a sufficient quantity of Wine given to the sick (from 2 glasses to a pint, daily).

6th. The food must be clean and well cooked by persons appointed for that duty: the meals should be almost daily inspected by Mr and Mrs Leitner. Good order must be preserved, but no cruelty or deprivation of food must ever be resorted to. The parties must be considered not as Convicts, but as Unfortunate. The School and Church should be encouraged, as so should industry as much as possible. As my visits to this Institution will be frequent I shall from time to time point out any necessary changes. Also Mr Leitner must write to me every week, as to the changes, success, difficulties &c.

These manuscript directions were the last straw for Leitner. Writing to his superior, the Reverend Halbeck, he attached a copy of these "certain Rules" and protested that "you will easily perceive that the author . . . assumes a power over me, which I cannot acknowledge." Leitner's sole concern was to have official confirmation that he was not subordinate to Barry. From Barry's point of view, the question of hierarchy was a side issue to the urgent need to improve conditions and save the lives of the lepers.

Leitner, however, consistently defaulted on Barry's instructions. By August 1823, Barry had had enough. He was despairing at the repeated failure of his attempts to institute medical administration and better conditions for the lepers. In a rigidly formal tone, Barry finally wrote to Somerset to lay the case clearly before him. Barry entitled his account "Drawing Conclusions Demonstrative of the Impropriety of Permitting Mr Leitner to Exercise Any Authority in the Management of the Leper Institution." Although objective in laying out the dispute, Barry's deposition was nevertheless laden with irony and heavy with sarcasm:

It appears that Mr Leitner supposes the Institution at Hemel en Aarde to be committed by His Exellency to his judgement and under his sanctions; and not that of the Colonial Medical Inspector (for I do not speak of myself personally but, of any Professional Gentleman who shall be placed at the Head of the Colonial Medical Department) with the option of calling upon the Colonial Medical Inspector as upon his Apothecary for a dose of Physic, thro' the medium of the Colonial Office when it shall please him to think such assistance necessary, either for himself, or for the Lepers—any thing so absurd and offensive needs no comment. But I do beg leave to remark that when in consequence of the wretched state of the Lepers, His Exellency the Governor did me the honour to place the Institution under my special care and Directions, HE also condescended to consult with me as to capabilities of the functionaries to be placed there, whether I thought they were equal to see carried into effect my Instructions as they were likely people to prevent the Patients being cheated out of their Rations etc; I of course thought they were and at the same time, explained to His Excellency that medicine alone could but little benefit the Lepers—that Diet, Exercise and Cleanliness were the principal points to be rigidly attended to.

Pointing out that this plan had been adopted, Barry went on:

> Without arrogating myself I can say, that the Health, situation and Circumstances of the Lepers, have been not a little ameliorated by the means I undertook for the Direction of the Institution— I have laid down General Rules in writing for the use of the Persons overseeing the Patients. . . . It is cruel to the unfortunate Lepers if means be not taken for their benefit, and comfort, as well as to prevent the spreading of a Disease, the most loathsome and horrible inflicted upon the human species.

Barry's is the voice of the humanitarian crying in a wilderness of bureaucracy and self-interested personal gain. Where was the care for the plight of the lepers? Barry was also asking Somerset to take sides. He had clearly imagined that Somerset's endorsement would be forthcoming, and had no understanding of the fact that Somerset was trying to mediate by handling the battle with diplomacy. Barry concluded his deposition with an attempt to offer an olive branch, but he still refused to back down on the essential question of effective administration:

> Mr and Mrs Leitner are excellent People, sober, honest, and well calculated for overseers but are very much in want of an active steward, who could in Person see carried into effect the Instructions which the Colonial Medical Inspector thinks necessary to give; this man should write; and in fact be capable of taking the fag and responsibility upon himself, of course being subject to Mr Leitner.

Somerset refused to take Barry's part. Barry and Leitner were issued a compromise in which Leitner was required to assist Barry's inspections and listen to his recommendations, but was not required to send the weekly reports required by Barry. Bird then made it absolutely clear that he intended to keep Barry and Leitner apart:

Leitner's journal is to be received at my office and if any thing occur therein necessary for the Inspector to be made acquainted with, it will be communicated to him by me, or if there be any case, on which Mr Leitner desires Medical advice, by sending the particulars to me, an answer will be given as soon as possible.

Barry decided to rethink the whole problem. Dogged in his persistence, he refused to give up on the lepers. In September he wrote to Bird offering a new solution that caught the colonial office completely unawares, outmaneuvring Leitner in one stroke:

> The number of insuperable objections to the present local situation of the Leper Hospital renders it impossible to ever carry into effect any Plan for the benefit of the Patients there. That many of the difficulties are insurmountable has been fully proved, as during the space of ten years little has been done either to ameliorate the personal conditions of the Lepers, or to prevent the spreading of this Horrible Malady in the Colony.
>
> It is melancholy to observe (and it has frequently been my lot to do so, in making my Reports relative to this Institution) that the common necessities of Life have not yet been able to be procured in a proper, or wholesome state. The distance from the Seat of Government is much to be lamented; as a Public Institution of this nature should ever be under the Eye of Government.

Barry proposed that the leper institution be moved to Simon's Town, which was on the Cape peninsula and afforded "ample means of Bathing daily" in the sea, which, Barry stated, "is one of the principal points necessary to effect a cure of the disease." He had already instigated a routine of daily sea bathing for the lepers at Hemel-en-Aarde. While popular with the lepers, Barry's views on swimming in the sea were regarded with deep hostility and suspicion by the residents of Cape Town, as he was to later discover when he erected a bathing machine for Somerset near the beach.

Underwriting his recommendation to move the leper hospital closer to Cape Town, Barry offered a personal guarantee based on his own scientific opinion:

> I shall begin by promising that there is, and can be no dread of contagion (unless in direct personal contact with open sores or by inoculation) from Lepers; which is well proved by many Families having Lepers employed about them as Servants during years, without being in the least contaminated.

Barry was trying to remove prejudice against those who suffered from leprosy. But his pleas fell on stony ground. In the 1840s the leper colony was moved to Robben Island. Barry's argument that "fear of Contagion is an unfounded and capricious prejudice without any foundation" was far ahead of its time.

Measured against his own ambitions, Barry's attempt to reform conditions for lepers at the Cape had failed. However, in the longer term he had succeeded in making the colonial administration acknowledge the need for rethinking policy on the leper institution. The leper hospital was never again abandoned and forgotten, and although the management may have been in Barry's view inadequate, there was management.

Barry's reforms had two particular successes, both remarkable challenges to the status quo. In each case Barry succeeded in securing better treatment for people usually unprotected. In June 1823, Barry brought to the administration's attention his concern that "there are at present at the Institution a number of fine Healthy young Persons, from 2 to 15 years old; children of Lepers, but who have never had that Disease." Barry requested that "should it meet with the approbation of Lord Charles to remove these children from the Institution" they could be apprenticed out "in situations not *far distant* from the seat of Government; so as to be kept in view." Barry's justifications were his usual strategic mix of economic rationale and humanitarian responsibility.

Arguing that this measure would reduce government expense in caring for the lepers, he also pointed out that "the children themselves would be rendered useful Members of Society; whereas, now they are in a truly deplorable state." At a more practical level, this was yet another instance of Barry's particular care for the needs and rights of children. In his early years at the Cape he had shown a protective and nurturing interest toward privileged children: Emmanuel de Las Casas, the Rex children, Somerset's daughters. Now he turned his care to children who had nothing. He was successful in this petition, and secured the opportunity of a new start in life for several of the uninfected children at the leper colony.

Barry's other notable success was on a confidential matter that was decidedly between men. In 1824, Carel Friedrich Liesching applied to be permitted to practice as an apothecary. The only documentation he could provide in support of his application was a local certificate of apprenticeship. Carel Friedrich was the son of Dr. F. L. Liesching, one of the Cape Town prison doctors and the most powerful private doctor and wholesale trader in Cape Town. German by birth, Dr. Liesching had blazed a settler trail to the Cape and had been practicing as a physician and apothecary since 1800. As his responsibilities as a visiting physician grew, he left his apothecary shop in the hands of two shop managers, who held European diplomas. The young Carel Friedrich was apprenticed to these trained apothecaries for four years and thereafter became a partner in his father's business. Although he had not been trained in Europe, he had spent his whole life being trained by those who had.

Barry was asked to examine Carel Friedrich on August 3, 1824. But when he saw the young Liesching could only produce a certificate of apprenticeship signed by his father, he refused to examine him. On his father's advice, Liesching immediately protested directly to the governor, claiming that Barry, with whom he shared some "differences of a private nature," had demonstrated a "vindictive disposition" and "prejudged" him, even "before he had ever thought it worthwhile to let me pass a mock trial." Liesching claimed that on August 9 he had received a letter late in the evening summoning him to attend at "Dr Barry's quarters" the next day at noon. Liesching arrived punctually, expecting to "undergo an examination for which he was fully prepared." However, instead of examining him Barry asked him two questions: "1. Whether he had ever been in Europe. 2. Whether he had ever been in India." Having answered both in the negative, Liesching was asked to produce his certificates of apprenticeship and immediately dismissed. "Staggered at this proceeding" Liesching went straight to the colonial office, where he discovered from Mr. Brink that Barry's report had already been received and "the fate of myself and Family decided . . . before he had ever exchanged a word with me. . . . I now plainly saw I had been called for Mockery!"

Begging Somerset to decide whether under these circumstances Barry "can any longer be the arbiter of my fate," Liesching complained that there had been "no necessity for a Trial." Representing himself as "a child, if only an adopted child of Britanick Majesty's Government" Liesching begged for Somerset's protection, bemoaning "my wife and children doomed to poverty and disgrace and why? Because it was Dr Barry's pleasure."

Somerset chose to handle this sensitive situation by referring it to Chief Justice Truter for his legal interpretation of the requirements for certification. To Barry's fury, Truter found against his decision not to grant Liesching a licence. His interpretation of the revised proclamation was that apothecaries and chemists required certificates of apprenticeship, and to pass an examination in the colony a European diploma was not necessary for these occupations. Barry responded by assembling an impromptu board of medical officers to whom he presented his case. The board endorsed Barry's decision. Having secured their support, he then did something breathtaking in its lack of diplomacy and judgment—he wrote a letter to the colonial office questioning the competence of the Lord Chief Justice: "Sir John Truter, the Chief Justice can in no wise be a judge, or lay down the Law respecting the Medical Profession in any of its Branches."

Having questioned Truter's judgment Barry justified his own, pointing out that there had not been "one Instance since 1807 of any Person
being recommended to be allowed to practice . . . who has not been
regularly educated in some part of Europe." Barry remained obdurate
and refused to budge on his position, commenting archly in conclusion
that "the Cape is not a School for Medicine."

Somerset escalated the matter further by referring it to the most
powerful colonial dignitary at the Cape, His Majesty's fiscal, public
prosecutor Daniel Denyssen, who promptly upheld Truter's ruling.
On December 14, Sir Richard Plaskett, a senior civil servant of equally
high standing at the Cape, wrote to Barry to notify him that he was to
examine Carel Liesching on the governor's instruction.

Barry responded by completely ignoring Plaskett's instruction, as
well as the further representations that followed it when the civil servant received no reply. Barry also went to Newlands to argue with
Somerset in his private rooms. The tempestuous meeting between
them, recorded by an eavesdropper outside the window, became legendary:

A long, stout arm seized the little man who was near the window
and the same arm suddenly thrust the yelling Surgeon through
the window, dangling him over a bed of hydrangeas until he
prayed for mercy.

Whether truth or embellishment, this story had found its way to the
gossip-filled balconies of Society House before sundown.

By the end of December, Barry was almost entirely isolated on the
Liesching issue. Barry had come to see himself as a persecuted champion of scientific standards, carrying the torch for the humanitarian
treatment of patients whose safety he refused to see compromised. His
conviction extended to refusing to back down despite Somerset's direct
request. Utterly opposed to Somerset's position on this issue, Barry
rudely suggested that he would leave it to "His Excellency's consideration to dispense with an examination and grant to Mr Charles

Liesching a licence to practise or otherwise as shall seem meet to His Excellency." By now exasperated at Barry's refusal to budge, His Excellency himself constituted another medical board to examine Liesching.

Creating a final opportunity for Barry to save face over this issue, Somerset offered him a position on the examining board. Barry made himself a hostage to fortune by refusing to back down even at this end point in the game. Barry wrote this time to Plaskett to ask him to request of Somerset "that he will be graciously pleased to spare me a Duty, the performance of which I am anxious to avoid, for reasons which I feel confident will be appreciated by His Excellency the Governor." Somerset allowed Barry to demur, but Barry had made an enemy of Plaskett during the Liesching affair. Plaskett was openly critical of Barry, complaining that he wrote his official letters "in a tone of unbecoming warmth." Plaskett also disapproved of Barry's insubordination: "Even in his official intercourse with the Highest Persons in the Government [he] was quite unmindful of the respect that he owed their rank and station." Finding Barry overall "most impertinent," Plaskett cautioned Barry that "if he were not more cautious as to his expressions, he would certainly get into a scrape." This was a prescient warning.

The Liesching affair stands for a number of disputes Barry had with people to whom he refused to grant licences. But because of Carel Liesching's standing in the community, it was the most significant. During this episode Barry also made an enemy of the man who was finally to cost him his job.

Barry's intransigence on the strict interpretation of the law was another indicator of his overdetermined identification with the institutions in which he worked. He had the ideologue's belief that all must participate in the grand scheme of medical reform and modern scientific practice on a basis of personal sacrifice. As he remarked in one of his letters regarding the need for the exact application of the laws of medical examination, the needs of the many should always come before those of the few. But there was more to Barry's pedantic application of regulation than his own shortcomings in the field of human diplomacy.

Barry's sophistry in this regard was a defense mechanism masking a deep and troubled insecurity. He was almost neurotically overinvested in his identification of his own person with his institutional office: he had no confidence that he would retain his own authority if he deviated, even for a minute, from the processes and methods authorized by the institution. Barry's relationship with official institutions was contradictory. He would defy rules when they obstructed his purpose, but he also clung doggedly to those conventions that protected his professional image as an officer, surgeon, and gentleman.

In his official correspondence regarding the licensing of physicians, Barry chose to illustrate his argument by presenting the scenario of a man shipwrecked at the Cape, washed ashore bereft of all possessions and unable to prove his qualifications to practice as a medic. How "in a distant Colony, occasionally resort of worse than convicts" could people know who a stranger was, "unless Certificates be previously produced?"

> Suppose a case viz: a Man shipwrecked and destitute of every means of support except he be allowed to practice Medicine having lost his Documents; that he should be allowed an Examination to Qualify him. To this, I do reply, that there are some in Practice here who by their Profession cannot obtain Bread; and again, that there are Funds and other means to prevent actual starvation until the necessary documents should arrive from Europe. The People here are not so destitute of feeling as to permit an industrious man to starve for a few months—and under all circumstances it is better one individual suffers than many perish.

It is an odd example and a deeply revealing tale. The truth of the shipwrecked mariner's identity rests on his ability to prove his professional qualifications with authorized documents. Without the authority of the certifying institution, Barry argues, this person simply does not exist. Worse, he most certainly is not what he seems. Despite the extremity of the story, it is a natural example for Barry. Without the sanction of the institution, it says, there are no recognizable markers of identity or good character. Without this documentation, a person is merely a shipwrecked stranger on an alien shore. It is a fascinating figure for Barry's deep-seated fears about his own self-fashioned identity. It is also another demonstration of his talismanic belief in the power of pieces of paper to create people and secure their position in the world.

Chapter 5

SACRIFICED TO INFAMY

My more than father—my almost only friend.

James Barry in a letter concerning Lord Charles Somerset

If one tells the truth, one is sure, sooner or later, to be found out.

Oscar Wilde, *Phrases and Philosophies for the Use of the Young*

ON THE EVENING OF JUNE 2, 1824, DR. BARRY ACCOMPANIED LORD and Lady Somerset to the African Theatre in Riebeeck Square to see a new comedy by the Cape dramatist Mr. Boniface. Set against the backdrop of Table Mountain, the theater had a distinctive appearance, with its grand columned entrance and large buttresses tapering to the roof. When the doors opened at six o'clock, fashionably attired ladies in empire dresses swept up the steep flight of steps past the Malay sweet-sellers to the entrance. Only the governor and his entourage were permitted to enter by the back door, as they did on that Wednesday evening in June.

The painter and diarist Dr. Samuel Eusebius Hudson, who claimed descent from none other than Dr. Johnson himself, was as keen a visitor to the theater as the Somersets and Dr. Barry. He wrote:

His Lordship and Lady Charles and Dr Barry were at the play last night and were received with enthusiastic applause by the audience. I am glad they were at the theatre, it was doing what they might. Had he [Somerset] been as attentive to those constant visitations and made the public his friends that deep hatred would never have taken place.

Hudson, along with the other Cape Town notables, socialites, and military men who thronged to the theater that night, was not there primarily to see the play. The performance they had come to see was the public appearance of the sensational ménage à trois, the governor, Lady Somerset, and Dr. Barry, out together for an evening facing down their critics. When the stylishly dressed Lord and Lady Somerset and Dr. Barry stepped into the governor's box, a momentary hush fell over the gossiping audience. The brief and pregnant pause was drowned out in an instant by the cacophonous sound of the spectators bursting into spontaneous applause. Many stood as they clapped. Lady Somerset dipped her head in a courteous bow as she sat down, followed by her husband and Dr. Barry. All three turned to face the stage curtain, on which was painted "All the World's a Stage." The curtain opened. It was seven o'clock, and the three had just endured the most traumatic forty-eight hours of their lives.

The previous day a controversy had broken over the heads of the governor and the colonial medical inspector that had scandalized the entire town. Lord Somerset and Dr. Barry had been publicly accused of a homosexual relationship. As Samuel Hudson recorded in his journal, the accusation charging "His Excellency Lord Charles Somerset with unnatural practises with Dr Barry has thrown the whole Cape into consternation." It was the gravest crisis of Barry's young life.

TUESDAY, JUNE 1, BEGAN ORDINARILY FOR CAPTAIN JOHN FINDLAY, master of the *Alacrity,* harbored in Table Bay. He rose early to take his morning coffee on the stoop of his lodgings in the Heerengracht and waited for the sun to lift the misty tablecloth spread over the granite mountain. The Heerengracht was the perfect vantage point from which to scrutinize the maritime comings and goings of the early-nineteenth-century world from east to west. Like other merchant seamen of his means, the Scottish Findlay opted for expensive lodgings in order to be in sight of Table Bay, where his brig was docked. It was "a very foggy morning," and Findlay was straining his eyes through the mist on the lookout for ships plying illegal cargoes from the great trading marts of the east: Sumatra, Java, Macao, and Cochin. Their contraband was human—slaves. In the decades after the British technically ended their participation in the Atlantic slave trade in 1808, slavers from the east, sidling along the lush coast of southern Africa, ran the greatest risk of discovery of their illicit traffic in human flesh in the stormy waters of the Cape. Motivated by cash rewards, people would report these ships to the British authorities. Findlay did spot something illegal that morning, but it was not a slaver.

Looking out from his stoop, Findlay "saw a libel fixed to the right side of the Bridge." He put on his boots and "went to the spot to learn the contents of it." As he approached the bridge, Findlay saw two strangers reading the placard, "the one black of complexion and the other yellow, being at the post of the Bridge, in looking at the Libel the yellow person, being a boy of about sixteen years of age, mentioned to me unasked that it was something about Lord Charles. I then examined the paper. . . ." Findlay was not a man to harbor any squeamish scruples about local political gossip and the people it affected. However, this placard, with its contents leering out on to the busiest and most public street in the entire colony, contained a scandalous charge:

A person, living at Newlands, takes this method of making it known, to the public authorities of this Colony that on the 5th Instant he detected Lord Charles buggering Dr Barry. Lady Charles had her suspicions, or saw something that led her to suspicion, which had caused a general quarrel. . . . The person is ready to come and make oaths to the above.

Findlay's acquaintance and neighbor, Thomas Deane, "about sunrise having got up and opened the window," noticed activity in the street below. He described how he had seen "two slave boys with baskets in their hands and a person with a grey cloak on, looking at the post of the Bridge." Deane was close enough to hear the group whispering about the governor, and went down into the street to investigate. Finding nothing out of the ordinary, Deane recalled that:

> I thereupon returned to my bedroom and did not come down until 9 o'clock, and about half past 9 o'clock I met Captain Findlay, who having been asked by me whether there was any news, communicated to me the contents of a Libel which was placarded at the post of the Bridge, and which he had seen and read.

Asked to repeat the contents of the placard to the investigating authorities, Deane confirmed that it asserted that an unnamed witness had seen "Lord Charles Somerset buggering Barry."

By then Cape Town was awake and the Heerengracht bustling with morning traffic. News of the placard had already reached Society House, where merchants, politicians, and civil servants were discussing its contents over breakfast. Findlay and Deane agreed that they should report the placard to the police office, but by the time the official investigation was launched, lurid descriptions of the placard and its contents had already spread like bushfire around the town, though the placard itself had vanished. The disappearance of the source did nothing to silence the fascinated town.

We cannot know how Barry discovered the news of this sexually explicit libel. There is no doubt that the news reached him swiftly, but not soon enough for him to see the placard for himself; it was torn down and disappeared mysteriously into the milling crowds by the bridge. Thomas Thwaite, who had heard of the placard through office chatter, reported that "it was a young man on horseback passing by who had taken it down." Mrs. Saunders, purveyor of Psyche's buns, told William

Bridekirk, "as decently and politely as she could," that "Dr Barry had mentioned it to her." Told of the libel by his wife, Mr. Saunders declared it "a most diabolical accusation." Barry was determined to put a brave face on acknowledging the slander. He presented a stoical image, but inwardly he must have been thrown into emotional pandemonium. Sexual scandal breached the professionalism that he had sought to make impermeable. In the British colonies of the 1820s, sex between adult men was an offense punishable by death. Though Barry knew that Somerset had the power to quash the libel, he could not calculate the damage this public charge might do to his career.

The accusation sought to expose two of the most prominent figures in South Africa and on the larger European imperial stage. Barry had flown close to the wind in his flagrantly intimate relationship with Somerset. Somerset for his part had stubbornly rejected official advice that he distance himself from Barry. For Barry had secrets. These were not the ordinary secrets of petty irregularities and youthful indiscretions that most people carry with them. Barry's secrets were of a nature that placed him beyond the understanding of the society in which he moved. They were also the secrets of the impostor. In the years 1824 to 1827 Barry's relationship with Somerset was placed under almost unbearable strain over civil and political issues. Yet at no point does the bond between them seem to have been really dented. The endurance of this intense and ultimately unexplained relationship was summarized by Barry in a letter he wrote when Somerset died. Somerset was, Barry says poignantly, "my more than father—my almost only friend."

In fact, it was not the first time that the intimate relationship between Somerset and Barry had been a matter of public satire. A few months earlier, Josias Cloete, Barry's friend and onetime dueling partner, had brought him a broadsheet on which was printed a satirical quatrain about Lord Somerset and himself, probably written by Mr. Bishop Burnett, a bankrupt cleric who had been evicted from his farm, a friend of the free press, and one of Somerset's fiercest critics. Barry, the story went, had arrived a little late at St. George's cathedral one Sunday morning. Striding into the church, he saw that the governor's pew was empty and promptly spun about and left the church:

> With courteous devotion inspired
> Dr Barry went to the temple of prayer
> But turned on his heel and retired
> When he saw that HIS Lord was not there.

The imputation was clearly that Dr. Barry and Somerset were engaged in ungodly, clandestine activities. The unkind characterization of Barry as Somerset's adoring lackey was uncomfortably close to the truth. Barry's unstinting loyalty to Somerset made him suspect with all the governor's enemies. It also infuriated the political opposition to Somerset, who knew that Barry's politics were at variance with those of his adored lord.

Mr. Bishop Burnett bore a painful grudge against Barry that might have explained his witty doggerel. Suffering from acute toothache, Burnett had the previous year sent a polite note to Dr. Barry requesting his attendance for the purpose of removing the offending tooth. On receipt of the request Barry flew into a whirlwind of indignation, declaring in front of the anxious messenger, "What, does this stupid parson suppose I am a vulgar tooth-drawer? If he had personally made the application, his cloth would not have saved his ears." Barry then mounted his horse, went to the workshops of the Cape Town farrier Mr. Thomas, and asked if he had ever drawn the tooth of a horse or a donkey. Thomas replied that he had not, but did not anticipate it would be difficult were he employed to do so. Barry then instructed him to "proceed to the residence of the Rev. Mr. —— and draw the tooth of a donkey then suffering from acute tooth ache." The willing farrier, "with assistants and lots of formidable hand-vices, pincers, &c," turned up on the reverend gentleman's doorstep, explaining that "Dr Barry has instructed me to come, without delay, to draw the tooth of a donkey in the stable of your reverence." Incandescent with rage—and toothache—the cleric went straight to Somerset to complain. The governor made light of the elaborate insult, saying, "No one pays any attention to what the doctor says and does; you had better join in the laugh against you."

As Burnett's doggerel verse shows, the peculiarly close relationship between Dr. Barry and the governor was a matter of common knowledge and public comment. Burnett wrote bluntly that Barry "is, has been and if rumour speaks true, will remain single." By 1824, Somerset was facing an increasingly serious array of problems with his administration, a central issue of which was his uncompromising effort to stifle the birth of a free press in South Africa. Somerset was increasingly suspicious of the loyalties of all but a few close friends and advisors, particularly his colonial secretary, Christopher Bird, who had revealed himself to be untrustworthy. In this climate of suspicion and mistrust, it was evident that Barry was one of the few who remained an arch Somerset loyalist. The fact that Barry was known to support the cause of the free press only made this allegiance more complicated. It was clearly based on personal loyalty, from which Barry would not be deflected by his progressive friends. Barry, in his late twenties, was single, professionally successful, and, as even his enemies agreed, dashingly rakish. His intimacy with Charles Somerset predated the arrival of the second Lady Somerset in 1821, and a number of diarists—Samuel Hudson among them—had speculated privately on the odd nature of the triangular relationship that dominated the governor's household. Hudson was not alone in expressing pity for "poor Lady Somerset."

By the Wednesday morning after the libel was posted, a full legal investigation had been launched, and a proclamation posted at Government House and all around the town. Cape Town talked of nothing else. Mr. Richardson entered his printing offices that morning and told his colleagues: "We have a fine to do, somebody has put up a Placard, saying that Lord Charles Somerset and Dr Barry had been caught in a certain position. The government are making a great storm, and have offered in a proclamation a large reward for any person who will tell who did it." The compositor Thomas Hammond had been fetched from his house late the previous evening to print the proclamation, which offered a generous reward of five thousand rixdollars to anyone who could provide information leading to identification of the culprits. A further reward of one thousand rixdollars was offered for the recovery of the placard, to which Barry personally added another one thousand rixdollars of his own money to bolster the incentive for the placard to be turned in to the authorities. A public subscription at the commercial exchange had raised an additional five thousand by the end of the week. Describing his role in the affair, Hammond could not help adding that all who heard of the slander "expressed their horror at the idea, and would not believe it could be true." Moral outrage and self-righteous indignation, of course, provided the perfect opportunity for people to discuss the gossip endlessly.

On the same day, William Edwards, a Cape Town attorney of "vituperous tongue," wrote a letter from the town prison to Stephen Twycross, member of the commercial hall:

> Being this afternoon informed of the disgusting placard which has roused the indignation of all Members of the Colonial Society . . . I took some hours uninterrupted conversation to form any opinion before I resolved how to act; this convinced me that the odious placard emanates from someone who wishes to bring the press and the public feeling of this Colony into disrepute, or with a monster whom it would be impossible to describe. As I would not be capable of acting with men who would stab another in the dark, I write this letter without the least consultation with anyone, and I shall now proceed to Botany Bay and leave this place without regret, altho' there is one person whom I suspect as the writer of that infamous paper, a suspicion which will not be removed until the detection of the miscreant shews me I am wrong.

This deeply ironic letter was a breathtaking act of audacity, and the last act of a reprobate grifter who knew his game was up. The "miscreant" and "monster whom it would be impossible to describe" was in fact Edwards himself, who was revealed by a servant to be the instigator of the placard. Edwards, "who seemed to have come from nowhere," had quickly established himself as a controversial celebrity at the Cape. His theatrical court antics entranced the public galleries, and he was imprisoned for contempt on practically every occasion he set foot in court. When Edwards decided to align himself with the independent press, he did their just cause all harm and no good. Launching a series of personal slanderous attacks directly against Somerset, Edwards soon found himself arraigned in court for defaming the governor and his administration.

It emerged that Edwards had sent a number of libelous letters to Somerset containing a torrid outpouring of accusations against him and his officials, including charges of murder. Found guilty on all counts, Edwards was sentenced to deportation to New South Wales. His letters were pivotal to the political storm that developed over the press freedom in South Africa. It was because of his fear that these libels would be published that Somerset ordered the presses of the *South African Commercial Advertiser* to be sealed. From this act of censorship unrolled a tangled dispute that found its way back to the parliamentary debating chambers in London.

While Edwards was a maverick, the printers, writers, and intellectuals who formed the hub of the free press movement in early South Africa were educated and committed radicals taking a principled stand on the essential need for a democratic, open press in the rapidly burgeoning colony. They could not know that Edwards, who appeared to be "a professional man of ability and good standing," was shortly to be revealed as one of the most remarkable impostors to have arrived on Cape shores. Shortly after his deportation to Australia it was discovered that he was in reality one Alexander Low Kay, who had inveigled himself into marriage with an attorney's daughter in Chester, England. Moving to London with his moneyed wife, Edwards had "got connected with Sharpers and Swindlers" and after numerous scrapes been deported to New South Wales for theft. Edwards escaped from Australia on a ship bound for the Cape, where he had presented himself in the guise of a professional attorney. This, then, was the man who had conspired to reveal the homosexual relationship between Somerset and Barry.

At the time of the placard affair, Edwards was in Cape Town prison, awaiting deportation back to New South Wales. Although his colleagues in the free press were unaware of it, Edwards knew that his past was about to catch up with him. While his supporters decried the severity of his sentence, Edwards was enjoying his last curtain call on the Cape social stage. On June 4, an anonymous letter was delivered to Barry's house suggesting that Mr. George Greig and Mr. William Edwards "be summoned by the Fiscal and be examined before the Commissioners of the Court of Justice" on the question of the authorship of the placard. George Greig, a former printer in His Majesty's Printing Office and a freeman of the stationer's company, was the owner of the Cape's only commercial printing house, proprietor of its first independent newspaper, the *South African Commercial Advertiser,* and printer of the *South African Journal.*

Until 1824, Cape Town had had no established independent press. Since 1800 the government had published a weekly paper, the *Cape Town Gazette and African Advertiser.* Known as the *Courant,* this was a bilingual Dutch and English publication. Those with access to Society House or the public library could read newspapers and journals from England already yellowed from their long journeys from Liverpool and London, usually four to six months out of date. In 1824, two local journals had made their appearance: Greig's *South African Commercial Advertiser* and the *South African Journal,* run by the Scottish intellectual, poet, and "arrant Dissenter" Thomas Pringle. The *Commercial Advertiser* had stopped printing in May with its eighteenth issue when the Somerset administration had objected to the reporting of the Edwards case. Regarding the press coverage as sedition, Somerset had ordered the sealing of Greig's presses and ordered him to leave the colony within a month. By June 1824, Somerset was deeply embroiled in a storm over press censorship, and Greig was on his way to London to put a case against him before the British government. Somerset's stifling of the first privately owned newspapers at the colony, whose news content was negligible, alienated not only the printers and aspirant journalists but the free burghers of Cape Town, with their pockets full of complaints and nowhere to empty them.

The stifled would-be press barons, their presses confiscated, retaliated by circulating anonymous and amusing lampoons, caricatures, and doggerel verse around the city. A rash of scurrilous anonymous placards appeared. Flagrantly disrespectful of Somerset's administration and full of wit, these posters demonstrated a new spirit of civic resistance to the colonial administration. In this hothouse atmosphere it was only a matter of time before Barry's close relationship with the patrician governor became easy game for the political satirists.

Barry passed the anonymous letter he had received on June 4 to the fiscal, Daniel Denyssen, who was in charge of the commission of enquiry. The affair was the sole topic of conversation in the town: "Every corner of the streets are assembled with servants and proclamations for the discovery of the author of the placard suspecting the governor and Dr Barry." One of these servants, Daniel Lee, came forward to offer damning testimony against his master, William Edwards, in exchange for leniency toward his own role in the affair. Lee proved to be the commission's most crucial witness. He explained how, before his recent arrest, Edwards had sent him with a message to Mr. Bishop Burnett. After taking the note from Lee, Burnett disappeared upstairs, and, as Lee described in court,

> Shortly after came down with a large bundle of papers wrapped up in another paper, but not sealed, desiring me to take particular care and not to let any of them drop; but to deliver them safely to Mr Edwards, which I accordingly did. Mr Edwards then opened the papers and the first which he took out was the Placard con-

cerning Lord Charles and Dr Barry's wife, which when he read it, he laughed so loudly as to make me take particular note of what he read.

Daniel Lee's tantalizing description of the placard as being about "Lord Charles and Dr Barry's wife" underlines the way in which Barry was feminized by the sodomy scandal. Under cross-examination Lee was pressed on this point. He told the court that he had occasion to see the placard on a further occasion when he "found Mr Greig and Mr Edwards . . . both employed in reading the paper. Mr Greig then spoke to Mr Edwards about putting it up, but Mr Greig said it was better to wait till his third sentence was passed, which Mr Edwards then said was very good." The planning of the conspiracy was thus revealed. The placard had been produced by Greig, Burnett, and Edwards prior to the latter's conviction. It was agreed that once Edwards was in prison and able to claim a convincing alibi, the placard would be posted.

Lee was clearly offended at being deemed by his employers "too low to pin the placard up," which was not a reference to his menial status as a servant but to the fact that he was too short to reach the post on which they wanted the poster secured "before Gunfire in the morning." Lee was sent to arrange for a taller man named Benjamin Wilmot to post the libel. Summoned before the court, Wilmot admitted his role and referred to "the placard of Lord Charles and little Dr Barry's wife." These repeated references to "Dr Barry's wife" were the cause of Bishop Burnett's pointed remarks regarding Barry's obdurate bachelorhood.

By June 12, the public subscription for the reward had increased to fifteen thousand rixdollars,* and William Edwards was infuriated that he was not going to get his day in court. He attempted to prod the commission into summoning him, and he accused Daniel Lee of perjury. As Edwards was already awaiting deportation on a separate conviction, the colonial authorities decided that there was little point in risking his ap-

---

*Current value: $195,000 (U.S.).

pearance in court. As Samuel Hudson astutely observed: "I must think Edwards enjoys it as do what they will they cannot punish him more than their former sentence and I have a doubt whether they can do it at all as the paper was torn down immediately and Edwards may swear he did not do it." Cape Town was alight with rumors about the placard. One claimed that Daniel Lee, who said that William Edwards "had a copy of it in his writing desk," had made a copy of the lampoon and that this copy had been lodged with Denyssen. Others whispered that they would not be surprised if the affair was "all a trick by some of Lord Charles's friends to convince the people at home of the dangers of a free press." On Sunday, June 6, worshippers emerging from St. George's gathered in the Dutch East India Company gardens to trade hearsay on the matter; the latest word was that many thought the placard would not be discovered. This proved to be true. Government agents inspecting the premises of George Greig and Bishop Burnett did, however, find a caricature of Lord Charles "as the Devil flying away with the Fiscal in his possession." Burnett and Greig were arrested for this cartoon. It was a mark of Somerset's power that he had ensured that within a fortnight all those suspected of being involved in the sodomy libel had been detained, without any of them being charged for the offense of producing the placard. Somerset would not countenance a public debate in which the contents of the libel would be placed under further, embarrassing scrutiny.

The process of gathering the depositions of witnesses had already led to persistent interrogation on the question of what exactly the placard claimed had taken place between Somerset and Barry. The flustered court recorder had stumbled over the frequency with which he was required to write the word *buggering,* or rather, as he initially wrote it, "bugguery." His spelling error having been quietly pointed out to him, he proceeded to spell the word with more confident accuracy. As the testimonials continued, witnesses were gently nudged toward more allusive reference to the "certain position" in which Somerset and Barry had allegedly been discovered. Some themselves asked if they might be permitted to "suggest the particulars delicately," or referred generally to "unnatural practices." Clearly there were those who felt nervous about impugning the governor, such as Thomas Thwaite, who when asked to repeat "the exact words" floundered:

> I cannot exactly say the identical words, but it conveyed to my mind, that it represented His Excellency and Dr Barry as being caught in that situation as was unnatural. It had that impression on my mind.

While William Edwards and his cohorts were fingered as the authors of the placard, the identity of the "person, living at Newlands" who claimed to have "detected Lord Charles buggering Barry" was never publicly revealed. Either the story was a fiction, or Somerset dealt with the betrayal behind closed doors.

Meanwhile, Daniel Lee found himself the target of bounty hunters eager to claim the reward for the discovery of a copy of the placard. Roger James O'Grady, an Irish sailor, was particularly persistent in his attempts to dupe the swaggering Lee. The mellifluous O'Grady later amusingly described to the court how he had taken Lee to The Sun, a public house near the barracks, and plied him with alcohol in the hope of further information:

> The bottle of wine came in, I filled the two glasses. The first conversation was about a sweetheart, but I questioned him about the Placard, when I found him to be a little warm from the wine; but I could not get him to tell me anything about it. He was continuously introducing his sweetheart into the conversation. But I was always wanting him to tell me about the Placard of which he told me the day before he had a copy. He told me he could not get it, but he promised to get it for me tomorrow (this day) at 2 o'clock.

Once thoroughly in their cups, O'Grady flattered Lee into confessing that "it was Mr Edwards and his good many friends" who had been the "clever fellows" who were behind the placard. In the early hours of the morning, the two staggered back along the Heerengracht, pausing under the bridge at the crossing of Hout Street: "Dan!" exclaimed O'Grady. "Is it not somewhere here where the Placard was stuck up?" Lee then proceeded to choreograph O'Grady in a drunken dance until the exact position was identified, after which the two collapsed in a heap. When Lee failed to produce the placard the following day, O'Grady took his irritation and hangover to the authorities and announced his wish to testify against Lee.

Though unwilling to declare their criticisms publicly, there were many in Cape Town who felt that Somerset had only himself to blame for the libels against him and his favorite. The merchants and commercial leaders of the colony made a great show of supporting the government; those who supported the cause of the free press and objected to Somerset's "Reign of Terror" felt that Somerset and his supporters deserved the discomfort they were experiencing. People were also insatiably curious as to whether the rumors of a sexual relationship between Somerset and Barry were true. In an age hostile to homosexuality, many were undecided as to whether Greig, Edwards, Burnett, and their cohorts had gone too far with their sexual libel against Barry and the governor. Samuel Hudson summed up this climate of opinion in his private journal:

> How galling it must be to the friends of Lord Charles and Dr Barry. There are many who will enjoy to see these arrogants humbled. But if miscreant, the scheme is a diabolical one. . . . Lord Charles surely deserves all he suffers and it remains to be proved whether the whole thing is without foundation. The Doctor is one of the dupes. . . .

Hudson, who felt particularly sorry for Lady Somerset's embarrassed status in the whole affair, clearly felt that there was some foundation in the charge made against Somerset and Barry. Determined not to make any contribution to the public subscription, he concluded smugly, "The laugh is completely against the whole of them."

News traveled slowly from the Cape to England. The affair was not discussed at Westminster until June the following year. Parliament was already waiting for the report of the commission of enquiry, which had been sent to the Cape in 1823. Led by Mr. J. T. Bigge, a former judge in the West Indies, and Major W.M.G. Colebrooke, the commission was appointed to investigate the affairs of the colony. Bigge and Colebrooke arrived in the Cape in July 1823 and were received by Somerset in "the most courteous manner." Somerset continued to fully cooperate with all diligent investigations of the inquiry, although it was a constant source of bemusement and frustration to him over the following years that he could not persuade Mr. Bigge to accompany him to the hunt or on one of his notoriously vigorous rides over the Cape countryside. Despite Somerset's frequent and eager invitations, "Mr Bigge seemed quite as eager to avoid such violent forms of exertion as Lord Charles was to offer them."

Somerset's boundless physical energy and love of blood sports were always among his most defining characteristics. An aristocrat of an already receding age, it never seemed to occur to Somerset that prioritizing hunting and sporting activities over matters of state might be regarded as inappropriate. In one of his earliest letters to arrange a meeting with Mr. Bigge, Somerset pointed out that Friday would not be convenient as it was "fixed for hunting."

On June 16, 1825, Henry Brougham declared in Parliament, "Lord Charles ought not to be the sport and victim of charges loosely ventilated in the house." The hunter had become the hunted. Somerset stood accused of "the most arbitrary and tyrannical oppression," of misgovernment, maladministration, and of being excessively "hostile to the press." And in his unusual relationship with James Barry, Somerset's pursuers scented blood. Bishop Burnett presented a personal petition, read out in Parliament by Brougham, protesting the unfair treatment he had received at the Cape. Tried (on an unrelated libel charge) and convicted to banishment from the colony for five years, Burnett made it clear that he believed himself persecuted because of his imputed involvement in the placard libel. In his petition, Burnett described how:

> His house was invaded by HM Fiscal, and attendants, under the sanction of His Excellency's warrant, and his papers seized for the avowed purpose of implicating him in the promulgation of a charge against his excellency, of having committed an unspeakable atrocity with his reputed son, the physician to his household.

Thus a charge of incest against Charles Somerset and James Barry was heaped on top of that of homosexuality. This claim led some in the twentieth century to speculate, rather literally, that Barry might have been Somerset's son. In reality, what the accusation underlines was the public awareness of the way in which the young bachelor Barry idolized the middle-aged, physically and politically powerful Somerset as a highly eroticized paternal protector and, probably, initiator in the rites of sex. It was only after Somerset died, and in private, that Barry revealed himself to be acutely self-knowing about the way in which Somerset had become a symbolic father for him—the caring, protective, and charismatic father he seems never to have had.

In public, Lady Mary Somerset retained a dignified silence. What took place between the three behind closed doors can be only a matter of speculation. If there had been, as the placard suggested, a quarrel between the three protagonists in this very public drama, it remained private. Public sympathy was extended to Lady Somerset as the humiliated wife, but as the appearance of the three together at the African Theatre demonstrated, she was determined to present a public show of support for her husband and, perhaps more curiously, for the troublesome Dr. Barry.

Despite his love of the limelight, Barry would have taken scant comfort from knowing that his imputed sexual proclivities and relationship with Somerset were the subject of parliamentary debate. In 1826 alone, there were no fewer than three occasions when this affair was discussed in Parliament in debates on Somerset's governorship, led by such radical members as Joseph Hume, Brougham, and Francis Burdett. Lord Edward Somerset, member for Gloucester, defended his relative in Parliament:

> Anonymous publications had been circulated against his noble relation, and the utmost pains had been taken to diffuse such slander throughout the Cape. Some of these charges were of the most atrocious nature; but at the same time, their inconsistencies with each other destroyed the credibility of the whole of them.

In May 1826, the commission of enquiry finally presented its first voluminous report to Parliament. It was the commission's opinion that while there were evident errors of government and administration at the Cape, Burnett's charges against Somerset were "grossly exaggerated." Somerset decided to return to England and face his accusers in Parliament. Burnett's was only one among a number of complaints that had been brought against him, including corruption, mishandling of land grants and, always his greatest Achilles' heel, his suppression of the press. It was, however, to be a while before Somerset would depart for England, and in the interim another crisis concerning James Barry would erupt at the Cape.

While Barry continued to weather the storm in Cape Town, he also had to contend with the fact that Somerset's attitude toward him had become complicated by the affair. When the senior commissioner of enquiry, Mr. Bigge, fell from his horse on his way back from Grahamstown on the eastern frontier, Somerset wrote him a considerate letter:

> Permit me to entreat you that . . . you will give a week or 10 days up exclusively to repose. . . . Barry (absurd in everything else) is the greatest physician that I have ever met with and would completely set you up.

Somerset continued to support Barry professionally while taking the precaution of distancing himself from him personally. Barry was still a welcome guest at the governor's private residence at Newlands, however, and seen frequently in the company of Lady Somerset and her stepdaughters.

Nonetheless, the placard affair, the very public trial that followed in its wake, and the governor's increasingly controversial political position brought a sea change in Barry's relationship with Somerset. Somerset was politically besieged, and Barry's position became vulnerable. Somerset had not withdrawn his personal friendship from Barry, but he realized that publicly he needed to be more circumspect in how he endorsed the colonial medical inspector's position. Tragically, it took longer for Barry to understand that Somerset was trying to protect both of them by instigating some professional distance in their relationship and encouraging him toward greater diplomacy. Whatever the truth of the libel, Somerset was shaken by the public charge of his indulgence in "unnatural practices." Sodomy charges were not to be taken lightly. Barry's fears that the sexual scandal would damage his professional standing proved well founded, although it would take several more years before he finally left the Cape. His activities in defense of the sick, the poor, slaves, women, lunatics, and criminals had already made him unpopular in conservative quarters, and he had made many enemies. Despite his waning popularity, Barry's manner continued to be forthright and uncompromising. For the first time in his life, he would hold fast to a difficult position alone and without powerful mentors.

A dogged critic of prison conditions and the treatment of prisoners, Barry had made particular enemies of the officials responsible for the prison system. In August 1825, Barry received a request from Denyssen to authorize the transfer of a prisoner, Aaron Smith, to the lunatic asylum in the Somerset Hospital. A sailor detained in prison after a drunken binge, Smith had been certified as "deranged in his mind" by Dr. Liesching, apparently at the request of Denyssen, whose property Smith had damaged. Somerset requested that Barry investigate the case and report back to him. Barry sent his report, as appropriate, to Sir

Richard Plaskett, acting secretary to the government, who in 1824 had replaced Christopher Bird. Barry was utterly uncompromising and, ill-advisedly, deeply sarcastic in reporting his findings:

> I am decidedly of the opinion that Aaron Smith is perfectly sane in mind; and by no means a subject for the Somerset Hospital. Dr Liesching appeared to be of the same way of thinking. But, probably, His Majesty's Fiscal's application for Aaron Smith's admission to that Establishment has been in the spirit of pure Charity, for the benevolent purpose of having the wounds inflicted on this poor Man (on the day of his admission to the Tronk) by the Dienaar [policeman], professionally attended to. However, upon inquiry I find that Aaron Smith had laboured under temporary insanity, the effects of hard drinking; in which state he was committed to the Town Prison, and upon which occasion, the Dienaar exercised his Brutality; to the horror and Dismay of the Prisoners, who loudly exclaimed against it. I beg leave here to say that it is by no means an uncommon event, to find Prisoners beat in the most savage manner by these good people—the Dienaars.

Barry concluded that Smith had merely gotten drunk, and that normal diet and much sleep had proved adequate treatment: "I think it expedient to enter into this Detail for the purpose of explaining that the absence of Viscious [*sic*] and Spiritous liquors was sufficient to restore Smith to his senses—such as they are." Smith was not mad, he was the victim of extreme reprisal for an inebriated escapade in which he had the misfortune to damage the property of a senior official. It was a courageous and unguarded protest. In one short letter Barry defended Aaron Smith; implicated Denyssen, the highest officer in the Cape colony, in corruption; and branded the prison service violent thugs. Barry was magnanimous but misguided in defending his old adversary Dr. Liesching. Seeing an opportunity to settle an old score with Barry, Liesching dissimulated and deliberately provoked him to challenge the fiscal's decision. Barry's spirited defense of a common sailor and his protest against the brutal treatment of prisoners continued unabated. Several weeks later, on September 12, he objected that Aaron Smith had still not been released from prison and was being unfairly detained. Exasperated, Barry reported that Smith had now *become* ill and "partially deranged" as a result of his extended detention in the violent prison. Finding him now "ill and weak," Barry recommended he should now be sent for "professional treatment" at the Somerset Hospital, "although not" he pointedly added, to the "lunatic asylum." Doggedly, Barry continued to draw attention to the cruelty of the Dienaars, recording that Smith showed further evidence of having been beaten since his first visit.

While Barry worked on behalf of the prisoners, a trap was being set for him. Plaskett, whom Barry had alienated over the Liesching affair and several of his other public campaigns, maliciously took it upon himself to show a copy of Barry's damning report to its key villain, Denyssen. On the same day that Barry wrote his second report complaining about Smith's delayed release from prison, he was shocked to be issued with a summons to appear before a commission of the Court of Justice. The summons ordered him to attend the court to defend his criticisms of the fiscal and the prisons department.

Realizing that he had been betrayed, Barry tore up the summons, threw it in the face of the messenger, and "threatened to cut off the Fiscal's ears with his sword!"—a fact solemnly recorded in the court proceedings. Issued with a second summons, Barry turned up in court. Once everyone settled in their seats, he took the stand and announced dramatically his insistence that an "order on him" should be issued by the colonial secretary. Barry was effectively saying that he refused to recognize the right of the court to try him. Until the colonial government endorsed his summons, he said, he would refuse to take an oath or comment on his or anyone else's reports. In fact, he would refuse to say any further word at all. Denyssen rose and, rejecting the right of the colonial office to intervene in the judicial proceeding, requested that

Barry's objections be overruled and that if he continued to refuse to answer questions, he be arrested under Article 117 of the Crown Trials
Procedure and a decree of civil imprisonment passed against him.

Satisfied that he had the upper hand, Denyssen sat back to watch the
unusually silent Barry writhe in discomfort. At this point a messenger
entered the court and a letter was passed to Barry notifying him that
Lady Somerset was ill and required his immediate attention. Thus having trumped Denyssen, Barry flounced out of court. The following day,
however, he was back, persisting in his silent refusal to recognize the
court's authority. When he adamantly refused one final opportunity to
answer questions, the sentence of civil imprisonment was passed
against him.

Barry's antics had potentially cost him his freedom. Backed into a
corner, he did the only thing he could—he appealed directly to Somerset. In a beseeching reminder to Somerset that he had just been carrying out his order to investigate the case of Aaron Smith, he laid out his
predicament:

> In consequence of this my Report, I have been summoned to ap-
> pear before the Sitting Commissioner of the Court of Justice this
> day, at the instance of HM's Fiscal to answer Interrogations
> touching the facts therein. Having acted in obedience to your
> Lordship's Commands, I declined answering any Questions aris-
> ing out of a Report ordered to be made by Government as tend-
> ing to introduce a dangerous principle by shackling its powers and
> preventing Public Officers from stating in their reports acts which
> they conceive ought to be brought to the cognisance of your Ex-
> cellency. From this refusal I have been sentenced to Civil Impris-
> onment, and am advised to throw myself upon your Lordship to
> protect the Liberty of a Public Officer who has not transgressed
> the Law—and the only charge against whom is that of having
> conscientiously discharged a public duty impressed upon him by
> your Excellency.

Barry's view was uncompromising: his honest report had been confidential. By breaching that confidentiality, Plaskett and Denyssen were trying to muzzle the truth in government reports. Trusting no one, Barry personally delivered the letter to the governor's office, first taking care to report his actions to Mr. Bigge. Somerset summoned Judge Kekewich and Daniel Denyssen, and behind closed doors a deal was cut. Barry's sentence was suspended on condition he withdraw his criticisms of Denyssen. Smarting under the requirement to stand down on what he considered to be the truth, Barry nevertheless accepted the terms to avert imprisonment. Yet even at this severe point in the crisis, Barry continued with his cavalier attitude. Sir Richard Plaskett later reported to the commissioners of enquiry that during this meeting about his prison sentence Barry, in a final act of defiant and impertinent behavior, "set up a kind of Horse Whistle" directed at the unfortunate Denyssen.

Barry had overstepped the line. Still relatively inexperienced, he was confused by Somerset's growing impatience with his behavior. His frank reporting and actions in the Aaron Smith case were no different than in hundreds of others he had investigated as colonial medical inspector. But he had not understood until now how politically besieged Somerset had become, and that diplomacy was required for them both to survive. Barry idolized Somerset, and simply could not imagine him weakened. Surrounded by spies, under investigation in Cape Town and in England, Somerset was fighting for his political skin. It is telling that he took the risk of intervening to protect Barry at all over this issue. Somerset instructed Plaskett to send Barry a warning. The letter was a coded instruction to step carefully. It also very fairly conceded that Barry's charges against the prison authorities were probably true. But the sensitive Barry interpreted it as a direct reprimand from Somerset. Plaskett, disappointed that Barry had avoided imprisonment, relished writing the letter:

> His Excellency desires me to say that what ever appearance there may have been of ill-treatment of Aaron Smith, or the probability

of such ill-treatment having been occasioned by the misconduct of one of the Dienaars, H.E. cannot refrain from remarking on the very great impropriety of your indulging yourself in reflections on the character of H.M. Fiscal—reflections which were quite irrelevant to the investigations.

For his part, Somerset seemed genuinely saddened by Barry's predicament. In a weary and sad letter to the commission of enquiry regarding the affair, he wrote:

On more than one instance Dr Barry has written officially in terms so indecorous and inadmissible that had I not (from my personal regard for him) pressed upon him the necessity of withdrawing his communications, I should have been compelled to notice them, in a manner most unpleasant to my feelings and disadvantageous to him.

This was a startlingly frank admission of Somerset's desire to protect someone personally where he could no longer do so politically.

Barry decided to call upon Richard Plaskett to ask him to look over the terms of his sentence and documents relating to his trial. Barry still questioned the authority of the court set up to try him. He had consulted the military authorities about his position as a British officer threatened with civil imprisonment and, believing he was gravely wronged, decided to present his case to the commissioners of enquiry. Plaskett "declared that if Barry did so, he should be dismissed from office, and that he would recommend it." Barry was astonished to be threatened in this way by Plaskett, but determined to follow through on his course of action.

Plaskett, meanwhile, had been building a case against Barry. Now with access to government papers, he dug up the protest from the Merchant Importers against Barry's high-handed tactics in curbing their commercial powers through the regulation of patent medicines. Plaskett also compiled a dossier of other complaints made against Barry, particularly those that illustrated his personal influence with Somerset. The conniving and duplicitous Plaskett then presented his case to the anxious and increasingly irritated Somerset, and put it to him that the Aaron Smith case was the final evidence that Barry's powers needed curbing. Somerset was cornered. In the process of being investigated for corruption, he could not afford to be seen to be protecting Barry out of personal favor. Failure to act could result in yet another accusation of malpractice being reported against him to the commission of enquiry. On October 4, Barry received a bombshell from Plaskett:

> The contents of your letter of yesterday's date, added to other circumstances which have lately passed with reference to your duties as Colonial Medical Inspector have impressed upon H.E. the Governor the impropriety of any one Individual being entrusted with the sole management and control of the Colonial Medical Department here, and he has therefore felt it necessary to propose to Council that the duties of that Department be henceforth carried on by a Committee according to the original intention of the Colonial Government in 1807, when the Supreme Medical Committee was appointed.

Barry was notified that the office of colonial medical inspector would cease to exist from the first day of November and a medical board appointed in its place. Barry was invited to sit on the reconstituted Supreme Medical Committee, but as an ordinary member, not as president. A rumor designed to reach him alerted him to the fact that two of the members of the new committee were to be senior officers. As Barry's military rank was still assistant surgeon to the forces, he knew that he could only be invited to sit on the board in a junior capacity. It was an utter humiliation, an instant demotion, and an arbitrary stripping of all the powers he had accrued in nine years of committed service. The ignominy and unfairness of the decision were too much to bear. Badly shaken, Barry wrote a letter directly to Somerset on October 13. The tone was stiffly dignified, but the uncharacteristically large, untidy scrawl with its crossed-out amendments indicated Barry's distressed state of mind:

> Having been informed this morning by Sir Richard Plaskett of an arrangement that is proposed for the future Establishment of the Department that has hitherto been under my Superintendence I lose no time in requesting to intimate to your Lordship that it will be impossible for me to reconcile to my feelings the acceptance of any subordinate place in the proposed Establishment should it have received your Lordship's approval that such a place should be tended to me. In this event I beg respectfully to tender my resignation too of the Civil Situations that I hold under your Lordship's appointment. And I request to be honoured with an early communication of your Lordship's final intentions, and before they are made Public in order that I may decide on the arrangements that will become necessary under such an alternative.

Barry would have agreed to the reestablishment of the medical board if he had been nominated as its president. It was not the reorganization that he objected to but the clear insult of the junior position he was offered. He may as well have been dismissed. No doubt sensing the genuine despair in Barry's letter, Somerset wrote to him directly and tried to explain the delicacy of the situation:

> In answer to your letter I feel it necessary to state to you what has precisely taken place with regard to the Colonial Medical Inspectorship. The very improper language in which you couched your official communications, and the imputations you unsparingly and unreservedly cast upon officers of this Government so greatly embarrassed the Government that Sir Richard Plaskett felt it his duty to submit to me the expediency of restoring the Medical

Committee. I observed that it would be certainly beneficial, and that the only obstacle was my apprehension that it might hurt your feelings, as Dr Arthur must be a Member, and as you are a Military Officer, of course he must take place of you.

So saying, Somerset then tried to defuse the bristling enmity between Barry and Plaskett. Telling him that "Sir Richard conceives from his conversation with you yesterday that you impute to him personal motives of hostility towards you," Somerset offered his own guarantee. "I can venture to assert he has not." Somerset would not budge in his remonstrances with Barry over his injudicious behavior, but he continued to try to encourage him to accept graciously the offer of a position on the new board. But Somerset's attempts at reassurance were to no effect. Barry already had first-hand evidence that Plaskett had conspired against him. His response to the final invitation from the governor's office, written by Plaskett, to join the committee was terse, immediate, and emphatic:

In answer to your communication of this Day's date, I have the honour to state for His Excellency's Information that I beg to decline accepting the situation of Member of the Supreme Medical Committee about to be re-established.

It was October 29, 1825, just over nine years since Barry had arrived at the Cape, and he was now back in exactly the same position in which he had started out: assistant surgeon to the forces. His salary was seven shillings and sixpence a day. After nearly a decade of campaigning to improve civil conditions, Barry did not hold a single civil office.

Deeply wounded, Barry understood finally that Somerset's hands were tied. There was no question of accepting the humiliating demotion. Barry also knew that Plaskett was an implacable enemy and would continue to pursue him until he was hounded out of the colony. Deciding that attack was the best form of defense, Barry continued with his application to the commission of enquiry to investigate his unfair dismissal. On Somerset's recommendation Barry had treated Mr. Bigge when he fell from his horse. Barry applied personally to Bigge, and the commission agreed to investigate his case. The detailed and labyrinthine enquiry into the "Case of Dr Barry," now a voluminous tome on the shelves of the Public Records Office, took five months.

Barry requested permission from the commissioners to write directly to Earl Bathurst to defend himself against the negative rumors reaching London. In his letter he objected to the manner in which he had been informed that the office of colonial medical inspector was to be terminated:

> Thus, in the midst of public and important duties, scarcely yet completed, I was disgracefully, virtually, dismissed out of my office . . . and I must here repeat, to the utter ruin of my professional character, and prospects in life. As to the temporary inconvenience of pecuniary matters—I have not, I do not—give them a thought. I had indeed flattered myself that I was bartering my time, my health and my talents (such as they are) to the public benefit, for honest fame, not sacrificing them to infamy.

The report from the commissioners of enquiry on the case of Dr. Barry arrived in Downing Street on March 14, 1826. "We have not been able to discover any well-founded complaints of the manner in which the very invidious duties of the office have been executed by him," declared the commission. On the issue of the inspection of newly imported medicines complained about by the Merchant Importers of Medicine, the commissioners found that Barry's remedy of recommending a board to vet his findings was commendable and had resolved the situation. The board of enquiry also vindicated Barry's conduct over the Liesching affair, finding that his objections had been "of a very conscientious nature" and quite correct in their "wish to preserve inviolate a rule of admission that the usage of 20 years had in his opinion established." Liesching, in their view, should not have been certified for practice, and although some of Barry's official letters on the matter had been written in a "tone of unbecoming warmth" and his manner could "raise some suspicion on the impartiality of his judgment," the board nevertheless felt that Barry's feelings had been unfairly "excited by indiscreet and discreditable solicitations by friends of Liesching." Barry should not in the board's opinion have been "induced to sacrifice his opinion and his sense of public duty to the interests of one individual."

The board reported that "Barry has said it was his bounden duty to the public" to report on the abuse meted out to Aaron Smith, and to draw the government's attention generally to the abusive practices of the prison constables. Barry, they suggested, would have been more successful in obtaining the correction of abuses "which we believe generally to have existed" if his written and verbal representations had "not been mixed with reflections upon the motives of individuals." These personal attacks had led the government to believe that Barry's motives were rather "to expose their conduct than to point out the error of the system that they conducted." It was their opinion that had his official communications "been of a more temperate nature" Barry would have been more effective in seeking proper remedy for Aaron Smith's plight. Although critical of his behavior, this conclusion was a particular victory for Barry, for Denyssen had been forced to admit to the enquiry that the behavior of the Dienaars was "less respectable than their duties require." The commissioners were, however, stern in their finding that "the ironical and contemptuous expression in which Dr Barry reflects upon the Fiscal's motives was one that deserved the severest reprobation," although they conceded that Plaskett's action in passing the confidential report directly to HM fiscal "probably irritated the latter against Barry."

The commissioners understood the official desire that "Barry should be precluded from causing further embarrassment to the government" by sharing his power and responsibility with an expanded medical board, but concluded that the measure of abolishing his position as medical inspector had been taken from fear of possible abuse rather than conclusive evidence of actual abuse. The town council that relieved Barry of the inspectorate should have examined the professional state of his department, allowed him a hearing to explain "the indiscreet or intemperate language of his official communications," and, most important, "considered whether his wants of temperament and discretion with which he was charged was not in some nature palliated or counterbalanced by his integrity or zeal in the exertions he had made to bring about the reform of abuses."

In short, the commission found that although he was clearly temperamental and wildly undiplomatic in his official communication, Barry had been unfairly treated. Out of respect for his contribution, "there should have been an arrangement in the constitution of the new Board to enable Barry to accept without tarnishing his reputation or losing his income." The commission saw no reason why Barry should not have continued "holding the executive office of Inspector" subject to "prompt and vigilant superintendence" by a medical board when deliberation was necessary.

Barry was vindicated. The sum total of the findings against him were that he was undiplomatic in the manner of his communications. The truth of his criticisms, exposures of injustice, and hard work were beyond reproach. The commissioners warmly found that "no exertion professional or personal had been spared by him to render his services useful to the community." They observed that Barry had many amicable relationships with senior officials as well as hostile ones, and that "his professional talents and reputation were universally acknowledged."

The young medic's name and notoriety were now known throughout Westminster. And for all his indiscretions, his professional talents as a uniquely talented medical pioneer were never questioned. But it was too late. The new medical committee had already been established, and no moves were made to reinstate him in his former position. Vindicated, Barry characteristically did not entirely give up hope.

But by the time the commission had reported, in March 1826, the storm over Somerset's administration was at its zenith, and dolefully Barry realized that his own problems were lost in the clamor to depose the governor.

Moreover, before the commissioner's report had arrived in London to clear his name, Barry had already suffered an even greater loss. What use was the commissioner's vindication when his "more than father" and "almost only friend" had left the Cape?

The *Cape Town Gazette* carried an advertisement for the sale of Barry's "furniture and effects" on December 23, 1825. It was a strange time of the year for a Christian to sell all his worldly goods. Barry was to remain in Cape Town for another three years. Why would he want to sell all his possessions? One possibility was that he needed the cash. Back on military pay since November 1, Barry had lost the benefits of his civil salaries and was quite possibly hard up. A further possibility also presents itself: he may have expected to accompany Somerset when the governor returned to England to face his accusers. Although officially the story was that he would return to the Cape once he had cleared his name, it was clear to those in political circles (not least Somerset himself) that he would not be returned as governor of the colony. Barry appears to have anticipated being asked to accompany Somerset and his family in his capacity as the family's personal physician. Perhaps Somerset privately proffered the invitation before realizing how unwise such an arrangement might seem to the colonial authorities back in London. As with his eager anticipation of sailing to join Miranda in Venezuela, Barry's hopes were dashed once more.

It was damp and overcast in Cape Town on the morning of March 5, 1826. Cloaked figures and horses had been trotting through the mist since the early hours to Government House: well-wishers anxious to take their farewell of Lord Charles and his family. Somerset was destined never to return to South Africa. Lady Somerset and her step-daughter Georgina were reported to have been "deeply affected" by the public display of support. Somerset and his staff thundered out of Government House on horseback, passing through the main thoroughfares of Cape Town before alighting on the foreshore:

> His Excellency, Lady Charles and Miss Somerset then entered the Government barge . . . accompanied by Lady M Fitzroy, Lady C Bell, Lt Colonel Fitzroy, Lt Rundell, Mr C Blair and Dr Barry. In two other boats followed Commodore Christian, Sir Richard Plaskett, Mr P G Brink, Mr Perceval, Mr D van Ryneveld, Mr Horak, Mr Muller and Mr J Brink.

There was poetic justice in the order of the waterborne procession. Barry was on the prow of the barge with Somerset, while behind trailed two boats filled with all the enemies he had made in loyal service to the governor. Barry had endured some hard days during his decade at the Cape, but this day of his separation from Somerset must have been the hardest. The *South African Chronicle* reported that "the visitors lingered on board as long as it was possible and did not leave the ship till the Captain announced that she was under weigh."

Dudley Percival remarked pithily in his diary that the pageant of Lord and Lady Somerset's final departure was:

> Quite theatrical. Table Bay in its finest style of scenery. Clouds on the mountains, sun on the water. . . . Shore thronged with spectators, cheering the Governor with the greatest goodwill. No small sore for his enemies that the first effect of their conspiracy had been to prove *themselves* liars by showing *his* popularity.

The theatricality of Lord Charles and Lady Somerset's departure was emphasized by a final, unexpected change in the weather:

> At a quarter past eleven . . . His Excellency Lord Charles Somerset embarked on the Atlas China Ship. At that hour the sun which had been obscured during the earlier part of the morning shone

forth with more than usual brightness like the far fame of an up-right man which the floating breath of calumny may dim but cannot tarnish.

But for Barry the dramatic graciousness of Somerset's departure held neither brightness nor solace. As Barry watched the *Atlas* unfurl her canvas and disappear onto the horizon, he knew that he was also watching the curtain drop on a particularly momentous drama in his own life. James Barry had lost his lord.

Chapter 6

"MY GOOD NAME"

*Why, Sir, your Julius Caesar, who gave the operation a
name;—and your Hermes Trismegistus, who was born so before the operation had a name;—your Scipio Africanus; your
Manlius Torquatus; our Edward the Sixth;—who had he
lived would have done the same honour to the hypothesis:—
These and many more who figured high in the annals of fame,
all came side-way, Sir, into the world.*

Laurence Sterne, Tristram Shandy

*How very dear to me, my good name is, and how very anxious
I am to make every human effort in order to avert the heavy
calamities consequent to the loss of it.*

James Barry

IN 1896, MARK TWAIN VISITED SOUTH AFRICA ON ONE OF HIS
final "tramps abroad." Invited to dinner at "one of the fine old Dutch
mansions" that so distinguish Cape colonial architecture, he was
struck by "a quaint old picture which was a link in a curious romance." Drawing closer to the lamp-lit image, Twain saw "a picture
of a pale, intellectual young man in a pink coat, with a high, black
collar":

It was a portrait of Dr James Barry, a military surgeon, who came out to the Cape fifty years ago with his regiment. He was a wild young fellow, and was guilty of various kinds of misbehaviour. He was several times reported to the headquarters in England and it was in each case expected that orders would come out to deal with him promptly and severely. Once he was called in the night to do what he could for a woman who was believed to be dying. He was prompt and scientific and saved both mother and child. This child was named after him, and still lives in Capetown. He had Dr Barry's portrait painted and gave it to the gentleman in whose old Dutch house I saw it.

The child who had Barry's portrait painted and was named after him was James Barry Munnik, born by a dangerous and almost unprecedented cesarean section on July 25, 1826. His father, Thomas Frederick Munnik, was a wealthy snuff manufacturer descended from a settler dynasty whose records at the Cape dated back to 1716. His wife, Mrs. Wilhelmina Johanna Munnik van Reenen, came also from an old colonial family.

By July 1826, Barry had been without his lord for nearly six months, politically left out in the cold. The difficult labor of Mrs. Munnik was to provide him with a remarkable opportunity to rehabilitate himself in the eyes of Cape colonial life. Barry took the chance with both hands, in an inspired act of breathtaking, even reckless, genius. Barry's training as a surgeon had tutored him in how to operate on the extremities, not the cavities, of the body. Because of the lack of effective anesthesia, these parts of the body were regarded as closed to the surgeon. "The abdomen, the chest and the brain," opined John Erichsen, "will be forever shut from the intrusion of the wise and human surgeon."

The month of July is midwinter in Cape Town, and the nights are often wet and windy. Wilhelmina Munnik was in excruciating pain. In labor with her first child, something had gone badly wrong. When it became clear that her life was in danger, Thomas Munnik decided to call in Dr. Barry, whose skill as an accoucheur was known to be "un-equalled." One of only twenty-three licensed accoucheurs in the colony at this time, Barry's methods were considered unorthodox but highly effective and invariably successful. Gathering his instruments, Barry lost no time in riding through the wet and gusty night to the Munniks' mansion. Entering the stuffy bedchamber where the ago-nized Wilhelmina Munnik lay surrounded by female friends, relatives, and the anxious midwife, Barry quickly took charge of the situation.

Diagnosing the state of Mrs. Munnik's perilous labor, Barry made a dramatic decision: to perform a cesarean section. To attempt a cesarean in 1826 was an enormous risk, as both lives were endangered. The Munniks were a formidably powerful family, and Barry was still politi-cally disgraced. Medical convention of the time required that the doc-tor act to save the life of the mother before the child. Most surgeons of the day would have opted to sacrifice the life of the child and perform a craniotomy, a horrific procedure that involved extracting the fetus piecemeal from the mother with sharp hooks, knives, saws, and for-ceps.

In Europe and America the new breed of male childbirth techni-cians—dubbed "man-midwives"—brandished an array of shiny metal instruments and were dismissive of the skills of ordinary midwives, "bemoaning their tendency in a slow labour to tug upon a hand or a foot, sometimes yanking it off altogether." Perhaps due to the need to share scant resources, the relationship between male doctors and fe-male midwives was more amicable at the Cape. A small training school for midwifery had been established in 1810, and by 1813 seven pupils were sworn in as midwives, two Malay women and five Europeans. By 1825 there were sixteen qualified midwives in the colony. Two more women were licensed to practice without examination. One of them was a freed slave named Hanna, whose freedom had been bought by Barry.

Despite the increase in man-midwives, women remained largely in charge of childbirth. Expectant mothers advertised in the local news-paper for wet nurses, and childbirth remained an all-female event run

by a midwife and female friends and relatives. Male surgeons were generally only called in to use their forceps when a labor became difficult,
or—all too commonly—to extract a dead fetus from a mother's womb.
On that July night, Barry's arrival at the Munnik household would
have been seen to herald doom. The best anyone would have hoped for,
including the fearful Thomas Munnik, would be that perhaps one life
might be saved.

IN THE 1820S, CESAREAN SECTION WAS REGARDED AS MORE OF A
hypothetical, mythical possibility than a surgical reality. Surgeons were
fascinated by the theoretical possibility of the cesarean but wary of the
dangers of the procedure. Medical histories generally maintain that
throughout all of Europe, only six were known to have been accom-
plished prior to Barry's attempt in 1826, and numbered among these
were operations that had resulted in the consequent death of either the
mother or the child. Dyre Trolle suggests that "until 1800 only 19 Caesarean sections had been actually performed in the British isles; two
mothers and seven children survived. Not until 1834 was a third
woman saved." William Smellie's treatise on midwifery, published in
the mid-eighteenth century, summed up the common view that the
section should only be tried "if the woman is strong and of a good habit
of body," but if the woman was weak or in a difficult labor "ought to be
delayed until the woman expires, and then immediately performed
with a view to save the child."

Like Tristram Shandy's father, educated laypeople regarded the operation as a philosophical wonder, likely to produce genius in the child,
whose soft head was protected from the pelvic pressure exerted during
normal parturition. Even among the foremost medical pioneers, understanding of the female reproductive system remained relatively
rudimentary. Medical science was still mystified as to the function of
the ovaries, and the myth prevailed in some quarters that the pelvic
bones separated during labor to expand the birth canal.

The cesarean operation was on the far side of futuristic medical possibilities. As for the women who were the subject of all this medical speculation, they, like Mrs. Shandy, would "turn pale as ashes at the very mention of it," a response hardly surprising in an age long before anesthesia or asepsis.

The earliest cesarean in which both mother and child survived is attributed to a Swiss sow gelder, Jacob Nufer, who in 1500 performed the operation on his wife. Two surgeons were reported to have achieved the operation in France and Holland during the eighteenth century. In 1738, a successful cesarean operation, believed to be the first in Great Britain, was reported by a female midwife. Male medics who considered it "a matter of good luck rather than good judgement" rather predictably undermined her remarkable accomplishment. There was also a strong element of moral disapproval regarding attempts to perform this procedure. The French surgeon François Mauricean argued, "I don't think that there has ever been a law, Christian or Civil, that lays down that the mother should be tortured or killed in order to save the infant." And in an age before the discovery of anesthesia, torture it was.

The pioneering father of modern surgery, John Hunter, attempted two cesareans in his life, one in 1769 and another in 1774, but on both occasions failed. In 1793 the operation was again attempted in Britain, but with a dead baby. On the other side of the Atlantic, it was not until April 1827 that the first successful cesarean would be reported in the United States. Thus, when Barry decided to attempt this procedure, he was spontaneously throwing himself headlong into a perilous operation that was known for certain to have succeeded only on a handful of previous occasions.

Soporific opiates had traditionally been used to produce local anesthesia, but they were liable to induce life-threatening sickness and vomiting. Wilhelmina Munnik would have been given little more than a liberal supply of Cape brandy to ease her excruciating pain. Many surgeons advocated "compressing the nerves that supply the parts upon which the operation is to be performed," a practice at best rudimentary in reducing the suffering of the patient. Franz Anton Mesmer had introduced pain control by hypnosis—or "mesmerism"—in the mid-eighteenth century, but by the early nineteenth century physicians relied largely on whiskey, gin, and rum to induce some numbing of pain. In practice, as Victor Robinson described, "the reduction of pain depended upon the skill of the surgeon." In the early 1840s, some American medics experimented with the use of ether and nitrous oxide for tooth pulling, but it was not until 1846 that Robert Liston successfully used anesthesia for invasive surgery in North London Hospital.

The experience of surgery could be as terrifying for the surgeon as for the patient. Many otherwise bold practitioners experienced extreme fear when confronted by the need to operate. As a medical student, Sir James Young Simpson was so traumatized by seeing the "terrible agony of a poor Highland woman under amputation of the breast" that he left the classroom immediately and "went to Parliament to seek work as a writer's clerk." Valentine Mott summed up the fearful conditions under which surgeons operated:

> How often, when operating in some deep, dark wound, along the course of some great vein, with thin walls, alternately distended and flaccid . . . how often I have dreaded that some unfortunate struggle of the patient would deviate the knife a little from its proper course and that I, who fain would be the deliverer, should involuntarily become the executioner, seeing my patient perish in my hands by the most appalling form of death.

What medical knowledge equipped Barry to undertake such a dangerous operation? He had never watched anyone perform a cesarean section, and had only read about it as a possibility in his medical textbooks. Dr. James Hamilton, one of his tutors at Edinburgh, wrote a detailed lecture on the operation, which Hamilton had twice tried and disastrously failed to complete successfully. It is possible that Barry may have witnessed or performed a postmortem cesarean section. Surgeons were urged to perform this where possible whenever mother and child had died. Canon law insisted that the child's soul could still be saved by baptism even after physical death. Barry was a confident cutter. His highly specialized training in morbid anatomy and dissection meant that, in theory, he had expertise negotiating the terrain of the body. However, as any medical student, now as then, would confirm, cutting into a dead cadaver and a live body are entirely different propositions.

Barry knew that bedding, linen, and curtains carried infection, making it unlikely that he would attempt the procedure in Mrs. Munnik's stuffy bedroom. The kitchen would have been the best place in a domestic house to serve as an improvised surgical theater, the kitchen table providing a makeshift operating table. As he worked under extreme pressure, the odds were stacked high against Barry. Recollections of somber professional indictments against even attempting the operation must have encouraged him to hesitate, summed up in the words of obstetrical authorities like Percival Willoughby, who declared: "As for the Caesarean section I do not like it. It hath proved unfortunate to severall, under whose hands the women have perished . . . a rash piece of work, and to do it in a living woman, a practice to be abhorred." But Dr. James Barry *was* rash, and notoriously contemptuous of received opinion on both surgical practice and the proper treatment of women in childbirth.

The performance of a cesarean section required the bladder to be previously emptied and the patient placed on a firm surface, with her shoulders slightly elevated. A seven-inch incision was made in the abdomen and a small opening then made through the sheath of the rectus, exposing the muscle. Fingers and surgical instruments were introduced into the external wound, bringing the uterus into view. The intestine had to be pushed aside, so that the position of the placenta could be ascertained. An incision of about five inches in length was made into the uterus, revealing the fetus enveloped in membranes. When these were ruptured, the surgeon could attempt to remove the fetus. Once the placenta had been also extracted, the surgeon could attempt to suture the wound, securing the repair with "adhesive straps" and applying a compress and bandages over the whole. The textbooks warned that women were usually overwhelmed by nausea and vomiting immediately after the operation, potentially fatal in their vulnerable condition. Solid opium was recommended to alleviate these symptoms.

The day after Barry attempted this daring operation, his was the name on everyone's lips. Wilhelmina Munnik had been successfully delivered of a son by cesarean section; both mother and child were alive and, people marveled, likely to survive. Cape Town feted Barry's achievement, journalists made haste to write up the dramatic event, and many letters sailed to Europe the following week informing friends, relatives, and colleagues of the amazing operation. Barry's medical friends, particularly Samuel Bailey and Mr. Poleman, congratulated him on his achievement. Mrs. Sandenberg and Mrs. Saunders shared the story with practically everyone who passed along the Heerengracht, and basked in the reflected glory of their personal acquaintance with Barry. Josias Cloete and his family sent their congratulations. Barry was the toast of Society House, where he had once been the subject of scandalized gossip. Most happy of all were the Munniks.

Thomas Munnik offered Barry a handsome fee, but despite the fact that he had hit hard times financially, Barry politely declined. Instead Barry, single, unmarried, and apparently without any relatives of his own, asked if it was possible that the child could be named after him. The grateful parents agreed, and furthermore asked the delighted Barry if he would be one of the sponsors at the child's baptism. From a family of the Munniks' lineage and family pride, the concession of naming the child after Barry and inviting him—an Englishman—to stand as a godfather was considerable, and a measure of the marvel in which they held the risky cesarean that had saved the family from tragedy.

James Barry Munnik was baptized in the Evangelical Lutheran Church in Cape Town on August 20, 1826. Barry attended the christening, "which was a riotous affair as the whole town was in a ferment over the operation." Dressed in full military uniform with a dress sword and white gloves, Barry was a guest of honor and gentleman hero of the day. The Munniks were unstinting in their gratitude to Barry, and in their pride that their son was not only one of the first children in the world to have been born in this way, but the first in South Africa. Barry remained a close family friend and corresponded with his godson as he grew up. The two spent time together in 1837, when Barry's ship was quarantined in Table Bay on his way to St. Helena. One of the few personal letters from James Barry known to have survived was written to his young godson in the same year. Discovered by June Rose, this letter—still in the possession of the Munnik family—is testimony to Barry's affection for his godson, as well as to his brusque style in personal correspondence:

> My dear James Barry
>
> I was much pleased with your letter and it was well written and it does you and your master great credit. I should have written to you before but I hoped your watch would have arrived from England. I expect it daily—you have a young friend of mine Mr Baker at your school. I hope you and he are friends. Write to me by every opportunity. Remember me most kindly to your father and to Mrs Sandenberg and Basham and his Lady to my dear old friend his mother, Mrs Cloete. I trust she is quite well. I have not time to say more than God bless my Dear Boy and prosper you.
>
> James Barry

One wonders how Barry felt, addressing a letter to "James Barry," a fine young man who owed his very life to his namesake. Barry had essentially created the young man in his own image—a striking example of the godlike persona of the surgeon, but also a more intimate reflection on Barry's own deeply felt narcissism. The "stalwart" James Barry Munnik grew up to be "a fine, tall, broad shouldered man" who inherited the family business and became South Africa's foremost tobacco and snuff manufacturer. The personal relationship between the two drifted as Barry's postings grew more distant, but the Munnik family convention of naming the male firstborn James Barry persisted for over a century. It is a curious twist of history that Barry's name was inherited by one of the central dynastic families of the apartheid regime. General J.B.M. Hertzog, well remembered as the prime minister of the first Afrikaner Nationalist government and a key architect of the apartheid state, inherited his name, James Barry Munnik Hertzog, from his god-father, grandson of the first James Barry Munnik.

And what of Barry's views on his own achievement? Although he never wrote on cesarean, Barry's interest in the procedure possibly went back to his early days as a medical student. Barry's fascination with all things medical related to sex and reproduction had continued in London when working with Astley Cooper. Cooper had an abiding interest in reproductive organs, genitals, and genito-urinary functions; he was to become the first to publish medical treatises on diseases of the female breast and male testes. Cooper had also declared a public interest in hermaphroditism, although he did not have the opportunity to develop his research more practically until the 1830s. Aside from his seminal work on diseases of the testicles, Cooper was most famous for his groundbreaking work on inguinal hernia. His high-risk operation had transformed this type of hernia from a potentially fatal condition to an operable disorder. There was an element of self-interest in Cooper's preoccupation with this subject—he suffered himself from a hernia that he successfully self-treated.

Barry's successful cesarean entered the history books, and medical students in Edinburgh are reminded of his achievement to this day. Yet Barry's medical innovations within the field of surgery were only one aspect of his prodigious scientific abilities. He also made another significant contribution to medical science that is less well remembered. In February 1827, seven months after performing his famed cesarean, Barry published his research on a possible treatment for syphilis and gonorrhea. This remarkable work, entitled "Report upon the *Arctopus echinatus* or Plat Doorn of the Cape of Good Hope," offered a new treatment for these ubiquitous diseases using a plant unique to the Cape.

There was a marked consistency in Barry's medical specialties. A pioneer in improving childbirth for women, he was also experimenting with possible cures for sexually transmitted diseases. Syphilis and gonorrhea were virulent throughout the nineteenth century. Described as "one of the new plagues of an age of conquest and turbulence," syphilis was spread by warfare, urbanization, changing lifestyles, sexual behavior, and migrations of soldiers, sailors, and traders. These were endemic diseases suffered by both sexes, and Barry was anxious to provide relief for both women and men.

It is clear from his report that Barry had been experimenting with the practical treatment of gonorrhea and syphilis for some time. With so many of his administrative duties removed in November 1825, Barry had more time to pursue his research. His work in this field is intriguing because it stresses his obsessive focus on all things sexually, genitally, and reproductively related. Equally striking is what this work tells us about Barry's interest in indigenous medicine. Politically and economically, life in the Cape colony was increasingly segregated along racial lines in the early nineteenth century. Nevertheless, white patients continued to seek advice from black practitioners in search of indigenous healing methods, just as black patients would request assistance from white doctors. Despite the general popularity of local treatments, licensed white doctors tended to ignore indigenous practitioners and their knowledge. Struggling to establish their credentials as professional gentlemen providing specialist services rather than just drug salesmen, licensed doctors were keen to detach themselves from apothecaries and folk medical practitioners. Barry, as ever, was different. A pioneer of modern biomedicine, he was nevertheless fascinated by indigenous, traditional medicines and the properties of local plants.

Known in the pharmacopeia by its anglicized Greek name *Arctopus echinatus,* the medicinal plant that captured Barry's imagination is more easily remembered by its Dutch name, Plat Doorn: literally, "Flat

Thorn." "Sieketroos" is the vernacular name by which the plant was known then as now, describing its general effectiveness as a remedy providing comfort for the sick. In his "Report," Barry explains that the *Arctopus* "flourishes abundantly on the hills and flats at the Cape, and for pharmaceutical purposes should preferably be collected during the months of October, November and December." Tramping around the Cape wilderness with his friend Mr. Poleman, an apothecary and amateur botanist, Barry had learned the ideal places from which the plant should be selected, and warned that if selected from the wrong location the plant would not be efficacious. Barry had experimented with preparations made from the plant and found them extremely successful in the cure of syphilis and several other diseases. In his "Report," Barry is insistent on the benefit of the cure as an alternative to mercury, the established remedy for most venereal diseases at the time. Confirming his own experience in experimenting with the treatment, Barry does not, however, claim the discovery of the benefits of this medicine as his own:

> With reference to the diseases in which the Arctopus has been beneficially resorted to. In Syphilis, it has been esteemed by the Natives of South Africa a specific, as also in Gonorrhoea. It is much to be depended on as a remedy in Lepra, Elephantiasis, and some of the obstinate Cutaneous Diseases incident to this climate.

Providing instructions for the administration of the medicine, Barry also suggested the treatment regime that went along with it should include a diet that was "plain and nutritious in almost equal proportions of animal and vegetable food," and recommended that "a moderate quantity of old wine" be allowed to patients if they also took "gentle and regular exercise." The state of the bowels, he sternly admonished, should be carefully attended to. Barry concluded with a call to develop *Arctopus* within mainstream European medical practice:

I shall conclude with expressing my most sincere wishes and ardent hopes that this plant may be admitted to a fair trial in Europe . . . and, perhaps, be appreciated as a resource in some of the most loathsome and awful scourges inflicted upon the human race, such as Leprosy, which is often considered incurable, and Venereal cases of long standing, where from idiosyncracy or other peculiar circumstances the use of Mercury cannot be persisted in, and every other species of practice has failed to produce an effectual cure.

Venereal diseases were particularly rife among the military. The *Arctopus* remedy continued to produce positive results in the Cape, but was not taken up in Europe as the cure-all he proposed it might be. Nevertheless, Barry gained a reputation as an expert in treating and alleviating the symptoms of venereal diseases, which was to become increasingly significant to the development of his future career.

Barry's achievement with the cesarean section gave a fillip to his self-confidence, still badly dented by the events that led up to the loss of his post as colonial medical inspector. By November 1826, he was keen to get back on track, but remained seriously worried that the "cruel, disgraceful and . . . unjustifiable" manner in which he had been deprived of office would block him from promotion. Barry wrote to Earl Bathurst explaining that he had waited patiently: "trusting that when Lord Charles Somerset reflected upon the circumstance coolly and dispassionately, his sense of justice would induce him to see me righted. . . . I have waited—nothing has been done."

Barry was deeply dejected when, a few days later, a letter reached him from Bathurst that had been written back in June. The decision had been made months before. Bathurst saw "no reason to doubt the propriety of the arrangement which has been recently made by the Governor of the Cape for resting in a Medicine Board the execution of the duties which had previously been assigned to the Colonial Medical Inspector." Galvanized by desperation, Barry took up his pen and wrote an immediate reply to Bathurst begging him for redress. "I do not complain of the abolition of my office," he wrote "or of its duties being transferred to a Medical Board," but, he reiterated, "I do complain of the unprecedented and to me injurious manner in which it was done, and in which I was so abruptly removed." He begged Bathurst to consider the circumstances:

> It is needless for me to enforce how dear, how very dear to me, my good name is, and how very anxious I am to make every human effort in order to avert the heavy calamities consequent to the loss of it. I therefore deem it my bounden duty to vindicate my integrity and to rescue it as soon as possible from the unworthy imputations which have been heaped upon it; and to manifest my honourable transactions to the World—without which even my claims to and anxious expectations of military promotion may continue to be obstructed, if not totally annihilated.

Barry's worries about his "expectations of military promotion" came to an end on November 22, 1827, when he received a promotion to staff-surgeon to the forces. The colonial office conceded that Barry had been unfairly dismissed and misrepresented. Barry had succeeded in rescuing his good name.

Somerset, for his part, received a letter "absolving him from all imputations upon his character" and was informed that all the charges against him had been dropped. The resolution was a fudge. While it was clear that Somerset had been subjected to some trumped-up charges of personal corruption, his political failings as instigator of the "Reign of Terror" weighed heavily against him. A year later the government conceded the right of a free press to the Cape colony, and George Greig and John Fairbairn recommenced publication of the *South African Commercial Advertiser,* which had been banned in 1824. Charles Somerset turned his back on politics and committed himself to a full-time life of horse-racing and socializing.

Based on the findings of the commission of enquiry that had exonerated Barry's actions, the Cape colony went through an intensive period of political restructuring. The role of the fiscal was abolished, and Barry's old nemesis Denyssen was sacked without pension. Many of the Cape's public institutions, such as the prisons, hospitals, and leper colony, underwent far-reaching reforms, all based on the practical recommendations Barry had made in his copious reports as colonial medical inspector.

Barry received notice that his next posting was to far-flung Mauritius, a hot and unhealthy tropical island in the Indian Ocean. Making preparations for his departure, Barry requested permission for his servant to accompany him. On September 10, 1828, permission was granted to "Dantzen, Dr Barry's servant, to proceed to Mauritius." Nothing is known of Dantzen's origins. Barry was accompanied by a black servant for the rest of his career, and many years later was photographed in Kingston with a black man who may have been his servant. Was Dantzen the man who appears in the photograph with Barry and Psyche? And was Dantzen the same servant, later dubbed "Black John," who was reported to have escorted Barry everywhere in his final years of retirement in England? Frustratingly little is known about the man who appears to have been Barry's companion for the remainder of his life, yet the possibility cannot be ruled out that it was this same Dantzen.

When Barry departed for Mauritius, he left as many friends who were sorry to see him go as enemies who were glad to see the back of the meddlesome and contumacious doctor. By the second week of September 1828, Barry had packed his belongings once and for all, and awaited passage east. The Cape press reported that by way of "marking their high opinion of his merits and their regret at his departure to Mauritius on promotion" the friends of Dr. Barry "invited him to dinner at George's Hotel." "Amongst the Company," the article noted, "might be seen many distinguished Civil, Military and Mercantile Gentlemen":

The evening passed harmoniously, the dinner and wines were excellent. Health and prosperity to Dr Barry was repeatedly drunk with enthusiasm, and the impression excited on Dr Barry was evident. He returned his acknowledgment for these last marks of attention with great taste and feeling, and the party separated at a late hour.

Barry took up his new post in Mauritius on October 9, 1828. He left behind at the Cape his youth and a legendary reputation and indelible imprint that has prevailed ever since. In 1910, an extravagant pageant was held at the Cape to celebrate the Act of Union uniting the four provinces of South Africa. The pageant was a high imperial folly: the whole of Cape Town was transformed into a public theater given over to the reenactment of the Cape's colonial history. Olga Racster, visiting from England for the first time, remarked on the "first rate episode about Lord Charles Somerset's attempt to muzzle the Press," a show that clearly went better than the attempt to restage the landing of the 1820 Settlers, who, due to the high winds, "simply could not get to shore." But Olga Racster reserved her finest praise for a romantic figure who walked out of the early nineteenth century to capture her twentieth-century imagination:

> Occasionally the wind did drop for a breath . . . and in one of those moments of quiet I saw a natty young Georgian officer, as stiff as a telegraph pole. His red uniform coat was skin-tight, his breeches ended in dandified top-boots with red heels; the hand holding the reins of his dapple-grey horse was gloved in white, and by his side walked a Malay holding an immense orange umbrella over him. This irresistibly attractive, adorable young blade was the pageant representation of Dr James Barry.

The pageant was stage-managed and filmed by Frank Lascelles. A former circus master, Lascelles was one of the first filmmakers in South

Africa, and his "topical" film of the 1910 Cape pageant numbers among the earliest examples of documentary cinema in the country. Across the grainy frames of this silent, barely edited footage, can distinctly be seen astride his horse led by Dantzen "the pageant representation of Dr Barry." Psyche trots pertly alongside.

Chapter 7

DOCTOR JAMAICA

Right is of no sex.

Frederick Douglass, *The North Star,* July 28, 1848

If slavery is not wrong, then nothing is wrong.

Abraham Lincoln, address to the Federal Army
on the benefits of allowing black people
to serve in the military, 1864

BARRY SAILED INTO THE CLEAR WATERS OF THE SARGASSO SEA IN June 1831. Still hundreds of miles from land, mariners recognized this temperate sea by the long trailing masses of yellowish weed that floated on its surface like streams of golden hair. The weed was the color of the sun, the sea sky blue; Barry had his first glimpse of the dazzling tropics. The death of Somerset, his patron, protector, and friend, lay behind him; ahead a prestigious but challenging appointment to the most politically sensitive and disease-ridden post to which the British laid claim. Barry had also lost his great educational patron, Lord Buchan, in April 1829.

Barry's desire to go to Jamaica was professional as well as personal. Grieving over the death of Somerset and feeling isolated by the loss of Buchan, he wanted to stay out of the confines of England. The

Caribbean offered not merely escape but an opportunity for adventure and advancement of his knowledge of tropical medicine.

Barry had arrived back in England in December 1829. He was in London when he received the letter of commission notifying him that Jamaica was to be his next posting. It was a somber, dark winter's day in January 1830. Psyche was listless and depressed in the wet cold. Barry would have welcomed the opportunity to return to the warmth. Beyond its climactic enticements, Jamaica was a challenging and intriguing posting. He was to become staff surgeon to the forces in this famous island. When Barry was a student at Edinburgh, Jamaica had been central to his dreams of intrepid doctoring in steaming jungles, vanquishing the most dangerous and mysterious diseases known to mankind. John Hunter, the father of modern surgery, had been posted to Jamaica early in his career as superintendent of military hospitals in the 1780s, and his subsequent publication *Observations on the Diseases of the Army in Jamaica* was studied and admired as the founding text of tropical medicine. Hunter trained Barry's own tutors, Henry Cline and Astley Cooper, and at Guy's and St. Thomas's, learning about Hunter's unflagging experimentalism had inspired Barry.

The chain of circumstances that led to Barry's being posted to the Caribbean was characteristically irregular. Barry had been in Mauritius when he received the disastrous news of Somerset's illness: "I . . . was recalled in consequence of the serious illness of Lord Charles Somerset upon whose death I proceeded to Jamaica. . . ."

Somerset, now retired, was living in England. Barry's terse official statement that he was "recalled" to attend Somerset was wholly disingenuous. In fact, he had left Mauritius on the next ship as soon as he received the news, "without making any official application for leave of absence." In claiming that he acted on official instruction, Barry was attempting to cover up a flagrant professional indiscretion. He had in fact gone absent without leave, a grave military offense.

The account of Barry's life published in Dickens's journal *All the Year Round* ironically depicts Barry as going absent without leave for a reason more sartorial than solicitous:

He would chuckle as he related the story of his unlooked for re-appearance before the director-general of the medical department in London.

"Sir," said the director, "I do not understand your reporting yourself in this fashion. You admit you have returned without leave of absence. May I ask how this is?"

"Well, said James, coolly running his long white fingers through his crisp sandy curls, "I have come home to have my hair cut."

While it is doubtless true that Barry would have traveled far for a fashionable haircut, the real reason that he once again "defied the rules of the service with impunity" was to care for his ailing and adored Somerset. Barry's fiercely loyal instincts and uncalculating generosity were characteristic of his style of friendship. He was ever a consistent ally to his friends. Opinionated, he was also forgiving. Rifts caused by political or personal disagreements—particularly in his earlier years, before he had learned to curb his outbursts of temper—were often swiftly healed. And a helping hand was never forgotten. Those who assisted Barry earned his lifelong allegiance.

Thought to be at death's door when Barry rushed to his bedside from Mauritius in 1829, Somerset rallied considerably under Barry's personal ministrations. As had been the case when Barry saved the life of Georgina Somerset in Cape Town, the family invested well-placed confidence in Barry's talents as a personal physician. The strained professional relationship between Lord Charles and Barry that had clouded his departure from the Cape seemed resolved, and Barry became once again a confidant of the aristocratic couple.

However, while Barry's success with Somerset healed old personal wounds, it presented a problem in other quarters. The longer he extended the life of his patient, the longer the army medical services had to wait for their surgeon to take up his commission to Jamaica. It was not until after Somerset's death, in Brighton in February 1831, that Barry finally took up this posting. The power and direct influence of the Beaufort family—of which Somerset and his younger brother were so prominently members—no doubt lay behind Barry's evasion of court-martial and the military authorities' acquiescence to Barry's repeated requests to delay his departure for Jamaica. While Lord Charles himself had fallen from grace in parliamentary circles, the Beaufort family continued to wield social and political influence in the military, and in Barry's career.

During his long illness, Somerset stayed in London, where Barry was with him constantly. Early in 1831, Somerset—ailing though he was—insisted that he wanted to return to Brighton and go riding on the Sussex downs. Barry begged him to stay in London, but Somerset was obdurate and would not even countenance taking the journey in stages. The Somersets and Barry took up residence at the Bedford Hotel, and the weakened Lord Charles persuaded Barry to go riding with him. A few days later, on February 20, in Barry's presence, Somerset died. Nearly 160 years later, Somerset's great-grandson discovered a revealing letter written by Barry to Lady Mary Fitzroy Somerset, Lord Charles's sister-in-law, shortly after Somerset's death:

Dear Lady Mary

There is indeed a melancholy satisfaction in relating what took place during the last moments of poor Lord Charles who was to the last a kind, a sincere and an indefatigable friend, and had been so thro life to many, some of whom did not appreciate it. We who have known him for years in other climes and under the most trying circumstances can conscientiously before God and man declare he was a man more sinned against than sinning.

Since my arrival in Europe (now about 14 months) I have been almost always with him and during the last few weeks day and night I have been near him.

Poor Lord Charles, during his sufferings, and he suffered much, he never for one moment forgot the interests of his friends. Poor Lady Charles, and during the last month Miss Somerset, closely watched him. Lady Charles laid on a couch near him for weeks, so that his every aportance [*sic*] and the consolation of being surrounded by his family and friends.

With what joy he hailed the arrival of Colonel Fitzroy and your Ladyship. Knowing the pleasure Colonel Fitzroy's company gave him, I anxiously watched his daily arrival and it was not among the least of my regrets that Lord Charles would lose his society by persevering in quitting London, alas before he ought to have done so. But it is not for man to say what ought to have been.

Poor Lord Charles made the journey to Brighton pretty well. He could not be persuaded to remain in town any longer, or to divide his journey. He arrived on the Monday evening and from that moment began to get weaker.

However he mounted his horse and I as usual accompanied him. He was weak and nervous but felt so pleased to be in the open air. Tuesday, Wednesday and Thursday we rode, after which

Here Barry's account breaks off in midsentence. In the words of the great-grandson who discovered the document, "regrettably the following page of the letter is missing." However, Barry's introductory cover note to the missive survives. Responding to Lady Mary's request for an account of his death, Barry writes his most passionate and revealing words on Somerset:

I have entered into detail as you wish, but I am unable of doing justice to my more than father—my almost only friend, and am here to be quiet today. Tomorrow I go remain [*sic*] till the earth covers a true Christian. J.B.

Somerset's funeral took place at St. Andrew's Church, Hove, attended only by his closest relatives and friends. The *Brighton Gazette* particularly noted in its obituary Barry's presence at the head of the family cortège. The long and eulogistic obituary that appeared in the

London *Morning Post* made no direct reference to the scandal concerning his relationship with Barry, but remarked that his feelings were "lacerated by the attacks of which he was the object into a state of nervous sensibility, which latterly hastened his decline."

Following Somerset's death, the grieving Barry sailed to Jamaica aboard the sloop *Guardian*. After three months at sea, the approaching end of the voyage must have been a welcome relief to Barry. Although he crossed four continents and lived the majority of his life within earshot of the changing tides, he never found his sea legs. Seaborne life was closeted, uncomfortable, and particularly arduous for Barry. Not only was there the problem of his perennial seasickness, but the forced intimacies and constraints of space on board were inimical to his physical requirements and what he called his "peculiar habits."

Although his professional status afforded him some measure of privacy, he was nevertheless obliged to share quarters with other officers that were uncomfortably intimate. Barry seemed strangely physically reticent among his fellow officers. Lieutenant Edward Rogers, occupying the same cabin as Barry on an intercolonial steamer cruising among the Caribbean islands sometime later, recalled his impatience, explaining how "in a harsh and peevish voice" he "ordered me out of the cabin—blow high, blow low" while he dressed in the morning, shouting, "Now then, youngster, clear out of my cabin while I dress."

Approaching Jamaica through the clear waters of the Sargasso Sea, Barry would have seen for the first time flying fish skimming the surface of the water, and often flying onboard. As well as encountering a new realm of natural flora and fauna, Barry was entering a territory still synonymous with adventure in the English imagination. These were the waters in which the freebooting buccaneers and pirates of the sixteenth and seventeenth centuries had plied their unregulated trade, Edward Teach—the infamous Blackbeard with his plaited beard and three pairs of pistols—being the most famous. Later the Caribbean had become the cradle of the Navy, reputed for the deeds of sailors like Benbow, Vernon, Hood, Rodney and, most famously of all, Horatio

Nelson. Fresh out of naval school, Nelson's first posting had been to Fort Charles, the military barracks around which Port Royal had originally sprung up in the seventeenth century. Two years later, in 1779, the twenty-year-old Nelson was put in command of the batteries at Fort Charles to guard against a potential French attack. Nelson returned again to Port Royal in 1780 suffering from yellow fever and dysentery and was nursed back to recovery by the black nurse Couba Cornwallis. As Barry was to discover, Jamaica numbered some unusually skilled doctresses among its daughters.

The region was, however, perhaps even more renowned for the exploits of those who sailed its waters on the wrong side of the law. The Caribbean had long been the world center of piracy. The popular history of profiteering on the high seas teemed with tales of masquerade, risk, deception, and disguise. Piracy had a tradition of cross-dressing and effeminacy, and the pirates of the Caribbean West Indies were famed for being dandies who adored ornate, satirical, unconventional dress. Male pirates loved strutting in "feathered hats, wigs, silk stockings, ribbons, and other garments." Dressing up was an essential part of pirate behavior, a factor that worked to the advantage of the many women who cross-dressed as pirates, such as Anne Bonny and Mary Read, the duo whose nefarious exploits were recorded by Daniel Defoe in his *A General History of the Pyrates.* In the eighteenth century, cross-dressed female sailors, soldiers, warriors, and cabin boys were a favorite theme in the pages of broadsides, and celebrated in ballads and folksong. Like every other gentleman of his class arriving in the Caribbean, Barry knew well this popular tradition, peopled by escapees from the conventional confines of gender, adventurers living borderline lives in crossover occupations.

The Watchman and Jamaica Free Press reported the arrival of "Dr Barry of the Staff" at Port Royal on June 12, 1831. For over two centuries a bustling trading port, Port Royal was once regarded as the wealthiest city in the New World. Later, it earned the moniker of "the wickedest city on earth," succumbing to piracy, prostitution, and privateering.

Port Royal was subjected to successive earthquakes and fires. It succumbed to both, repeatedly, and like the succubus it was it bounced back, although each time a little more submerged. As it slid inexorably beneath the Caribbean its shadowy architecture could still be seen by the many ships, fishing boats, and ferries that crossed the harbor between Port Royal and Kingston.

The placidity of the Sargasso Sea through which Barry passed on his approach to Jamaica belied the fact that he had landed in a political cauldron. Although he did not know it then, he had arrived in Jamaica during a turning point in the history of the British empire, to a posting that was to prove one of the most tumultuous of his career. Jamaica was a fairy-tale tropical island only in the storybook of empire.

Jamaica in the 1830s was a world of extremes, a colonial fantasy spun from sugar built upon the violence of slavery. Where the Cape colony retained the flavor of the frontier and struggled for the consistent attentions of the home Parliament and exchequer until the discovery of diamonds and gold later in the century, Jamaica was the epicenter of Britain's economic and political attentions. For the sugar barons, Jamaican colonial society was a landscape of palaces, social intrigue, extreme indolence, and excessive indulgence.

Although those growing fat on sugar and slavery lived in luxury, slaves and soldiers experienced very different lives. This brittle façade was about to crack under the weight of its own iniquity—rumors about the activities of the antislavery abolitionists were beginning to reach beyond the ports of Montego Bay and Kingston Harbor and spread into the interior to the plantations. The human misery upon which this edifice was built was about to experience its first major tremor—one that sent aftershocks rippling back to the colonial center. Within a year of Barry's arrival, the hinterland would explode into an unprecedented uprising that was the founding moment of a struggle toward decolonization that would last over a century.

Port Royal lies at the tip of an elongated peninsula extending from the mainland like an extended thumb. The gateway into Kingston Har-

Two portraits of James Barry
as a youthful military surgeon.
Wellcome Library, London

Self-portrait by James Barry, R.A., uncle to Dr. James Barry. Also depicted on this canvas are the artist Dominique Lefevre and the architect James Paine the Younger. *Picture Library, National Portrait Gallery, London*

Barry's revolutionary mentor Francisco de Miranda, imprisoned in Cadiz. Known as "El Precursor," Miranda was the first leader of Venezuela after its liberation from Spanish rule in 1811. *The Hulton Getty Picture Collection Limited, London*

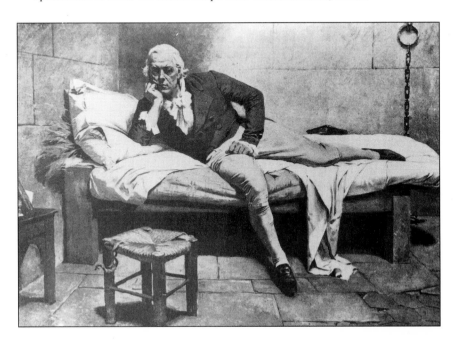

Portrait of Sir Astley Cooper, professor of surgery at Guy's Hospital.
Royal College of Surgeons

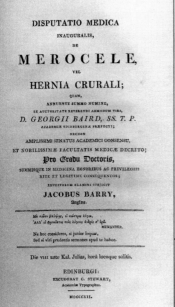

Frontispiece of James Barry's thesis on hernia, submitted to the University of Edinburgh in 1812. The quotation from the Greek dramatist Menander reads, "Do not consider whether what I say is a young man speaking, but whether my discussion with you is that of a man of understanding." *Edinburgh University Library*

James Barry's registration as a pupil dresser at St. Thomas' Hospital in 1812. *King's College, London*

Cape Town in the first half of the nineteenth century. *Mary Evans Picture Library, London*

Drawing of the African Theatre in Cape Town by Lady Anne Barnard. *Cape Town Archives Repository*

Cartoon of Lord Charles Somerset, governor of the Cape Colony. *National Portrait Gallery, London*

Romantic portrait of Somerset as Barry knew him at the Cape, by Richard Cosway. *The Earl of Devon, Courtauld Institute of Art, Somerset House, London*

Engraving of Ngqika a Mlawu, paramount chief of the Xhosa, whom Barry met on a diplomatic mission to the eastern frontier in 1817. *Cape Town Archives Repository*

James Barry at the height of his success. The inscription in his hand reads, "I have certainly striven to do my duty towards God and Fellow men." *Percy Ward Laidler and Michael Gelfand, South Africa: Its Medical History, 1652–1898*

The burning of the Roehampton Estate at Montego Bay during the January 1832 uprising in Jamaica. *National Library of Jamaica*

Kingston Barracks, Up Park Camp, where Barry was stationed. *British Library*

Cartoon of an elderly James Barry at Corfu, attributed to Edward Lear. *Wellcome Library, London*

Barry's gravestone in Kensal Green cemetery, London. *Photograph by Nathan Kelly*

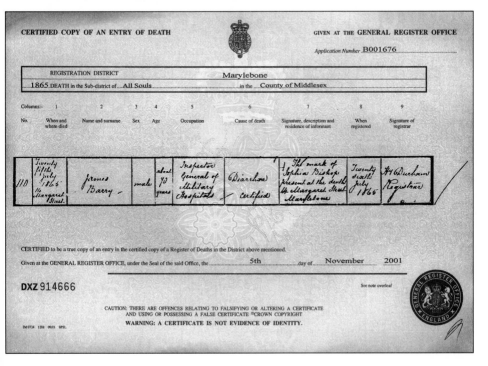

A copy of Barry's death certificate, recording his sex as male, and witnessed by Sophia Bishop. *General Register Office for England and Wales, Southport, England*

James Barry in old age, accompanied by the man Dickens nicknamed "Black John" and Psyche, Barry's dog. The photograph was taken at Duperly's studio in Kingston, Jamaica. *Wellcome Library, London*

bor from the Caribbean, the military fort and its port guarded both Spanish Town—then the administrative and business capital of the region—and Kingston, with its wide boulevards and lofty mansions, then largely the residential playground of colonial society and its diversions. Overlooking the harbor, Kingston lay with its back nestled against the feet of the Blue Mountains—in whose velvet foothills some of the wealthier colonial magnates built exaggerated baronial mansions and cultivated the land as much as possible after the fashion of English country estates.

Barry was sent to Jamaica to replace Staff Surgeon Dr. Wilson, who was retiring from service. Fitzroy Somerset, Lord Charles's younger brother, personally authorized his commission. This is the first of a series of key interventions Fitzroy Somerset made to facilitate Barry's career following the death of his elder brother. While he gave no reason for his protection of Barry's career, it was assumed that, as the doctor had served the Somersets well as their brilliant family physician, Fitzroy Somerset was honoring a debt of gratitude. Barry had saved the life of Georgina Somerset in an age where even minor infirmities could quickly prove fatal. Although certain of his exceptional skills as a medic, Fitzroy Somerset was also taking a calculated risk on Barry's ability to handle an appointment as staff surgeon to the forces of a politically sensitive region. Jamaica was a highly prestigious posting; long established, excessively lucrative, and socially complex. Barry would be expected to execute his duties with some diplomacy and composure, qualities for which he had not hitherto been noted.

It is unclear if Barry arrived in Jamaica alone. "State whether you wish conveyance for any person(s) to accompany you," requested the director general when confirming approval of Barry's new appointment and instructing him to prepare for embarkation. The conventional retinue for a surgeon to the forces of Barry's age (about forty-one) posted abroad would typically include a wife, children (if not yet old enough to be boarded in England), one or two servants, and sometimes a particularly favored horse.

Barry usually set sail with a far more atypical entourage, comprising the latest incarnation of Psyche and a goat for fresh milk during the crossing. Among his possessions was an abundance of linen and pillows, which Barry insisted were "requisite in a long voyage" and described as being "of a particular description necessary to me under the peculiar circumstances in which severe accidents have placed me." On later voyages his retinue included a monkey and a parrot. As Barry's response to the director general is lost, there is no record of whether or not he requested passage for a servant on his way to his posting in Jamaica. Dantzen had followed him to Mauritius and accompanied him back to England, but there the documented trail ends. Nevertheless, from the time of Barry's arrival in the West Indies, he is recollected as head of a mobile household of three—the diminutive white military doctor, his statuesque and silent black manservant, and the irrepressible Psyche, the ever-present poodle.

On arrival at Kingston, Barry reported to Governor Somerset Lowry-Corry, the earl of Belmore, and was garrisoned to Up Park Camp, first in importance of all the Jamaican stations. The Jamaica garrison was modestly sized at about four thousand—composed mainly of white troops and a small detachment of the black West India Regiment. Following Barry's death, some said that the manservant who accompanied him for the remainder of his life had been assigned to him from the West India Regiment. Situated two miles north of Kingston at the eastern end of a fertile plain, Up Park Camp was canopied by trees and cushioned from the punishing heat by strong sea breezes by day, and by gentle night winds from the Blue Mountain ridge, by which it was overlooked. The wind blew through the raised arches of the brick-built barracks and hospital, providing ventilation that in theory gave Up Park Camp advantages over lower-lying, marshy stations. The apparent benefits of the site were not, however, reflected in the health of the troops. When Barry arrived in 1831 the mortality rate among the troops was running at an average of 110 deaths per 1,000 men. "The fevers" were the principal cause of sickness. Malaria, the ubiquitous yellow fever—dubbed "yellow jack"—and typhus were the biggest killers. Lung, liver, and bowel diseases followed closely in menace, with chronic dysentery and diarrhea also proving fatal conditions.

The troops were ill-equipped and completely untrained for tropical warfare. To a large degree this was of little consequence, as they were far more likely to die from disease and the ravages of the unfamiliar tropical conditions than as a consequence of armed service. They lived in badly positioned low-lying barracks, stifling in the heat, fetid with damp in the rain and buffeted by gales when the trade winds blew. The year before Barry arrived, a report from the army medical department about the state of the barracks and hospitals in Jamaica had summed up the situation: "sickness and mortality amongst the Troops in that Colony continues to be of the most distressing extent, that it is attributed, chiefly, to the state of the Barracks and the Hospital accommodation."

Between the hottest months of December and August, the troops were confined to quarters between nine and five—their extreme boredom aggravated by unwholesome rations of salted meat and dry biscuits. After they had stumbled outdoors to drill listlessly in the oppressive afternoon heat, they headed for oblivion at the price of one-and-a-half pence a pint: rum. Jamaica's infamous and aptly named "white lightning" was the only thing that struck life into the dulled senses of the troops and unleashed their frustration in drunkenness and disorder. Their pay of one shilling a day was reduced to a few pence once deductions for their risible provisions and accommodation had been made. Their funds were insufficient to pay for the attentions of prostitutes, and although they were shared around, soldiers' wives were in short supply, their ratio strictly controlled by the military authorities. The troops thus lived a twilight existence dominated by rum, sodomy, and the lash. All else was endemic disease and death.

Barry enjoyed the comforts of the roomy and better-ventilated lodgings given to senior military officers. These were "upstairs houses" with balconies safely suspended above the pestilential ground levels in which the less fortunate assistant surgeons lived. The assistant surgeons fared little better than the regular soldiers. Their mortality rate caused one official to state anxiously:

> I need not say here, where life is so precarious, and death so imminent, every available means ought to be put into operation to protect the lives of men who are constantly by day and night doing their best to save the lives of others.

Life so precarious, death so imminent. These were the challenges that confronted Barry in Jamaica. And they were compounded by another encounter with his old enemy from the Cape: endemic corruption in an unregulated medical fraternity whose primary interest was their own self-enrichment. "This is a superb country for physicians," expostulated the entrepreneurial Dr. Cynric Williams; "a customary fee is a doubloon, and the inhabitants are all sick in their turn; for there are very few who escape a seasoning; and a great proportion die." Rich pickings indeed for medics more interested in cash than cure. There were no professional medical schools, civilian hospitals, societies, or learned journals. Here Barry was at the frontier of tropical medicine, his modern methodology in sharp contrast to the humoral-climatic and miasmatic theories of medicine to which less progressive colonial practitioners still clung. Their advocacy of bloodletting, purging, vomiting, blistering, sweating, and overdosing with opium, mercury, and antimony proved as fatal to their patients as did the climatic conditions and disease itself. The sale of medicines imported from Europe made up the largest part of the average doctor's income. As at the Cape, Barry continued to crusade against this medical profiteering, enhancing his reputation as a missionary of modern medicine.

In August 1831, shortly after his arrival, Barry was sent to deal with an epidemic outbreak of yellow fever at Stony Hill barracks, nine miles north of Kingston. Incidence of death was high, but the one in seven fatality rate recorded at the end of the outbreak was regarded as a success, as this disease usually killed 25 percent of its victims. The authorities noted Barry's achievement, and agreed to his irregular request that he be allowed to retain his quarters in Stony Hill. Barry liked this rugged, verdant station with its elevated vistas situated in the foothills of the Blue Mountains, and he now adopted the routine of driving down to Up Park Camp in a small brougham, "even in the hot season." The rough road wound precariously down to Kingston, and Barry's eccentric commuting was regarded by even the locals with a mixture of humor and bemused awe. Like Phaeton, child of the sun, Barry would arrive to attend to his duties at Up Park Camp breathless, hot, and dusty from his precarious descent. At night he returned to Stony Hill, daring the overgrown and indirect road in the heavy tropical dusk.

Mrs. Magnus, a Jamaican woman who lived in Stony Hill village and served the officers at the barracks, recalled that in addition to his arduous commute, Barry was the only officer who ever refused her entry to his rooms. He was "very peculiar in his habits," she recalled, "never allowing a woman to attend him or to even enter his quarters." Years later, Mrs. Magnus told a Captain Dadson, by then living in Barry's old rooms, that she was always struck by the "delicacy of hands and smallness of his feet." Only his manservant and Psyche were permitted freedom of access to Barry's otherwise closeted chambers.

Barry was a familiar figure at Up Park Camp. So firmly did he become associated with Kingston that people were later erroneously to claim that he had died in Jamaica and been buried in Up Park cemetery. Another medical innovator famously associated with Up Park Camp was Barry's contemporary, Mary Seacole. Born in Kingston in 1805 to a free black woman and a Scottish army officer, Seacole's medical career rivaled Florence Nightingale's. Her mother ran a boarding house frequented by army and navy officers and their families, a place where people often convalesced, as it was healthier than the hospital. Seacole married a successful English businessman and, with the extensive knowledge of herbal remedies learned from her mother, fought the cholera epidemic at Up Park Camp in 1853, and later served in the Crimea, where her path was again to cross with Barry's. Like Couba

Cornwallis, the black nurse who had restored Nelson to health, Mary Seacole had extensive knowledge of herbal cures that often proved more effective than the remedies applied by European physicians.

Barry continued his interest in local pharmacopeia and the methods of indigenous practitioners that had begun at the Cape. The military was a close-knit culture, particularly in the upper ranks, and Barry knew many officers and their families who spoke enthusiastically of the restorative convalescence they had received at the establishment of Mrs. Grant, Mary Seacole's mother. There is no record of the two having met, but given their mutual standing in the Kingston community, there is no doubt that they were professionally aware of each other. Barry may have been inspired by the examples of Mrs. Grant and Mary Seacole in 1837, when he controversially hired a black matron to attend on the troop hospital in St. Helena.

As well as meeting with success in containing the Stony Hill yellow jack epidemic in 1831, Barry made a significant impact on the health of Up Park Camp. The mortality rate at the station dropped between 1831 and 1834, Barry's period in office. In the year of his arrival there were 110 deaths per 1,000. By the time of his departure in 1834, this had gone down to 70 per 1,000.

Barry's success established him as part of a new medical elite whose application of modern science was revolutionizing medicine at precisely the same moment that European colonization was tightening its grip over Africa, Asia, and the Americas. His role as staff surgeon made him responsible for eight military hospitals: four on the north side and four on the south side of the island. All were located in inhospitable and unhealthy locations.

It was one of Barry's characteristics that he was never far behind the trailblazers who had so inspired him to become a surgeon. In Jamaica he was following in the august footsteps of John Hunter, the leading surgeon-physiologist of his age, younger brother to William, and the man credited with turning surgery from a debased manual craft into a scientific discipline. Hunter had been the first person to hold the post of staff surgeon in Jamaica, and his essay *Observations on the Diseases of the Army in Jamaica,* based on his experiences of the military hospitals there, was one of the founding texts of tropical medicine, a discipline that became synonymous with the imperial mission of civilization and subjugation. Hunter was the first to highlight "the dreadful mortality that has always accompanied military operations in the West Indies." He realized that there were many similarities among the diseases of warm climates and drew connections between Africa, India, and the Caribbean that became the starting ground of tropical medicine.

Hunter's early work confirmed what Barry soon realized—that heat, moisture, and decaying animal or vegetable matter in combination cultivate fever. Hunter in particular highlighted the unhealthiness of Kingston's position, although he insisted on the social causes of disease: rum, "causing excesses and irregularities," hard labor, and bad diet. Barry could not have been a more fervent apostle. Crucially, what medical pioneers like Hunter, Cooper, and Barry came to understand was that the effectiveness of modern medicine lay in overcoming the diseases of poverty and social inequality. Although half a century apart, Hunter and Barry insisted that clean water, sufficient food in a healthy, balanced diet, adequate ventilation, and sanitation were absolutely essential to preventing and resisting disease. To progressive philosophers, thinkers, and politicians of the day, these elements were among the core entitlements of man, not to mention woman. Within two decades, all of Europe and North America would be in revolution to secure these rights. Barry translated these rights into the practical business of medicine. He was fiercely passionate about giving succor to the soldiers, and made representations to the army medical department suggesting the restructuring of the Jamaican medical staff. A letter to the army medical department from Barry's acquaintance the marquis of Sligo, written when Barry was home on leave, pointed out that patients recovered more quickly when treated by local practitioners than by the military surgeons. The letter recommended that a large permanent medical staff was required at the key hospitals on the island, and that local doctors should be invited to practice there alongside the regimental surgeons, all of whom should be compelled to attend in the hospitals. These recommendations bear the strong stamp of Barry's own innovatory regimes, and it is likely he lobbied Sligo to send the letter.

As always, Barry enjoyed the social expectations that accompanied his role as a high-ranking military officer. King Sugar was a degenerate and indulgent monarch, and the British settler society over which he ruled reveled in decadent excess. Jamaica's social life revolved predominately around the large houses on the various estates. There were frequent balls at King's House, the governor's official residence, complemented by an annual schedule of events on the grand estates on other parts of the island—St. Anne's Bay, Falmouth, Montego Bay. Even the smallest military maneuvers provided excuses for expensive celebrations, and there was a full schedule of regimental dinners to which the governor and his retinue were invited.

However, King Sugar's society was not restricted merely to the genteel provincialism of balls and military dinners. Spanish Town, Kingston, and Port Royal regarded themselves as a golden triangle of urban sophistication, and were in truth laced with a harder edge of indigence bred of limitless alcohol and narcotics, whose consumption was then regarded as palliative and medicinal.

Yet Barry experienced Jamaican high society at a time when the absolutist sway of sugar was reaching its end. "There were only three topics of conversation in the island: debt, disease and death," noted a historian of the terminal decline of Jamaican settler society. For two decades the impact of the 1807 abolition of the slave trade had progressively undermined the economic supremacy of the Jamaican sugar industry. Some plantations had been abandoned, the price of sugar had plummeted, and by 1830 it was becoming impossible for men of once-unimaginable wealth to borrow against their properties. From the metropolitan standpoint, this was a shrinking economy, and cheaper sugar could be bought from India and Brazil.

The West Indian trade system was going bankrupt, and the settler society was infused with a barely repressed hysteria and disbelief that their gilded, privileged world spun from sugar and human pain was on the verge of collapse. With an edgy frenzy covered only by the veneer of social convention, they desperately held on to the rituals of their elite society. Barry found himself a frequent guest of a social order whose primary concern was the frenetic keeping up of appearances.

Barry had arrived in the West Indies in search of another horizon and fighting off a shadow self—the overconfident, newly qualified Young Turk who had overplayed his political hand at the Cape. He was reconciling himself to living with the memory of Somerset, cloaking his bereavement in professional distance, ceaseless energetic activity, and constant movement. It is in the Jamaican period that Barry's persona became so markedly defined by detachment, so expert in keeping social intimacy at arm's length—while deeply involved and passionate about social justice. He translated his progressiveness into doctoring. Fixing, mending, restoring, making whole, alleviating, succoring, respecting. His charismatic personality was a contradictory compound of the aloofness of the idiosyncratic loner with a natural gregariousness and exhibitionism expressed in his love of argument, entertainment, and fashion. Barry was not without friends, but he did not suffer fools and his acquaintances were select and few. Moreover, they were drawn from the civilian classes as much as from his military peers.

The belles from Kingston and Spanish Town flocked to the annual regatta at Port Royal in their best frocks, intent upon obtaining an invitation to join the distinguished naval officers on board their pleasure boats. The horse races at Kingston and Spanish Town were another key meeting point, and there were regular meets in five other regions of the island, including the nostalgically named Bath, Manchester, Clarendon, and Vere. Defined by indulgence, this society spared itself no luxury, even when it could no longer afford it. The Jamaican colonials determined to provide themselves with diversions from the increasing precariousness of their political situation. In March 1832, Kingston society buzzed with excited talk about the "Phantasmagoria," a fantastic, dreamlike show of exhibits "from the size of the miniature to five times as large of life" held at the Kingston Theatre. The exhibition boasted subjects including the "Turkish Ambassador, Head of A Giantess, London Bridge with processions of the Lord Mayor's Royal Barges, Babes in the Wood and Burning of Mt Vesuvius." The surreal dimensions of this show captured the essence of this moment in Jamaican colonial society. All out of proportion to itself, this once-exaggerated, absurdly wealthy culture was shrinking back to the size of its diminished humanity.

Barry's hard-won seriousness was in great contrast to this colonial excess. Now a devoted surgeon and exacting administrator, Barry used his position as he had at the Cape—to assist the sick, disadvantaged, and oppressed. His abolitionist views were well known, and off-kilter with many of the social butterflies who were intrigued by the rather reticent new officer.

As in Cape Town, Barry found that the theater was a focal point of settlers' socializing and entertainment—and the key public place to see and be seen. Musical entertainments offered full if rather tropically damp orchestras. Light-hearted comedies were favored fare, and with actresses in short supply audiences tolerated understaffed casts such as that in which an actress called Miss Lane took the parts of no less than five characters.

Edward Bradford, who met Barry socially in Jamaica in 1832, found his appearance and manners "most singular." Bradford recalled that Barry "sought every opportunity of making himself conspicuous, and wore the longest sword and spurs he could obtain. . . . He delighted in scandal and gossip, and told me that on one occasion he had gone out with some one at the Cape, and had shot his whiskers off." As at the Cape, Barry's sedulous attention to the most beautiful wives and daughters of the local military men was remarked upon—and complained about—by his colleagues. An officer at Up Park Camp objected vehemently to "the little doctor visiting his wife during the hours when he himself was absent in the orderly room." This reputation, combined with his flair for dashing dress, of course only increased Barry's standing with the bored and enervated military women, who actively sought out his company.

Despite his new air of gravity, Barry retained his weakness for flamboyant dress, a predilection that drew the attention of the theater reviewers, who observed his frequent presence at the theater "crowded with the fashionables of our city." Barry was a noted figure on the politically charged occasion when "Sir Willoughby Cotton, attended by a brilliant staff, entered the Theatre" following the Christmas uprising of 1831. "His Excellency had scarcely time to take his seat," recalled the correspondent, "when the audience greeted him with three hearty cheers. . . . such a compliment indeed is not often paid by a Kingston audience."

This rare demonstration of public approval for a military leader was offered by Kingston society for a deadly serious reason—Cotton had recently returned from Montego Bay, where he had suppressed the slave insurrection that came to be known as the Sam Sharpe Rebellion. Although quelled, this uprising in fact signaled the imminent overthrow of King Sugar and his barons by the forces of emancipation.

The tension that exploded into this mass protest had been building throughout 1831. Earlier in the year the more radical members of the Anti-Slavery Society led a campaign to mobilize popular support and lobby parliamentary candidates. Unsettled by this activism, the Jamaican settlers protested, claiming it was incitement to rebellion. In fact, the sugar planters themselves did the most to fuel the uprising, by holding public meetings around the country at which they aired their litany of grievances against Westminster. As had been the case on other Caribbean islands, the slaves were well aware of the political divisions among their oppressors. In this instance, the vehement opposition of the planters was interpreted to mean that emancipation had in fact already been declared in Britain but that the benefits to be conferred on the slaves were being withheld by the Jamaican Assembly, in league with the plantation owners. The slaves determined to claim the rights they believed already to be theirs.

Samuel "Daddy" Sharpe, a charismatic Baptist preacher and slave, led a strike during the Christmas week of 1831. Thinking they had been freed, slaves refused to return to work after the brief Christmas holiday. This triggered the rebellion. It was the largest uprising the island had ever seen, involving twenty thousand slaves throughout western Jamaica and causing damage to 226 estates at an estimated cost of £1,154,000. Sharpe and the protest leaders intended passive resistance, but the campaign escalated into a violent rebellion when a breakaway faction of slaves stormed a rum store and drunkenly proceeded to set fire to mansion houses and sugar factories. Colonel Gignon, who commanded an incompetent local militia comprised of planters utterly unable to contain the situation, retreated swiftly into the hills without even attempting to engage the rebels. Gignon was later court-martialed for his part in leaving the countryside in the hands of the slaves.

As soon as he heard of the "extensive and destructive insurrection," the governor, Lord Belmore, declared martial law, and ordered Sir Willoughby Cotton and Admiral Sir Arthur Murray Farquhar to mobilize a campaign to bring the situation under control. Belmore prepared to dispatch ships to Montego Bay and Black River. He sent word to Barry at Up Park Camp, notifying him that he must prepare immediately for departure.

The troop ships arrived at the northwest coast on January 1, 1832, with Barry accompanying Cotton in the commander's flagship. As Barry sailed into the harbor, he could see the smoking hills around Montego Bay still ablaze with the "lurid glare" of destruction. It took less than a week for Cotton's forces to repress the uprising, but martial law stayed in place until February 8, while slaves believed to have participated in the rebellion were hunted down, flogged, tortured, or summarily executed. Barry was witness to cases of extreme brutality in which he had no power to intervene. Four hundred slaves were killed during the fighting and subsequent reprisals. The loss of life to the colonists was conversely small—"ten killed, two murdered, and one or two burned in houses."

Barry's first task was to take care of the injured redcoats. The slaves fought with knives, rocks, and fire. Only a small number had firearms, and they were badly outflanked by the grimly superior firepower of the soldiers. Barry dealt with knife wounds, burns, and a few gunshot injuries. The troops were, however, overrun by a far greater foe than injuries sustained by combat: the tropical maladies. Yellow fever, dysentery, malaria, and diarrhea challenged Barry's expertise under very crude conditions, while his innovative approach to hygiene helped preserve his own immunity from infection.

In order to deal with this crisis, Barry reopened the Montego Bay barracks hospital. The location of the station was so unhealthy that it had been closed and the station disused for some time. The abandoned hospital was a rank stone building devoid of light and ventilation. Under Barry's supervision it was scrubbed and sluiced and its small wooden shutters and door opened for a largely futile airing. Low-lying and almost enclosed by an amphitheater of mountains, Montego Bay was known as one of the hottest places on an already sizzling island. Its location meant that the scorching heat was unrelieved by wind. Fresh water supplies were limited, and despite Barry's efforts to increase them for the sick, food rations were insufficient. It is hardly surprising, then, that Barry's ability to protect the lives of the troops was limited, or that 40 percent of the troops stationed in Montego Bay in 1832 lost their lives. In searing temperatures, Barry did battle against the ravages of tropical disease in this tiny, ill-equipped and ill-serviced hospital, while around him raged the fierce retribution against the slaves. Not recorded in the official correspondence were the attacks on missionaries—both black and white—who were blamed for inciting the slaves to mayhem. Many of their chapels were also destroyed.

A key figure in Cotton's entourage on the night of the theater visit, as he had been during the campaign, Barry must have experienced a tumult of contradictory emotion as Kingston society applauded them as conquering heroes. On the one hand, he could revel in the increased stature of the campaign hero, his masculinity enhanced by the fact that he had been on the front lines. But the glow of this social approval, which he otherwise so often craved, was tempered by the knowledge that his first taste of active service was bitter with the betrayal of his own principles. Pro-emancipation, Barry had gone into the field of battle to restore and protect the lives of soldiers whose job it was to destroy the lives and spirits of the slaves whose bid for freedom Barry so keenly understood.

In this, his politics were in keeping with those of his somewhat reluctant commander. Settler society had hissed with the accusatory rumor that Cotton had shown tardiness in his willingness to fight against the slave rebels, and newspaper editorials openly challenged his allegiance:

> Sir Willoughby's firmness of character as a soldier has never been questioned, but it remains to be seen whether he is what a Lieutenant-Governor of Jamaica ought to be, or whether he is a servant of Mr Stephen, of the Colonial Office. . . . We shall reserve our opinion with characteristic highland simplicity, "until his deeds show themselves."

This editorial expressed exactly the crux of the contemporary political situation in Jamaica. The settlers had long opposed the right of Parliament to enact legislation for the colonies. Their persistent argument throughout the great controversy that raged over emancipation was that all legislation relating to slaves must be left to the colonial legislatures. The slave owners described abolition as "a direct violation of the rights of private property to which they were entitled as British subjects." They had enjoyed legislating for themselves for over a century, and resisted centralized rule from England. The home governments were nervous and tired of the reactionary demands of the plantation owners, whose reductive bottom-line capitalism—their chief argument for the maintenance of slavery—was increasingly out of step with the hot winds of republican revolution and the cooler drafts of liberalism blowing across Europe. The planters were an embarrassment to a Parliament that was at the same time too weak to move against the interests of capital.

By the time the Act of Abolition was passed, in August 1834, Barry had served at Jamaica's key outposts. His duties took him to Port Antonio, Maroon Town, and Falmouth, with repeated stays of duty at Montego Bay. All of this involved arduous traveling on horseback and by sea around the coast. His travels around the island had given him a broad view of the condition of slavery and the brutal attitudes and behavior of the unrepentant plantation owners. When he was at the Cape, alongside the scandal of his relationship with Somerset, the issues that had brought Barry the most criticism were his progressive attitudes toward matters of race and slavery. This reputation had followed him to Jamaica.

Barry had, of course, intervened in the treatment of slaves in prison at the Cape, but as two exemplary cases demonstrate, Barry kept a sharp eye out for evidence of maltreatment of slaves elsewhere in the colony. In 1822, a Mozambiquan slave had died following "a domestic correction with the birch" by the Reverend Gebherd of Paarl. The district surgeon stated in his report that "the slave was a big eater in life and suffered from bulimia with occasional faintings." Barry scrutinized the report, and was appalled, declaring it to be "most incorrect and unprofessional." He then asked if the body had been dissected. Dr. Tardieux, the district surgeon, said that he had not conducted an autopsy because everyone knew that "bruises could not occasion death, only cuts." Barry declared that bulimia as a cause of death was utterly ludicrous and that beyond a shadow of doubt the Mozambiquan had died as a result of the flogging.

In another instance, in February 1824, Barry received a letter from the assistant colonial secretary, P. G. Brink, containing an anxious request for medical information and advice from a regional landdrost. Its contents were confidential, a mixture of anxiety and reproach. The previous year, Barry had ordered the release of a slave called Cathryn from the Hemel-en-Aarde leper colony on the grounds that she had been misdiagnosed. Cathryn was returned to her owner, who shortly afterward raped her. The landowner's letter made it clear that he had also forcibly made Cathryn's sexual services available to his friends and colleagues. Only subsequently realizing that Cathryn was the slave whom Barry had sent back from the leper colony, her master became fearful that he would contract leprosy from his sexual intercourse with her, and that, moreover, he had unwittingly exposed a circle of his male friends to a similar health hazard. Unwilling to admit his error to them, he bought Cathryn's silence with gifts and money. He then wrote to Barry in confidence to find out if, as he feared, he had now contracted leprosy. Deflecting from the morality of his own behavior, Cathryn's owner attempted to question Barry's wisdom regarding her release from the leper colony in the first place. Barry was having none of it: in his reply he made it clear that he regarded Cathryn as a victim of venality. Mimicking the slave owner's pompously formal tone, Barry played him at his own game of presenting himself as benevolent, charitable slave owner:

> I beg to assure you that the Landdrost's regrets respecting the Slave Cathryn are perfectly unnecessary; as no danger can be apprehended (as even possible) to result from any communication, or connexion that this Gentleman, or any other Person is likely to have had with Cathryn. My views in discharging this poor Woman from the Leper Institution were, and still are, to prevent her being wantonly or unnecessarily exposed to the filth, horrors, and other miserable scenes, which in the present situation of the Hospital are unavoidable and to give the poor Woman an opportunity of recovering her Health—she has a bad Breast, from injudiciously suckling her Baby: thus never could get well at the Institution. Her Master who has shewn a most excellent and benevolent Disposition which does him great Credit, has arranged for the comfort of his Slave. I am decidedly of the Opinion that no mischief can ensue, on the contrary good, and therefore hope His Excellency will be pleased to order that the Slave Cathryn be not annoyed by any interference from prejudiced or capricious individuals.

This was an age in which men took no responsibility for their sexual behavior: they made women vassals of their own disease, and then blamed them for spreading it. More than half a century later, the Contagious Diseases Acts would still be criminalizing women as agents of sexual disease. Barry's dry sarcasm illustrates his critical stance on male sexual hypocrisy.

Sir Jahleel Brenton, the naval abolitionist who used his extensive wealth to assist the emancipationist cause, was frequently heard to praise Barry for his care for slaves, and on his travels around Africa, India, and the West Indies he would tell how at the Cape Barry had bought the freedom of two slaves, Sanna and Hermes, at his own expense. Sanna, a hermaphrodite, Barry saved from a cruel master. Hermes was just about to be sent to prison for a petty theft committed on the property of a Dutch householder. Barry paid his ransom and placed the "Hottentot boy" safely in the care of Jahleel Brenton's household as a paid servant, where he became a family favorite.

Throughout his career, Barry always identified with the plight of the dispossessed. The humanitarian education bequeathed by his mentors had coached him from an early age in the political and moral philosophy of the eighteenth century that so defined their progressive milieu. Mary Wollstonecraft, a personal friend to James Barry, R.A., and so admired by Lord Buchan in his profeminist publications, had famously compared the oppression of women to the condition of slavery. Another philosopher whose work influenced the circle of James Barry, R.A., and whose opinions were much discussed amongst the abolitionists, Alexis de Tocqueville, drew attention to the rootlessness and alienation that was so central to the condition of slavery:

> He remains halfway between . . . two communities, isolated between two races; sold by the one, repulsed by the other; finding not a spot in the universe to call by the name of country, except the faint image of a home which the shelter of his master's roof affords.

Tocqueville's words resonate with Barry's own condition of being always halfway between. A military doctor, he was in the pay of an institutional machine central to the maintenance of colonial supremacy. Yet his radical education and dissident views on humanitarian issues placed him always on the outside of conformity. Joined to this philosophical and political radicalism were his own peculiar physicality and mysterious, parentless origins. An agent of empire, he was also its detractor, reforming from within.

Barry's chosen path enabled him to escape the habit of servitude, but however much he excelled as a surgeon and medical innovator, he could not escape the confines of his own unconventional identity. Betwixt and between, belonging nowhere, Barry faced the problem of self-orientation alone. His own and only hope of emancipation was to confront constantly the task of reinventing himself and making himself at home in an existence devoid of fixed points of support.

Acting with the precision of the scientist in the execution of his duties, Barry disguised the enigma of his emotions with frenetic activity, movement, and the work through which he expressed the core of his beliefs. His constant evasion of rootedness, however, was not entirely a matter of choice. However far he traveled, he remained the prisoner of a personal mystery known only to himself.

Chapter 8

INSULAR OBSESSIONS

*Islands are the quintessential example of the impression of free-
dom without its actuality.*

Paul Kauffmann, *The Dark Room at Longwood*

TO JUDGE BY THE AMOUNT OF TIME HE SPENT ON THEM, JAMES
Barry liked islands. Either that or the military authorities thought he
was particularly suited to island postings. Firing off a letter of complaint
against what he regarded as early retirement in the 1850s, Barry loftily
reminds his superiors that he "has continuously served to the present
time at the Cape of Good Hope, Mauritius, Jamaica, Trinidad, St Helena, Barbados, Antigua, Malta, Corfu, the Crimea, and Canada."
Scored with amendments, asterisks, and marginalia ensuring that he
has remembered all his postings, this letter itself looks like a map, plot-
ting the routes of Barry's twenty-year odyssey through the islands of
the Indian Ocean, the Atlantic, and the Mediterranean. All of these islands were hybrid, creolized places. Barry liked his islands of indeter-
minacy.

By their nature, islands encompass a dichotomy. They represent simultaneously freedom and eternal entrapment. Finite, knowable, and
encircled by sea and sky, islands had for Barry the appeal of being just
beyond the reach of the traffic of the mainland. Yet in reality, as he

quickly discovered, they remained subject to the economic and political whims of their far-distant mainland rulers.

Islands had traditionally offered the traveler the possibility of starting anew, of self-invention in an environment set apart from the mainlands of the world. Some of this promise still remained, but as Britain's islands were colonial possessions, they were fast becoming subject to interfering patterns of politics and travel that harnessed them more securely to the life of the mainland. Parts of the global map of the British empire, they were also set apart from its imperial center.

Like Barry, islands were paradoxical places made up of disparate elements. To a loner with secrets, the clearly visible boundaries of islands made them appear safe and knowable. News took a long time to travel, and trouble could be seen approaching from a distance. Yet at the same time the impermeable borders of islands were illusory. On every tide, ships could unexpectedly bring an interesting stranger, an unwelcome friend, or a new disease. Islands were indeterminate, holding out promises of unexpected encounters with people from all points of the globe. The social intensity and intimacy of island life made it easy to gain a foothold and become upwardly mobile—an important consideration for a snob like Barry. On the downside, the same intensity also made them risky and dangerous hothouses.

From the unrelenting heat of the tropical West Indies to the sun-scorched Mediterranean isles, Barry traveled with an almost inhuman vigor. The high temperatures, inhospitable afflictions, diseases, and various other discomforts of island life that had other colonials fainting under their parasols seemed to galvanize Barry into a frenzy of energy. The robust and disputatious Barry was never sick, or too hot to argue. By the same token, he shrank from the cold and had an animated aversion to wintry climates. Receiving orders at the end of his career to depart for Montreal, his first northern posting, he protested grumpily to a friend that he was being sent to Canada to "cool off."

In 1836, Barry was posted to the most famous island of all: the fortress of St. Helena, which had played grim host to Napoleon while Barry was at the Cape. "A damned awful country," declared Napoleon as soon as he saw it. An ominous mass of mountains rearing out of the South Atlantic, vaporous and surrounded by banked sentries of cloud, St. Helena was no palm-fringed tropical idyll. Another visitor, Edmund Halley, was so fascinated by the changeability of the weather on the island that he ended up staying for two years in a self-imposed research exile that enabled him to identify the origin of winds.

Wedged into a ravine between two mountains, the capital, Jamestown, stubbornly persisted in evoking a look more Portuguese than English, despite the efforts of the English to soften its appearance with irises and daisies. George Thomas Keppel, earl of Albemarle, who had met Barry and Somerset at the Cape, discovered St. Helena to be "a gloomy little island," and thought the man a very bold adventurer "who first thought of settling in so uninviting a locality." He was equally unimpressed by Jamestown, "the only town in the island," occupying the bed of a "deep, narrow and almost perpendicular ravine." Overall, Albemarle found that the first appearance of the place "produced upon me a deep feeling of depression." Misty, storm-tossed, but ruggedly romantic, St. Helena retained an air of haughty self-possession, apparently impervious to the far-distant powers who tossed her between them as booty. Six months before Barry arrived on St. Helena, in September 1836, the island had been transferred to the Crown from the East India Company. George Middlemore had been appointed first governor, and civil government established on April 1. The military was sweeping clean with a new broom, and Dr. Barry was just the administrative bristle they needed.

Director General Sir James McGrigor selected Barry as the new principal medical officer for St. Helena with careful deliberation. McGrigor, a departmental reformer legendary for his level of personal knowledge of the officers he commanded, "selected judiciously for heads of the medical staff in each of the colonies those best fitted by previous service and professional ability." Contemptuous of the back-biting niceties of civil politics, McGrigor prioritized medical expertise above all else in the selection of his officers. When it came to stations vulnerable to epidemics he considered "only ability."

Barry had four essential qualities McGrigor needed. He was used to tough, rough colonial postings. As shown by his track record in the Cape and Jamaica, he had the experience to implement a medical infrastructure where, in the wake of the departing East India Company, none existed. Thirdly, St. Helena had a huge and escalating problem with venereal disease. Barry had built a reputation on his success with treating what he brusquely called "the Venereal," and McGrigor had undoubtedly taken note of his research work on syphilis and gonorrhea at the Cape. Finally, Barry was good at pretending that he had a thick skin. McGrigor knew that whoever took this job would encounter resistance. The unstinting support McGrigor gave the maverick Barry throughout this contentious posting suggests that the military had cottoned on to the strategic usefulness, under certain conditions, of Barry's pugnacious individualism. However idiosyncratic, Barry was a great stickler for regulations, seeing "not the slightest reason for a deviation from either the letter or the spirit of the rule." This exacting nature reassured the military authorities and went some way toward offsetting his unorthodox methods.

Barry arrived at St. Helena in a bad mood. His journey from England had been fraught with misadventure. Barry and his servant, for whom he had requested passage, had left England from Deal on the *Lord William Bentinck* in April. Sir Andries Stockenstrom, whom Barry had known at the Cape, turned out to be a fellow passenger on the voyage. Stockenstrom was amused to find Lord Somerset's old family physician embarking with his motley entourage: servant, Psyche, goat, and an extensive array of sea chests. Even Barry's excessively careful provisions proved inadequate for the ill-fated voyage. An outbreak of smallpox on board took five lives, and the remaining passengers lived in fear of contagion for the remainder of the two-and-a-half month voyage. Needless to say, Barry's expertise was sought ceaselessly throughout the hazardous journey.

On arrival at the Cape the ship was impounded and its passengers quarantined for six frustrating weeks. All their possessions were confiscated. Linen and bedding were either burned or steeped in lime to disinfect them. Letters and personal belongings were fumigated. In August, Barry wrote a long and indignant letter to the governor, demanding recompense for his damaged and destroyed property: "I am sure that it was not your Excellency's intention that beyond the requisite confinement to obviate the possibility of infection I should have been despoiled, and my property sacrificed, without positive necessity."

"Humbly" questioning the need for the extreme measures, Barry made it clear that the loss of his linen was catastrophic. His estimate of losses presented an exact account of all the items damaged, including "a horsehair mattress and pillow" and "four dozen shirts." His primary concern, however, was with the loss of three pillows whose function was deeply ambiguous:

> On our removal from the Chavronne my bedding was burnt, my linen, a large quantity requisite in a long Voyage, steeped in chloride of lime until so decimated that it fell to rags in washing, three pillows of a particular description necessary to me under the peculiar circumstances in which severe accidents have placed me which cost fifteen guineas each were wantonly and against my strongest remonstrance seized and destroyed making altogether unto me a most important Accident in loss considering that I am on my way to join the Station to which I am appointed.

Barry's demand for remuneration was waved aside by the government, which regarded it as the "most extraordinary claim" they had "ever seen," and "highly indelicate and unbecoming on his part." They did concede "the loss of the pillows however was a heavy one for Dr B—— considering his peculiar infirmity of body," and, while rejecting the rest of his claim, recommended he be reimbursed for these down pillows. The purpose of the "three pillows of a particular description" seems baffling. Barry did not clarify their use, nor the nature of the "severe accidents" that made them necessary, but the vehemence of his long letter of protest makes it clear that whatever their function, these mysterious pillows were crucial to him.

The fact that Barry was now overdue in taking up his new post and had missed his free passage to St. Helena on board the *Catherine* was worsened by the fact that the *Lord William Bentinck* had sailed on to India with the "principal part" of Barry's baggage still stowed aboard. There would be no means of replacing his clothes, crockery, linen and all manner of other personal possessions once on St. Helena; Barry knew he had to try to reequip himself at the Cape. In an attempt to cover his losses he tried to sell some of his damaged linen at public auction, but the proceeds were insufficient to replace all the things he needed. Out of pocket, furious that the government refused to recognize his plight, and presumably anxious as to how long his "pillows of a particular description" would take to be replaced from London, Barry found solace only in the daily visits of his godson, James Barry Munnik.

Barry arrived at St. Helena on September 4, 1836, to an outbreak of chronic dysentery. He was shown round the hospital, which was divided into separate wings for the garrison and civil patients, and briefed on the crisis by the regimental assistant surgeons, Eddie and McLaren. Filing his report to McGrigor, Barry said that as he had only been on the island "a short while" he endorsed the measures taken by the regimental surgeons and had little to add to them. Of course, Barry always had something to add:

> However, on the subject of the general health of the garrison, there seems but little doubt that the total want of fresh provisions has contributed greatly to the prevailing disease on the Island—namely fever, commencing with obstinate constipation and terminating in dysentery.

He noted with approval that the daily ration of a pint of Cape wine was a measure of "eminent utility" in combating scurvy. Impressed with surgeon Eddie's "clean and well arranged" organization of the military hospital, Barry praised his ability and appointed him as his assistant. It was a canny move—James McGrigor was a stickler for thorough docu-

mentation, and Barry anticipated correctly that there would be a considerable burden of administration in this new role.

All the same, these administrative requirements were a measure of
the level of responsibility given to Barry in his new post. In October
1836, McGrigor sent Barry an exhaustive letter outlining his new responsibilities in detail. The imperative to keep "correct accounts" for
this, and "another account" for that, ran like a chorus through the set of
minute instructions. Barry was also to plan "requisitions for supplies of
medicine and medical stores" eighteen months ahead, "always keeping
a similar stock in hand." One can almost hear the active, hands-on
Barry inwardly sighing at all these instructions for bookkeeping, although he would approve of the contingency for forward planning.
Barry was a vigorous and efficient administrator when he could see the
purpose of the paperwork, but was antipathetic to bureaucracy for its
own sake, especially when he had to duplicate the same accounts and
reports for both military and civil departments. Later he grouchily objected that the volume of accounts and reports required in England was
at a level "as if there had been a much larger Force in the Command."
But McGrigor had found the right man: Barry worked out a system and
delegated the keeping of accounts and inventory for the military hospital to Eddie, while he set about inspecting the civil hospital.

Barry's commendation on the existing management of the military
wing of the hospital was in direct inverse proportion to his condemnation of the state of the civil wards. Without hesitation, he cut straight to
the point. The civil hospital was in a "confused and disgusting state"
and required immediate reorganization. The insanitary and teeming
civilian wing was more like a city ghetto than a modern hospital: sailors,
low-ranking soldiers, prostitutes, and animals hustled together in the
overcrowded wards. The civil hospital was out of control, and from
whatever else its inhabitants were suffering, they all had venereal diseases. Yet Barry's refusal to scapegoat immoral women for the venereal
scourge was startling. Without casting judgment on prostitution, Barry
pointed out that the huge increase in the number of venereal cases was

"owing to the number of females left destitute on the removal of the East India Company's regiment from the island who were obliged to resort to prostitution for their support." Barry placed the blame for this female destitution squarely on the shoulders of the men who had changed the political economy of the island. His statement that these women were "obliged" to "resort to prostitution" in the absence of any other means of support was the model of idealist gentility. To a twenty-first century eye, Barry's diagnosis of the problem may appear as common sense. To the early nineteenth-century mind-set, it was an outrageous indictment of male reprehensibility over female lewdness.

Digging deeper into Barry's indignation, a clear sense of his disgust at the sexual economy of the civil hospital emerges. At one level this is the straightforward impatience of the scientist for the venal behavior of less informed social inferiors. Yet Barry's righteous anger at the "greatest irregularities" to which the female patients were subjected signifies a keen understanding of their extreme economic and social vulnerability, a vulnerability he was determined to correct:

> On my arrival I found a want of arrangement in regard to the Civil Department, more particularly in the disgusting circumstances of male attendants on the female patients—syphilitic and other diseases—and of course the greatest irregularities. I immediately hired a respectable woman of colour as Matron and requested the Military Chaplain to visit the civil side of the hospital as well as the military.

Barry asked Major General Middlemore "to sanction that accommodation for the Females (which it is always incorrect to treat in a Military Hospital) should be fitted up . . . in a waste Building near the Hospital called the Brewery." Middlemore agreed to his request. Consistent with his early concern for the plight of the insane, Barry also pointed out the need for separate accommodation "for maniacs who are in an awfully neglected state." In earlier years, he would have simply argued for better treatment for the insane on the grounds of natural justice, but Barry's strategy in justifying the need for these separate quarters demonstrates his increasing understanding of the need for a strategic approach. These arrangements were essential, he argued, because without them "we shall be at a loss to accommodate even the Troops, in the event of accident, or increase of disease in the Garrison."

Barry sent his initial report on St. Helena's medical institutions to the exacting James McGrigor even before the letter arrived asking for it. Having made his recommendations, Barry launched himself into a grinding routine of what he described as "laborious and important" civil responsibilities. He held a daily clinic for "paupers and indigent persons whose disease did not require Hospital treatment" at the out-patients dispensary from noon to three o'clock. He "attended the Prison," and established the first process of organized vaccination for St. Helena, "a matter of eminent importance to a Colony where vessels touched for water, from many parts of the world." All this and the daily superintendence of the Civil General Hospital too. Barry listed his patients:

> . . . prisoners and convicts, Lascars and Invalids of the B.E.I. Co. Service, Seamen of the Merchant Service—English, Dutch, French, American etc., who from Scurvy, Accidents (requiring capital operations) or acute diseases could not proceed on their respective voyages.

St. Helena was regarded as a challenging and difficult appointment. Within two months, Barry had clearly demonstrated his ability to make a difference.

Yet while these successes mounted, Barry was charging headlong into a bitter dispute with the army supplies division, known as the Commissariat. It was a matter of constant irritation to Barry—as it was to be later for Florence Nightingale—that this heavily bureaucratized department was run directly by the treasury and not the war office. Behind its foreboding title, the Commissariat was a supplies department staffed by civil servants whose real job was to keep down the costs of providing equipment and provisions for the army and to cut deals with private retailers in whom the government usually had a vested interest. The Commissariat, that is, was exactly the kind of obstructionist bureaucratic dinosaur that enraged Barry when he was trying to overturn old structures and build anew.

As principal medical officer, Barry was responsible for the requisitions to both the military and civilian sections of the St. Helena hospital. The withdrawal of the East India Company meant that there was no system of providing regular supplies for the civilian hospital. On the military side, Barry could see from surgeon Eddie's audits that the troops were not receiving their full rations and that the military hospital was being shortchanged on its entitlement to supplies. Bread, meat, candles, and coal had been provided, but other essentials like sugar, salt, tea, and milk—no doubt regarded as luxuries by the Commissariat—had been withheld and paid for out of the medical officer's own pocket.

Barry proposed a neat solution to this mess to the head commissar, the dour F. E. Knowles. The department should buy wholesale goods to supply both the military and civilian hospitals. Out of these consolidated supplies, Barry reminded him, the military hospital should be given the full range of items allocated to it. In response to this sensible request, Barry received an immediate and emphatic "no" from Knowles, who refused to supply the civil hospital for the reason that "the duties of purveyor to that establishment were not comprised in his Commission."

Clearly Knowles had not apprised himself of Barry's nature before he ran the risk of making an enemy of him. Checking McGrigor's "General Instructions for Medical Officers, Heads of Staff and others in charge of Departments," Barry fired back an immediate response that pointed out to Knowles that indeed it was his responsibility to supply the civil hospital, and that he had better get on with releasing "the stoppages" in rations to which the military hospital had been subjected.

Unaware that Knowles was smarting under his instructions, Barry continued to hurl his administrative thunderbolts, as well as offering the increasingly livid Knowles advice on the management of his own conscience: "I trust these considerations seconded by a desire to promote the good of the Service will prompt you to withdraw further opposition to my requisitions at the least until a reference may be made on the subject."

Judging that he could not resolve the issue through Knowles, Barry decided to go round him. At the beginning of the second week of November, he wrote a letter directly to the secretary of state at the War Office outlining the dispute between Knowles and himself, and requesting the direct intervention of the War Office secretariat. The letter is a classic piece of Barry self-sabotage. It starts well, by referring punctiliously to the specific military instructions at stake ("Article No 2 of the Instructions of the 28th Feb. 1835 for the management of Hospitals on Foreign Stations") and objectively outlining the problem. This done, the letter gives itself over to a characteristic burst of Barryesque verbal incontinence: "It will appear unnecessary to comment on the total absence of all rational objections on the part of the Commissary here to further the ends of the Service in this instance." Barry rounds off with due notice to the head of the War Office, a cabinet minister, that he will take it upon himself to proceed irrespective of the objections of the Commissariat and "take the most efficient means in my power of obtaining the necessary supplies, until favoured by your Lordship's instruction on the subject."

Before it reached the government dispatches Barry's letter had been copied by a malicious hand to Knowles, who in turn made sure a further copy found its way to General Middlemore's desk. Ignoring the central issue at stake concerning the supply of provisions to sick patients and troops, the military establishment closed ranks against Barry. Patients might be dying of hunger in the hospital, but Dr. Barry was regarded as having informed on a fellow officer to a higher authority, and that was entirely unacceptable.

On the morning of November 13, 1836, Barry was at his Jamestown villa preparing himself for a demanding day. Two patients had died at the hospital the night before, and another was dying who needed his immediate attention. Barry's servant interrupted him: Major Barnes was waiting to see him. A great lover of ritual and etiquette, Barry emerged to greet Barnes with due courtesy and great curiosity as to the cause of his unexpected morning call. To his surprise he found Barnes in an aggravated mood, accompanied by a military escort, waving in his face orders for Barry's arrest.

Barry demanded to know from Barnes whether the garrison general had been informed that he was to be arrested. Barnes faltered, and admitted he had not. Triumphant, Barry rejected the major's authority to arrest him, and left him and his entourage in a brew of confusion as he galloped off to speak directly to the governor at Plantation House. The dazed Barnes took off after him through the steep streets of Jamestown. Jamestown had only one large thoroughfare, so there cannot have been many who missed the spectacle of the town major on horseback in pursuit of the hurtling Dr. Barry.

The furious Barry was dragged home and placed under house arrest, pending orders to be called before the court-martial on the charge of "conduct unbecoming to an officer and a gentleman"—specifically, for the ungentlemanly action of sending to the "Right Honourable the Secretary at War" a report "opposed to fact and tending greatly to prejudice the professional character of the Assistant Commissary General in the estimation of the authorities in England." Barry argued with Barnes over his house arrest: he had a fatally ill patient to attend in the hospital, and urgent arrangements to be made for the two dead bodies. Barnes was immovable: Dr. Barry was confined to quarters. His servant might fetch him provisions, but he was assigned a guard. Left alone to stew for ten days, Barry impulsively decided to conduct his own defense and lodged a plea of "Not guilty on my Honour." Like Napoleon, another short innovator, Barry had become a prisoner on St. Helena, incarcerated by the British authorities.

The court hearing opened on November 24 and lasted for a fortnight. Throughout the rather absurd proceedings, the only thing that all parties, including the accused, seemed to be agreed on was that it was Barry's status as a true gentleman that was on trial. The petty level to which the debate stooped, particularly on the part of the slighted Knowles, leaves the distinct impression that the endemic tropical damp that rotted everything at St. Helena had seeped into the underexercised minds of the military elite. Whole days were taken up by Knowles taking the stand to complain about the grave insult that Barry refused to sufficiently recognize his rank. "The prisoner will tell you that I am only a Warrant Officer. I am the same rank as the prisoner, comparable to a Captain in the Army," he complained. Knowles demanded "an absolute and unqualified acquittal of the accusation alleged against me to the Secretary of War."

For his part, the prisoner obdurately refused to concede that he had in any way acted improperly. In fact, Barry grandly argued, "It was probably the first instance of an officer being brought to trial for the performance of his duty." Despite the weak case against him, Barry clearly was placed under great stress by the ordeal of the court-martial. He had only been on St. Helena for two months. Conducting his own defense, far away from his network of friends in London, the Cape, and Jamaica, Barry felt isolated. His vulnerability at this time is betrayed by the fact that he rather dangerously reached for the example of Somerset during his grandiloquent defense to the court: "the late Lord Charles Somerset . . . suffered much in mind and body from garbled statements from his persecutors, through which he lost his life but saved his honour." It was rather dramatic to claim that the calumnies against Somerset had killed him, but the statement provides an insight into the fact that time had not ameliorated Barry's sense of loss. Was Barry identifying himself as the inheritor of Somerset's mantle of suffering at the hands of petty politicians, or wishing out loud that his "only true friend" were still alive to help him and extract him from the mess into which he had got himself?

The trial exposed the degree to which Knowles had attempted to turn Governor Middlemore against Barry. Barry testified that he had had a meeting with the governor regarding the administration of the hospital. Middlemore had told Barry that Knowles had written to him regarding the hospitals, and volunteered to share this correspondence with Barry. Seeing the top line of the letter the governor handed him addressed in an informal personal style, Barry handed the correspondence back unread: "I looked no further—a gentleman ought not to do so." Middlemore refused to come to court to testify, leaving the irate Knowles exposed.

Barry's closing speech was the emotional high point of the trial. He had exposed the alleged intrigue between Knowles and Middlemore and insisted that he was justified in referring the matter to a higher authority. There were no half measures for Barry—the thing had to be seen through to the end, otherwise there was no merit in it. He shared with the court the background to this philosophy of persistence: "When I was a boy I was told that when I began a story, to begin at the beginning and continue to the end." This remark was the only time in his career that Barry referred in public to his childhood. Barry concluded with his most melodramatic statement of all. Not to be a gentleman was unthinkable to him. He would rather, he implied, take his own life than endure any self-doubt about his character and reputation as a gentleman: "If for a single instant I could imagine I have lost sight of the character of a gentleman I should have spared this or any other tribunal the task of investigating my conduct."

Barry's romantic notion of gentility was at variance with that of his military colleagues. For men like Knowles and the generally well-meaning Middlemore, gentlemen were trusted members of a cabal who played polite sport with the truth in order to defend each other's interests. What Barry defended as the character of a gentleman was in fact much closer to the notion of virtuous citizenry he had been taught by his radical mentors.

Middlemore's refusal to turn up and testify at the court-martial, combined with Knowles's bombastic self-justifications, significantly weakened the case against Barry. On December 7 the court, "having maturely weighed and considered the evidence in support of the charge against the prisoner," issued its ruling: "Dr James Barry is not guilty of the charge preferred against him." Acquitted and released from arrest, Barry was restored to his full rank of principal medical officer. The court confirmed that Barry wrote the letter upon which the charge was founded, "but is of the opinion that he was justified in so doing, and doth therefore fully and honourably acquit him."

Barry was ebullient. Unable to contain his delight at having vindicated himself, he attached a triumphant cover note to the court verdict:

> Subsequent to this Court-Martial the Lords Commissioners of H M Treasury ordered the Commissariat Dept. to provide for the Civil Branch of the Hospital by contract the same as for the Military, by which means the Government saved considerably and the patients were better provided for.

Although Middlemore never forgave Barry for exposing him, he demonstrated elsewhere a genuine support for Barry's hospital reforms, and pushed the boundaries of his own authority in order to secure the new building Barry had requested to receive female patients. Commissar Knowles, however, was unambivalent in his antipathy to Barry. He smarted under the yoke of having to fulfill Barry's orders. Knowles saw himself as exposed to ridicule by the uppity medical officer, and tried to exact his revenge by continuing a whispering campaign against Barry, trying particularly to undermine his relationship with his assistant surgeons, Eddie and McLaren, both of whom Barry had promoted.

Barry continued with his efforts to improve the state of the hospital, and by June 1837 plans were progressing for the establishment of the new hospital for women. Barry had also been involving himself in some local politicking. He was shocked by the extent to which the ordinary inhabitants of St. Helena had been left unsupported following the departure of the English East India Company. In April 1837 he got wind that the colonial secretary, Lord Glenelg, wanted to abolish the

General Hospital and force the local inhabitants to provide funds "for the support of the sick poor." As most of the island's inhabitants *were* the sick poor, Barry regarded this an ill-considered and offensive measure. He was one of the prime movers behind a public meeting of the islanders, who gathered together to write a petition to the government that was composed in Barry's own unmistakable style and contained some giveaway references to his previous postings:

> The inhabitants of St Helena respectfully appeal to HM Government whether, under the peculiarly distressing situation in which they are now placed, by circumstances over which they had no control, the same consideration and assistance should not be afforded them as, it is understood, have been, and still are, granted to the comparatively rich and flourishing colonies of the Cape of Good Hope and Mauritius, where a considerable part of the expenses is borne by HM Government.

Middlemore agreed that the "inhabitants evidently have a claim to some such accommodation upon the government" and forwarded the petition with his support to Lord Glenelg, who was becoming increasingly impatient with his concessive and, in his view, spendthrift St. Helenian governor. Glenelg also noted that whenever new recommendations requiring further expenditure on St. Helena arrived on his desk they invariably contained words to the effect of "the Principal Medical Officer having represented to me. . . ."

The last straw came when Glenelg discovered that Middlemore had authorized the payment of additional salaries to Dr. Barry and his staff, assistant surgeon Hopkins and the hospital apothecary, Mr. Courtney, in remuneration for their additional civil duties. In fact, these payments were a convention, made to military surgeons to compensate them for civil duties even prior to Barry's taking office. Knowles had taken it upon himself to look through the accounts and point out to the governor that the salary payments had not in fact been authorized by London. Middlemore apologized to Glenelg, who ordered him to stop any further payments of this kind. The decision was highly unfair. The arrangement of hospital services on St. Helena meant that military surgeons were expected always to treat the civilian population as well as troops. Measures implemented by Barry, like the vaccine programs and daily clinics for the poor, as well as all that accounting and inventory-keeping, added to the burden of responsibility on the medical team. Furthermore, Barry had promoted both Dr. McLaren and Dr. Eddie, and rightly claimed that they deserved salary increases. Glenelg was unbending. Not only must Middlemore cease any further payments, he must require Barry, Dr. Hopkins, and Mr. Courtney to return the "overplus" to the government. Surgeons McLaren and Eddie were granted their promotions, but no pay raise.

Middlemore ceased the salary payments, and the situation became serious for Barry. He had been short of cash since he left Jamaica, and he had received only one month's full salary since arriving on St. Helena—the month that Middlemore had signed off the additional civil salaries. On top of all this, hanging over him was the prospect of having to pay back to the government money he had not only already spent, but believed himself rightfully entitled to.

Barry was not good with money. To an honorable extent, he mortgaged his own income against expenses incurred doing his job, almost none of which were reimbursed to him. He spent far more time fighting to raise funds from various departments for his medical reforms and institutional reorganization than he did attending to his own personal exchequer. He lived on what he earned, and never made any effort to accumulate capital. As he grew older, this lack of financial care began to catch up with him.

The three-year dispute over payments due to him on St. Helena was the turning point in Barry's fortunes—or rather lack of them. Although he could not be blamed for Barry's lifelong impecuniousness, Knowles had exacted his revenge by contributing to Barry's financial struggles. While the battle over his pay raged on, it never occurred to Barry to withdraw from his civil responsibilities or to curb his energetic plans for reforming St. Helena's medical services. But all his efforts were cut short a few months into 1838.

The weather on St. Helena is exceptionally volatile. Squalls tumble over the basalt cliffs without notice, cutting off any view of the sky. Matching this mood, the colonial authorities on St. Helena seemed to be subject to equally arbitrary tempers. At the end of March 1838, Barry found himself once again under arrest and threatened with court-martial, a prisoner for the second time in less than two years. St. Helena was certainly living up to its history as a penal colony for the wayward. Napoleon had been humiliated by his exile to St. Helena. Later in the century, during the South African War, the British were to use it as a prison camp for six thousand Boer prisoners. The Boer leader General Cronje was deported to the island, and after him Chief Dinizulu and the Sultan of Zanzibar. The British only stopped sending prisoners to St. Helena in 1957.

"How I've fallen," lamented Napoleon upon his arrival at St. Helena. This was a sentiment that James Barry might easily have echoed. Regarded by many as another military martinet, Barry had so inflamed the St. Helenian government that they passed up the option of trying him on the island and arranged for his immediate deportation. Assembling his family trio of servant, pony, and Psyche, Barry attempted to make a dignified departure from St. Helena. His exit was seen by the author of the article on Barry's life published by Dickens in 1867:

> The writer of this article witnessed his departure from James Town. On one of those still sultry mornings peculiar to the trop-ics, the measured step of the doctor's pony woke up the echoes of the valley. There came the P.M.O., looking faded and crestfallen. He was in plain clothes. He had shrunk away wonderfully. His blue jacket hung loosely about him, his white trousers were a world too wide, the veil garnishing his broad straw hat covered his face, and he carried the inevitable umbrella over his head so that it

screened him from the general gaze. The street was deserted, but other eyes besides the writer's looked on the group through the Venetian blinds. No sentry presented arms at the gates, and the familiar quartet proceeded unnoticed along the lines to the ship's boat in waiting.

Like Napoleon, Barry sailed away from St. Helena under military arrest. Contained in the military dispatches aboard HMS *London* was a letter from General Middlemore to Lord Glenelg to inform him of the action he had been forced to take against Barry:

> I have to regret that Dr James Barry has so conducted himself that I have ordered him home under arrest. The proceedings of a court of inquiry with various documents relative to Dr James Barry's conduct have been transmitted for the Commander-in-Chief's information and guidance by the London, in which ship Dr James Barry has embarked.

What had Barry done this time? In fact, there is an unresolved mystery attached to his second arrest on St Helena. For while it is clear that Middlemore felt pushed beyond the bounds of toleration by his PMO, Barry's particular offense in this instance remains unknown. The War Office files on this episode are missing, and along with them any documentation on the court of inquiry that examined the charges against Barry, if indeed such a hearing ever took place. Is this gap in the records an accident of incorrect filing or a deliberate omission? Here as elsewhere, when a Somerset appears in Barry's story, official records disappear. All that is left is evidence that when the matter was referred directly to James McGrigor and Fitzroy Somerset, Barry's arrest was lifted and no charges were pressed. He was, however, punished with demotion.

Barry's time at St. Helena was over. However, as one chapter of his insular career closed, another one began. At the end of 1838, he was

back to the rank of staff surgeon, this time to the Windward and Leeward command in the West Indies. This was an appointment deliberately designed to be all disease and no politics. Barry was made
responsible for thirteen pestilential tropical islands dubbed "The Cradle of Death." McGrigor, it seems, had deliberately deployed Barry in a
place where he could concentrate on his exceptional skills as a surgeon
and try to avoid his predilection for causing political and administrative
havoc. Judging by the fact that less is known about Barry's activities
during his seven years in these islands than at any other time of his career, it seems that McGrigor's strategy to extricate him from meddling
in politics worked.

Barry's responsibilities on the West Indian islands would have been
overwhelming to anyone less energized by responsibility. The command included Barbados, British Guyana, Trinidad, Tobago, Grenada,
St. Vincent's, St. Lucia, Dominica, Antigua with Montserrat, and St.
Kitt's with Nevis and Tortola. In ceaseless motion, Barry became a familiar figure on the boats and steamers that traveled between the islands. Encountering Barry on one of these journeys, Dr. C. F. Moore
recalled: "In common with all on board I was struck with the peculiarities of this officer. . . . The diet and fondness for pets, the peculiar figure and appearance." Dr. McCowan, who served in Trinidad, recalled
Barry being always "a very bold person, and challenged one or two of
our officials for naming him a diminutive creature. He had a favourite
little dog which he always carried about with him, and it was currently
said that he had made a will leaving the dog all his effects and 'Sambo'
£100 as a legacy." The suggestion that he made a will in favor of his servant is unproven, but this rumor indicates that there was a noticeable
bond of intimacy between the two.

Forced to spend much time traveling by ship among his islands,
Barry jealously guarded his privacy. Edward Bradford, deputy inspector
of hospitals, was curious about the fact that, "when travelling, he carefully secluded himself from observation." Bradford had an unexpected
run-in with Barry in Trinidad:

I had, in the last named island, the misfortune to give him great offence by stating in an official report that he was probably 50 years of age. He had then been 33 years in the army, but he called the report a "base attempt to blast his prospects." Yet he forgave me afterwards.

Colonization spread disease: Barry had to battle dysentery, yellow fever, malaria, sleeping sickness, lung disorders, and excessively high rates of sexually transmitted diseases. He pointed out that on nearly all the islands the barracks were too small and the conditions unsanitary. In Barbados he introduced the use of washing troughs and arranged for convalescents to be encamped at some distance from the barracks. There was nothing glamorous about being a soldier on a sun-kissed tropical island. They were bored and listless and experienced great privation. Alcoholism was rampant among the regular troops and not a few of their officers. The increasing rate of deaths from delirium tremens in the Windward and Leeward Islands command alarmed the director general, who in 1842 sent a questionnaire to Barry and asked him to report on the subject. Barry replied instantly to "Circular No. 12378—Report on Delirium Tremens," stating that without doubt the primary cause of the problem was the "continued use and abuse of ardent spirits." Describing in detail the progress of the paroxysms experienced by the sufferer, Barry reveals his intimacy with the lurid sufferings of his patients:

In many cases every species of Blue Devils torment the sufferer inducing him if not watched often to commit suicide:—all stimuli cease to have effect, the stomach rejects everything and low mutterings are succeeded by stertorous breathing which precedes death, the final termination of this unfortunate Disease.

Having encountered the problem before in many tropical posts, particularly Mauritius, Barry was pessimistic about the ability of medicine to

cure what was in fact a social and environmental disease, a laconic opinion he freely offered to the Director General:

> But as it is almost impossible to cure the habit of Drunkenness,
> particularly in the West Indies where, to use a patient's own
> words: "The weather is always too hot, rum always too cheap, and
> a man always too dry," perhaps the only chance would be to em-
> bark the subject in a temperance vessel for a cold climate, with
> plenty of nutritious diet.

Barry attempted to keep his head down and concentrate on doctoring
in the West Indies, but he had not been either forgiven or forgotten by
his enemies at St. Helena. After the mysterious charges against him had
been dropped, on his return to England he had written directly to Lord
Glenelg from his lodgings in Great Ryder Street to pursue the matter of
his outstanding pay. It is a fine testimony to Barry's imperviousness that
he seemed undented by his recent experience of international deportation and impending demotion:

> Permit me here my Lord to observe, that having to establish some
> system, everything being in a most confused and disgusting state
> so far as the Military and Civil Hospitals were concerned on my
> arrival—it required great exertion and much ungracious and
> painful duties fell to my lot—from which although I have person-
> ally heavy suffered—yet I am proud to say the service has bene-
> fited considerably.

Barry's claim was referred to Middlemore, with whom the statement
that the hospital had been in "a confused and disgusting state" persistently rankled. Middlemore's own role in the requisitions row had
been left murky, and he now saw the opportunity to place the blame
firmly on the sacked PMO's absent shoulders. Constituting a medical
board of officers who had all been fed gossip by the unforgiving

Knowles, Middlemore placed Barry's letter before the board. Reporting their findings in February 1839, by which time Barry was already busy dealing with dystentery in Antigua, the St. Helena medical board found that the various civil duties on which Dr. Barry based his claim "were *actually* and efficiently performed" but not, as he states, by him. The board, including McLaren and Eddie, who owed their promotions to Barry, asserted that Barry "was daily in the habit of imposing upon them" the duties he lists in the letter as having performed himself. This was the first and only time that anyone tried to accuse Barry of being a shirker, and it speaks for itself that Barry's superiors—sensitive to the distinction between delegation and dereliction of duties—did not pursue this issue. Avoiding any mention of Barry's strenuous efforts in introducing a vaccinating program, providing daily care for the sick and poor, and his hospital reforms, the board then moved to their main point of contention:

> The Board is willing to hope for the sake of Truth and Candour that Dr James Barry might possibly only have intended an allusion to the defective state of the accommodation and not a reflection on the Administration of the duties of the Hospital, and the Board feels happily released from all necessity for further comment by the impossibility of its being believed His Excellency Major General Middlemore, or Lt. Colonel Anderson . . . could have tolerated a "confused and disgusting" administration to have existed for a day.

That was the end of Barry's hopes for fair remuneration. Despite the fact that James McGrigor had forcefully supported Barry's civil pay claims throughout the dispute, the treasury won the day. The colonial office endorsed the finding of Middlemore's medical board. The only concession they made was to relieve Barry of having to pay back the excess salary originally received as a result of Middlemore's "error." It was scant solace for the financial cost of Barry's turbulent stay at St. Helena.

He was in Antigua when he received a letter from the marquis of Normanby informing him that he was not entitled to receive "any extra remuneration." It was a grave disappointment—Barry's belief that he would be paid out was reflected in the fact that before he left for the West Indies he had sent a note to the colonial office asking, "Could such sum as is awarded be handed to Mr Thomas Powell Hayes, of 21 Bloomsbury Square, who will give a receipt." In retrospect, the arrangement looks pitifully hopeful.

There was no hope of recompense from the past. Barry provided a steely solace for himself by doing what he did best: innovation in the sphere of medicine and public health. Evidence of Barry's medical influence in the West Indies emerges through the official correspondence of the period. Shortly after his arrival, the governor of Antigua ordered an end to the "objectionable practice of detaining lunatics in prison" and requested a report on the conditions of the insane from the new PMO. Barry recommended that the insane should be transferred to the military prisons. In 1840, a proclamation was passed prohibiting the sale of medicines by unqualified persons throughout the Windward and Leeward command. Disbarring unqualified people from practicing as "either physician, surgeon or apothecary," Barry's measure had the familiar stamp of his reform and regulatory methods developed in earlier postings. He had by now applied these methods in South Africa, Mauritius, Jamaica, St. Helena, and the West Indian archipelago. In an age of slow communications and arduous travel, Barry's reforms had a global character, threading together the history of the care of the sick from the Indian to the Atlantic oceans.

However, toward the end of his time in the Caribbean, Barry himself fell victim to one of the diseases he had spent so much time attempting to prevent: yellow fever. Although he ultimately survived, the sickness was to profoundly affect subsequent perceptions of Barry. He knew a great deal about yellow fever. It was the most ruthless of the tropical diseases, causing violent hemorrhaging and acute jaundice before pushing some of those afflicted into coma and, usually, death. The

Christian churches of the Caribbean islands were crammed with plaques and tombstones to sailors and settlers slayed by the yellow jack, named after the quarantine flag flown from infected ships. Barry was taken with the fever in Port-of-Spain in Trinidad. Excepting the delirium and bouts of unconsciousness caused by the disease, Dr. O'Connor, who treated Barry, must have found him to be an impossible patient. William Chamberlayne, who knew Barry in Jamaica, recalled that he "always evinced a dislike of medical men." Edward Bradford, whom Barry had twitted for the slur on his age, was one of several officers on Trinidad at the time who were struck by Barry's request to be buried without examination should he die: "When ill he invariably exacted from the officer who attended him a promise that, in the event of his death, strict precautions should be adopted to prevent any examination of his person." Barry's passion for the sciences of anatomy and dissection were well known. His tutors, including Astley Cooper, had declared publicly their intention to leave their corpses to their colleagues for autopsy and dissection. Put in this context, Barry's repeated requests to be wrapped in the sheets in which he died and buried without ceremony were even more curious.

Barry, as his colleagues observed, was more than lucky to have recovered from his first bout of yellow fever. Many credited his dietary habits for his recovery: Barry himself claimed that vegetarianism, always keeping a goat for milk, and relatively modest alcohol consumption made the body more resilient when under attack from disease.

It was hard for Barry to confront the fact that his health was severely compromised by the yellow fever. The ravaging effects of the disease on his body are plain to see. The handful of paintings and sketches produced prior to the 1840s depict a figure with a thick mane of curly hair, robust shoulders, and a broad chest. Barry was never tall, but it was only after he succumbed to this extended illness that he became the thin, angular, and almost cadaverous figure that has come to typify his image. Accounts of Barry's brittle and waspish appearance rely on a set of images produced in his later life. Lieutenant Colonel Edward Rogers famously described him as "short in stature, angular in figure, with a long Ciceronian nose, prominent cheekbones, and a rather lugubrious expression of countenance." This is an accurate description of Barry after his near miss with death—Rogers met him for the first time in 1857, a decade after his first battle with yellow fever. Barry retained a "pale, sallow look" in later life, and while his "attenuated form" was in some quarters put down to his vegetarianism, this was in fact another indicator of the toll the yellow fever took on him. Yellow fever is remittent, and Barry was to endure relapses on several more occasions during his career. Commentators also demonstrate a tendency to shrink Barry after this turning point. Those who met him in earlier life recollected his height as being about five foot six. Those who met him after his illness insisted that "his stature scarcely reached five feet."

In 1845, Barry arrived back in England after seven years in the West Indies, during which he had taken no home leave. It was Christmas. London was smoke-filled, sooty, cold, and awash with mud. Barry, however, did not take much to the streets. Dangerously weakened, he spent his year of home leave languishing in London and convalescing from the degenerative effects of his bout of yellow fever. The dandified Regency playground of his youth had ceded to Victorianism: London had become an imperial capital ruled over by a woman for only the second time in its history. After so long in the tropics, Barry must have felt out of place. Barry himself makes only one brief but telling reference to his sickness. "Home, sick" he wrote, archly.

By November 1846, Barry had recuperated sufficiently to report himself ready for service. Perhaps mindful of the toll the yellow fever had taken on his health, the military authorities decided to post him to the Mediterranean. Barry began his Mediterranean odyssey in Malta with a promotion. His strenuous attempt to avoid controversy during his years in the West Indies had paid off. Barry had also, in 1840, impressed his superiors by stepping in to cover for an absent colleague and acted as temporary inspector general of hospitals and medical director without incident. Thanked in general orders for his direction of the department at this time, this temporary appointment proved highly significant to the pattern of his promotion in later years.

Barry arrived in the walled city of Valletta at the end of 1846 as principal medical officer. The cradle of the Mediterranean, with the world's biggest harbour, Malta was unlike any of the islands on which Barry had previously worked. Most novel to him were the wealthy visitors who thronged the island for purely leisurely purposes. Barry had never previously encountered tourism. A company called the Peninsular and Oriental Steam Navigation Company (P&O for short) had recently inaugurated a new concept: shipboard travel excursions around the Mediterranean for the wealthy English middle classes who wished to tour merely for the purpose of taking pleasurable time off. Two years before Barry arrived in Malta, P&O invited an ambitious young novelist, William Makepeace Thackeray, on an all-expenses-paid trip of the Mediterranean on *The Great Liverpool*. Thackeray favoured Valletta above all other island cities on his shipboard excursion, "by which, in the space of a couple of months, as many men and cities were to be seen as Ulysses surveyed and noted in ten years." Like Homer's Ulysses, Barry spent ten years in the Mediterranean, first in Malta and then in Corfu.

While Thackeray wrote enthusiastically of the wonders of Valletta and enthusiastic tourists dawdled to watch street theater on its arrow-straight cobbled boulevards, Barry firmly straightened his sharply tied cravat and set to work overseeing an unhealthy island ravaged by typhus and—most pressingly—a cholera pandemic. Previously localized to the Indian subcontinent, cholera first became a global disease in the nineteenth century. By the 1830s it had traveled through four continents and hit London and Paris, where mass hysteria and extreme violence, including public dismembering, were heaped upon its unfortunate victims. The common belief was that cholera was contagious and spread by "miasmata," a soupy and invisible poisonous air.

Barry experienced daily the extreme contrast between the idle pleasures of the well-heeled middle-class tourists visiting Malta and the poverty suffered by the island inhabitants. Visiting a swampy coastal village called Casal, situated just outside Valletta, Barry was shown a twelve-year-old boy "stretched on a handful of straw on the ground in an open yard under a stone stairs." Barry diagnosed the boy as suffering from "Typhus Fever." Next door, "in an adjoining hovel, or cell," he found an old woman "quite as scarcely provided for." Barry was deeply affected by the conditions he found in the overcrowded and poverty-stricken village: "These wretched beings were in the most deplorable plight, surrounded by filth and stench intolerable without sustenance or support. In fact, I feel inadequate to describe the scene, and shrunk from it with horror."

The Casal physician had prescribed the old woman "Calomel and Opium." "She perished," Barry wrote with bleak despair. Local doctors, fearing a new outbreak of cholera, wrangled over the cause of the old woman's death. Barry stood aloof. It was "not cholera; it was poverty and destitution. . . ."

It was not until the late 1850s that John Snow's theory that cholera was waterborne gained the endorsement of Parliament, although he had published his research *On the Mode of Communication of Cholera* in 1849, and it is possible that Barry, following the course of the pandemic in London for what he could learn in his own practice on Malta, was familiar with Snow's radical theories. Certainly he kept up to date on the latest work being done on the disease in London, as demonstrated in his report on cholera in Malta to the government in 1848, in which he cited, at great length, the "invaluable researches" of Dr. E. A. Park, "late a Military Medical Officer and at present Assistant Physician at the University College London," who was busy at work on the subject.

Working in a prebacteriological age, Barry's lifelong insistence on the connection between sanitation and health was ahead of its time. Although he still believed in the miasmatic theories of contagion, Barry's hunch that bad sanitation promoted disease was shortly to be discovered to be scientific fact. He had several interviews "with His Excellency the Governor on subjects touching the sanitary conditions of the Island" and

pointed out in particular his concern about the "deleterious efflu-
via...with which the atmosphere is impregnated from the many
sources around Valletta, particularly about the residences of the swine."
Fearful of the mass panic caused by outbreaks of the "most dreaded
Cholera" that often resulted in physical violence and torture of its sufferers, the medical men on Malta were anxious about confirming the diagnoses of the disease. Badly handled publicity might "excite panic among
the Troops, which could only drive them to despair, drunkenness, and
death: every Soldier looking upon a case of Cholera as a Forlorn Hope."

Even when they all agreed that the disease was cholera, the medics
jostled over their opinions of what specific *kind* of cholera they might
be dealing with. Barry reeled off a list of options longer than most, including "Bilious, Mucous, Diarrhoea and Sporadic Cholera," not for-
getting the finer distinctions between this last type and "Asiatic
Cholera." In truth, these arguments were born of ignorance—without
being sure what caused it, they couldn't effectively provide preventive
measures. Barry crossed swords in just this way with a fellow surgeon,
Dr. Richardson. When a Royal Artillery soldier died of cholera,
Richardson and Barry both conducted a postmortem examination. Because their disagreement hinged on the question of whether the soldier
had died of an epidemic or nonepidemic form of cholera (such distinctions were believed), the matter was referred to the Governor, who
asked Barry—for the sake of official consistency—to back down and
confirm Anderson's postmortem findings. Needless to say, Barry was
not prepared to concede the point. More interesting than his resistance
in this instance, however, were the tones of diplomacy in which he
couched his request that the governor reconsider his position:

> With the greatest deference and respect, I must beg to be excused
> from coinciding with His Excellency's view's or making any such
> admission:—"Tot Homines, quot sententiae."
>
> It is proverbial that all professions, whether legal, ecclesiastical
> or medical differ and seldom arrive at the same conclusion as to

the cause and effect of things; in fact the world in general disagrees . . . and I even presume to contend, that such equality of opinion would in no wise add to the credit of the Profession, or ensure the safety of the Public.

In other words, Barry was defending the principle of intellectual freedom, and characteristically resisting being foisted with a political solution to the problem. The tones were more conciliatory, but two court-martials, a parliamentary smear campaign, demotion, and endless boards of investigation had not succeeded in budging Barry from his implacable belief that a point of scientific principle was not something that could be bent to fit the needs of *realpolitik*.

Justifying his position, Barry took the trouble to lay down precedents from his own experiences where he had saved lives by acting in contravention to the medical opinion of others. Citing a recent success in Valletta where he had saved the life of the daughter of a Captain Rich, Barry also harked back to his triumph in saving the life of Lord Charles Somerset, "when I was young, very young." Describing the event, Barry told the governor that he "may refer to Lord Fitzroy Somerset, Military Secretary, to corroborate this fact."

Weather-beaten, tormented, and much traveled throughout the islands of the empire, Barry was beginning to assume the persona of the elder statesman who realized, wistfully, that he was "young, very young" no longer.

Chapter 9

THE LAST POST

The problem of all man's self-orientation ... is the task of making oneself at home in existence without fixed points of support.

Erich Auerbach, *Mimesis*

The most hardened creature I ever met.

Florence Nightingale on James Barry, in a letter
to her sister Lady Parthenope

EARLY IN 1853, THE BRITISH AMBASSADOR IN VIENNA RECEIVED A letter from Fitzroy Somerset, Lord Raglan, asking him "to show some civility to Dr Barry, who was passing through Vienna" after home leave on his way back to his post in Corfu. Barry was now deputy inspector general of hospitals, and his seniority meant that he could expect to be received at the embassy. Lord Raglan also advised the ambassador that "though his appearance was peculiar he was a most noble man, and had rendered excellent service in South Africa and elsewhere." Barry was duly invited to dinner at the embassy, an occasion remembered ever after by one of the envoy's small daughters, Rose Weigall:

When he arrived we saw a small man with small features, a very smooth though wizened face, very fair (*not red*) hair, and a most peculiar squeaky voice and mincing manner, the whole effect of which was so irresistibly comic that it kept all the younger members of the party in agonies of suppressed laughter all through the dinner. . . . My mother, whom he sat next to, however, said that in spite of his ludicrous appearance his conversation was most interesting, though his manner was that of a mincing old maid! We heard of him afterwards in Corfu doing good work.

A fashionable rake in his younger days who had captivated women and men from Cape Town to Kingston, the British empire's most infamous army doctor had become an oddity. Barry's dandified dress and manners were a throwback to a previous era. His eccentricities and what he called "my peculiar habits" were no longer softened by youthful charisma, and his intellectual passions made him seem cantankerous. It is painful to think of Rose Weigall and her brothers and sisters sniggering at Barry, but her mother's defense of his most interesting conversation perhaps reveals that Barry had not lost his touch with women.

Barry's dandified extroversion and peculiar habits and appearance became more pronounced as the century advanced into a more sober form of masculinity. In Barry's Regency youth, real men had been effete, highly tailored, fashionable dandies, raucous and expressive in their camaraderie, and modishly overflowing with intellectual passions and human sympathy. Wigs, stockings, stays, and make-up made the real man. While Barry spent the first half of the century traveling the tropics, Britain had been transformed by industrialization. On the handful of occasions he was in London on home leave between 1816 and 1853, Barry found that the size, shape, and style of men had changed drastically. Sentimental fops were no longer fashionable. Masculinity was defined by a new austerity and emotional repression. Although corsets were less popular, men were nevertheless more emotionally staid. The somber-suited men Barry saw in the gentleman's clubs of London were a new breed of muscular Christian empire builders, driven by dreams of commercial success and a disturbing belief in their own racial superiority. Barry's dandified ostentation, once so appealing, seemed ridiculous to a younger generation.

In 1851—two years before the young Rose Weigall encountered him in Vienna—Barry had gone directly from Malta to the Greek island of Corfu without home leave before taking up his new appointment. Sparsely populated and dotted with small villages of whitewashed limestone houses, Corfu had a rugged bucolic charm that belied its strategic importance to the military, an importance that was to become immediately more visible at the outbreak of the Crimean War in 1853. As so often in his career, Barry ended up being in a politically sensitive trouble spot at a critical time. His promotion to deputy inspector general of hospitals was a serious acknowledgment of his achievements. Barry had made it to the upper echelons of the military medical elite. He remained punctilious in his dress code, as illustrated by a cartoon of him sketched by Edward Lear when he visited Corfu in 1852.

Barry's appearance in this satirical sketch is defined by its orgy of accessories. On his head he wears a large cocked hat; from out of his high collar protrudes a starched cravat, over which his chin juts forward pugnaciously. The exaggerated epaulettes on his smartly tailored tailcoat are the size of Victorian lampshades, and from the heels of his built-up boots protrude absurdly elongated spurs. Behind his heels, mimicking his own stooped demeanor, sits a bewhiskered black cat dubbed "Ye Cat Rap." Barry props himself up with an ornate regimental dress sword that he holds in his left hand. From his right suggestively dangles a rather flaccid horsehair whip. A fellow officer, William MacKinnon, recalled that Barry kept "a lovely grey Arab" in Corfu, but the horsewhip is not a nod toward Barry's equestrian talents—considerable though they were—but a satirical reference to a "rather amusing rupture" that took place between Barry and Colonel Denny, who commanded the troops of the 71st Highland Light Infantry.

Barry was "at perpetual war" with the military authorities at Corfu over the practice of drilling the troops in the heat of the day, causing unnecessary sunstroke and dehydration and consequently pressure on

Barry's already overstretched hospital wards. When the authorities failed to act to prevent the practice, the exasperated Barry decided to take the matter into his own hands. At two o'clock on a searingly hot midsummer afternoon, Colonel Denny led his regiment out of the fortress over the drawbridge for drill on the esplanade. Barry intercepted him. In full view of the no doubt highly entertained troops, he arraigned their commander for taking risks with their health. When Denny refused to back down, a "wordy duel ensued, the doctor declaring that he would report the colonel to the commander in chief, at the same time vigorously flourishing his horse hair whip." Unluckily for the overanimated Barry, the whip struck Colonel Denny in the face:

> The enraged officer instantly snatched it from him, threw it into the moat, and was about to send the doctor after it when some kind friend intervened on his behalf.

Barry was not prepared to leave the matter at that, and determined to have his revenge. He reported Denny to the authorities and "declared the colonel to be mad." With the permission of the lord high commissioner and the troop commander, Barry "convened a medical board, which declared the colonel to be *non compos mentis.*" It was not long after this that the "gallant regiment" departed for the Crimea. Following after them, Denny "persistently applied to Lord Raglan to be restored to the command of the corps. His services, however, were declined, much to the satisfaction of the men." Barry might have been feared, hated, and cruelly ridiculed among his colleagues, but he clearly enjoyed the popular support of the soldiers whose health and interests he was always quick to protect.

Barry's apparently limitless appetite for public dispute was offset by many accounts of his personal consideration for the sick. Many who encountered him in Corfu commented on his attentive bedside manner. R. F. Hutchinson, a noncommissioned officer, said that Barry was "punctuality itself" when it came to his weekly hospital inspections and "insisted" on the medical officers' being ready and waiting "in uniform to meet him on his approach." Overweening in his love of pomp and circumstance, "to the sick, however, Dr Barry was the most kind and humane gentleman." Hutchinson received a detailed report from a relative of his who was nursing an old school friend dying from consumption in one of the Corfu hospitals. He was keeping him company, "writing a letter to his parents" and "now and then feeding the poor fellow with some comforts that had been ordered him." Barry came across this loyal friend on his rounds of the wards, and "complimented him on his good, and as he termed it, humane conduct." He sent his servant to the dying soldier with "five dollars and a dozen of blood oranges for the sick patient."

Following the death of the consumptive young soldier, Barry tactfully engaged the help of his grieving friend to distribute fruit to other sick patients. "The doctor received most of his fruits per the mail steamer from Naples and Sicily, and frequently ordered my informant to call at his quarters for a few choice oranges for some poor sufferer." Despite his own financial difficulties, Barry rewarded the soldier with a dollar for each visit. He took a lively interest in the soldier, quizzing him about the position of his family and proffering "his influence and material help" to place him in the medical profession, "but he being carried away by the unreasoning silliness of youth, and the splendid prospect of being shot at, much to the doctor's surprise, if not disgust, declined the gallant and considerate offer." Within his own means, Barry tried to offer patronage to young hopefuls in the same way that his uncle, Francisco de Miranda, Lord Buchan, and Charles Somerset had supported him. Yet it was one of the great sadnesses of his life that he never really found someone adequate to inherit the mantle of protégé.

Although Barry's high rank, eccentric manners, and advancing years made him "an intolerable bore" to some of the younger officers, none asserted that his professional powers were in any way diminished. He remained a maverick force, insisting that medical innovation was a key weapon in the arsenal of military modernization. When the government announced in March 1853 that Britain was going to war with Russia in order to protect Turkish independence, Barry instantly volunteered for service in the Crimea, probably nudging his superiors to remember how well he had performed in battlefront conditions during the Jamaican uprising in 1832. Filled with anger and amazement when his application was rejected on the grounds that there were no positions left available for officers of his rank, Barry formulated his own battle plans for contributing to the Crimean War effort.

If the authorities would not post him to the front lines, then they must at least send sick soldiers to his station at Corfu for medical care. He would, he guaranteed, make himself "as useful as possible to the army before Sebastapol." Meanwhile, Florence Nightingale was already at war with the entire military establishment and British government over the appalling lack of medicine, food, and basic provisions for the Crimean troops, who were suffering unimaginable horrors in the ill-equipped military hospitals of Scutari.

The military agreed to Barry's request, and in February 1855, HMS *Dunbar* transported nearly five hundred injured men to Corfu. Festering gunshot wounds were only one of the litany of afflictions from which the poorly prepared British troops suffered. Cholera, dysentery, malnutrition, and acute, disfiguring frostbite afflicted the exhausted soldiers, who arrived in a desperate state of deterioration to be treated under Barry's supervision. The hospitals were overflowing, and he had to oversee a complicated system of billeting the sick and dying in every available space. Private houses and administrative buildings were commandeered as temporary infirmaries, and Barry ordered a ruthless regime of cleanliness to be applied to all.

Barry's success was astonishing. Of the 462 sick and injured men brought to him from Scutari, 53 were ready for full duty after a fortnight in his care. A further 63 were ready to report for "slight duty." Of the remainder, 69 were hospitalized and 260 attended daily clinics at the hospital. The loss of 17 patients represented a 90 percent reduction in the death rate at Scutari. Having restored the troops to health, the army command was keen to have their manpower back to work. By April, Barry had passed 213 men as fit for duty, but he objected to the arrangements proposed by Major General MacIntosh for shipping them back to service. Barry wanted the troops sent back to Scutari on the Austrian steamboat so that they could rest and complete their convalescence on the journey. MacIntosh came up with more haphazard arrangements that involved cramming 93 of them onto two already overcrowded troopships on their way to Turkey, and leaving the remaining 120 awaiting orders on fatigue duties. As this meant that the men would miss their final period of recuperation, Barry was incensed.

His anger was no doubt considerably compounded by the fact that no arrangements were made for provision of the troops. Like Florence Nightingale, Barry objected vehemently to the way in which regular troops were shunted around, underprovided for and treated with scant respect. Barry's anger over the threat posed to the health of the troops by these arrangements knew no bounds. In the course of the ensuing row with MacIntosh, Barry threatened to take up his pen and inform Lord Raglan directly of the whole sorry affair.

It says much about how the times had moved on since Barry's early days that MacIntosh doubted Barry's claim of having direct access to Lord Raglan, who was, after all, commander in chief of the entire British army, and leader of the whole Crimea campaign. No doubt hoping to catch Barry out in a name-dropping bluff, MacIntosh wrote a telltale report in which he told Raglan of Barry's unlikely avowal "that he possessed more than usual influence with your Lordship, that he was a private friend of yours, and had resided 13 years in the house of your Lordship's brother." Raglan replied with a judicious letter that successfully arbitrated the situation yet, to MacIntosh's astonishment, made it clear that Barry was indeed well known to him:

> I am sorry to learn that Dr Barry, of whose zeal for the service I entertain no doubt, should have thought fit to interfere in a mat-

ter . . . which rested with you alone. You will be glad to learn that
he has not written to me, and I should hope that he may upon reflection feel that such a course would not only be highly improper, but would be utterly disproved by me.

The timing of the letter was poignant. Within five weeks, Lord Raglan
was dead; his heart, it was said, was broken by the decimation of the
British troops in the disastrous winter of 1854.

It appears that Barry may have only narrowly missed the appointment to Scutari that he so coveted. He seems to have remained expectant that Lord Raglan would bring him in nearer to the center of the
action. Inspector general was the most senior rank accorded to medical
officers by the military, and Barry's promotion to deputy inspector general had placed him on the inside track that put this position within his
reach. Certainly Sir John Hall, inspector general of hospitals, believed
that Raglan was considering replacing him with Barry. In December
1854, on the cusp of the onslaught of "General Winter," who was to
plough down so many British troops, Hall confessed to his diary: "It is
possible his Lordship wants to get rid of me and make room for his protégé Barry—if so well and good—but don't persecute other people on
that account."

Hall's diary bears eloquent testimony to the privations of that winter.
Depressed because he had to shoot his "best Arab" horse, who had been
injured in a skirmish, the inspector general was struggling desperately
for provisions for his staff and horses. "My position is one of utter misery," he despaired, "better dead than to start this." Hall's anxieties about
the condition of the soldiers proved prescient:

How the poor soldiers bear up against it is a wonder to me, but
this is only the commencement of the winter, and what will it be
in another month. When the intense cold sets in. Well might the
Emperor depend on his friend the climate to thin our ranks, and
break down the spirit of the troops.

But the winter was not the only implacable force that besieged Lord Raglan. "His Lordship's temper," Hall revealed, was kept "up to boiling point" with the unceasing letters and deputations organized by "Miss Nightingale." Both champions of the needs of patients and regular troops, and voluble in their criticisms of military and state bureaucracy, Florence Nightingale and Dr. James Barry had much in common—not that Florence Nightingale seemed to think so when she met him in Scutari. In her view, Barry was the enemy. In fact, as she wrote to her sister, Parthenope, Nightingale accorded Dr. James Barry the rare distinction of having subjected her to the worst "scolding" she had ever experienced. "I never had," she wrote with indignation, "such a blackguard rating in my life—I who have had more than any other woman—than from Barry." This encounter between two of the nineteenth century's most tireless medical reformers took place in the military hospital at Scutari sometime during 1855.

Ever unpredictable, in 1855 Barry had decided to take his leave in Scutari. Having thus decided to holiday in a war zone, he volunteered his services to the army while he was there. It is possible that he wanted to spend some time with the ailing Lord Raglan. The exact dates of his visit are unknown. Several officers, such as Surgeon Major Longmore, said that they had seen Barry with Lord Raglan in the Crimea. If these recollections can be relied upon, Barry arrived in Scutari before June 1855. Barry's own recollection was that "I myself proceeded on leave to the Crimea where I remained about three months with the 4th division before Sebastapol."

With Raglan's health waning, the renowned Barry posed less of a threat to the security of Sir John Hall's position, although the gossips were at work to try to predispose Hall against him. Dr. Cummings, a younger officer who clearly regarded Barry as an old curmudgeon, wrote to Hall warning him that Barry planned to pay him a visit:

> I may as well warn you that you are to have a visit from the renowned Dr Barry. He called on me yesterday and as I never met

him before, his appearance and conversation rather surprised me. He appears to me in his dotage and is an intolerable bore, so I would recommend you to be prepared for him as he seems to have the intention of quartering himself on you. He has with him his horse and his servant. He will expect you to listen to every quarrel he has had since coming into the service. You probably know that they are not a few.

Whether or not Hall found Barry to be "an intolerable bore" at the dinner table is unknown, but yet again Barry's personal disposition was overlooked in the face of his professional abilities. Barry said of his time on leave in the Crimea that he had made himself as "useful as opportunities offered which can be certified by Sir John Hall and the Colonel and officers of the 48th Regiment." Clearly Barry believed that he had earned Hall's good opinion sufficiently to rely on him for a reference. For his part, it seems that Hall's sense of rivalry with Barry, defused by Lord Raglan's death, was replaced by respect for his effectiveness in handling the sick, wounded, and dying.

Later, Hall consulted Barry for his opinion on the report of the Sanitary Commission, which was deeply critical of the state of the hospitals in the Crimea. Hall asked Barry to comment on these criticisms. Although a stickler for sanitation, there was nothing Barry liked less than civilians meddling in military matters, as demonstrated in his support for Hall on this matter. Is it also possible that for one of the first times in his life, Barry compromised his principles in order to curry favor for promotion? The shadows of his life were lengthening, and the death of Lord Raglan meant he had lost his chief source of influence in the higher army echelons. Thanking Hall for soliciting his opinion, Barry expostulated that over the matter of hospital sanitation, "the Dept has been treated in a most extraordinary manner." Barry went on to express his surprise and dismay that Hall had not been appointed to the Royal Commission enquiring further into the matter, and revealed his contempt for the politicking of government agents and civilians:

I hear they [the Royal Commission] are going to send a lot of Medical officers to India. Will the Commissioners and Civilians be despatched also?—they should all go in the same boat. Pray say all manner of kind things for me to Lady Hall. I should have liked to have seen your young ones especially the little Lord Chancellor if you had been in London.

Barry made a careful note of the recognition he received for his contribution to the Crimean war effort. "For my efforts on this occasion," he wrote, "I was thanked by the Director-General and the Officers Commanding 97th 3rd Buffs and 91st Regiments who consecutively received similar aid." Further praise was forthcoming also from Admiral Lord Lyons, who conveyed his "approbation" for "my zeal and services, having discovered the cause of the malignant fever on board [the *Modeste*] and for my successful treatment of the sick and the purification of the Ship."

Florence Nightingale, however, remained singularly unimpressed by Dr. Barry. Their encounter took place in the courtyard of the hospital at Scutari. This was Nightingale's domain, and one can only regard with trepidation Barry's audacity in taking it upon himself to come and inspect the state of the establishment. As Barry was officially on leave, his visit can only have been unofficial. More breathtaking is the fact that, having toured the hospital, Barry offered his unsolicited views on Nightingale's arrangements. Surely only James Barry could be foolhardy enough to tell Florence Nightingale how to run a hospital.

Recalling Barry's "blackguard rating" in her letter to her sister, Nightingale remembered that she encountered Barry, mounted on his horse, "while I was crossing the hospital square, with only my cap on, in the sun." Barry, no doubt, would have wondered why Nightingale had a reputation for pragmatism and medical know-how. No one sensible, in his view, ventured out in the heat of the day with only her cap on. Having thus intercepted this most infamous of women, Barry delivered his salvo to Nightingale without dismounting. It must have been quite a scene: Dr Barry kitted out in full military uniform on his horse, Florence Nightingale in her neat pinafore, billowing dusty skirts and insubstantial cap, the two surrounded by a most captive audience: Barry "kept me standing in the midst of quite a crowd of soldiers, commissariat servants, camp followers, etc., everyone of whom behaved like a gentleman during the scolding I received."

Praising the genteel behavior of the onlookers, Nightingale accused Barry of having "behaved like a brute." Nightingale concluded that Barry "was the most hardened creature I ever met."

For his part, Barry seemed to have regarded the encounter as beneath mention. While Nightingale was sufficiently irked by the episode to remember it in crisp detail over a decade later, there is no evidence that Barry was motivated to record his views on meeting her. Nightingale did not long have to contend with Barry's continued presence in the Crimea. Barry returned to Corfu, where he continued to contribute to the Crimean War effort. His final departure from Corfu was in July 1857.

Back in England on leave, Barry wondered where he would be posted next. Sir Andrew Smith had replaced his old champion James McGrigor in the role of director general. Smith and Barry had been contemporaries at Edinburgh medical school, where Barry was the more academically successful. Both had chosen to pursue medicine in the military. The two had met again in 1821 when Smith arrived in Cape Town and reported for duty to Barry, the most senior military medical officer. As well as confirming his duties, Barry had introduced his university friend to the medical fraternity and town society. In 1825, Lord Charles Somerset had granted Smith's request that he be allowed to establish the first officially sponsored museum in the colony. Smith—whose struggles with Florence Nightingale are legendary— was director general during the Crimea campaign. He was well aware of Barry's fulfillment of the precocious promise of his youth.

Barry spent a large part of his three months' leave as the guest of the unconventional earl of Lonsdale at Lowther Castle, a connection he had forged through Lord Charles Somerset. It remains unclear whether Barry idled away his time at Lowther Castle because of the fine conversation and entertainment or because he had nowhere else to stay. A labyrinthine warren of endless chambers and apartments, Lowther was the kind of place that made it hard to keep track of one's guests. There is no suggestion that Barry was an unwelcome visitor, but it is possible that he was in a painfully awkward position. After forty years in perpetual motion, Barry had the aura of the itinerant migrant. He had no house of his own in London, and he was ever anxious to avoid staying overlong in barrack accommodation. Barry was not poor. He had enough to sustain his mobile household and to meet his day-to-day needs. He had money to travel, buy gifts, and spruce up his wardrobe. But he owned no house, no land, no investments. Nothing, that is, that typified the solid Victorian gentleman.

Although sometimes embarrassingly short of cash, he was never short of friends. The fact that he was never in England for long also meant that he was protected from outstaying his welcome. Aside from the earl of Lonsdale, Barry spent time during this leave with the widowed Lady Somerset, who had not remarried. Perhaps each took solace in the other's recollections of the man they had both most loved.

Who can imagine Barry's response when he finally received notice of his last post? It was so antithetical to his preferences and expertise as to be almost absurd. Even the hot-blooded Barry seems to have been more inclined to greet the news with a wry and resigned humor rather than rail against it: "So I am to go to Canada to cool myself after such a long residence in the Tropics and *Hot* Countries." The man who probably had more accumulated knowledge and expertise in tropical diseases than anyone in the entire army was to be sent to one of the British empire's coldest colonial possessions. Having seen Barry at work in Cape Town, Andrew Smith may have thought him particularly suited to managing the rigors of a frontier colony. If Barry was grumpy about being sent north to the cold, his new rank was a significant compensation. Barry had been promoted to local inspector general of hospitals—only one step away from earning his full colors as inspector general.

The Canada command comprised both the north and south of the country. Barry was responsible for barracks and hospitals at Toronto, Quebec, Montreal, and Kingston. He was ordered to winter in Montreal—whose temperatures fell further below freezing than Barry could ever previously have imagined. Barry became a familiar sight on the streets of the city:

> One of the sights of Montreal in the winter of 1858 was a magnificent red sleigh that dashed along Sherbrooke Street every fine afternoon, silver bells jangling, harness glittering, a coachman and footman in glossy furs on the front seat. But eye filling though all this was, two things made the sleigh downright spectacular—the lunatic speed at which it was driven and the grotesque appearance of its solitary passenger.

Whizzing through the snow in his distinctive sleigh swathed in furs, Barry seemed already to have become a mythical, fairy-tale figure. As James Bannerman, author of these Canadian recollections of Barry, observed, "he was already surrounded by rumour and legend." Emaciated beneath his uncompromisingly elaborate uniform, Barry had something of the wizard about him. Despite his diminutive frame, neither his energy nor his ability to curse had left him:

> Not quite five feet tall he wore a tight-fitting dark-blue military uniform. His chin, half hidden by the folds of the greatcoat collar, was narrow and sloping; his mouth a tiny peevish slit under a beak of a nose. The yellowish cheeks had a kind of withered smoothness, and such of his thinning hair as could be seen under a gold-braided peaked cap was dyed scarlet. Every now and again, when the sleigh bounced and slewed in an icy rut, he was flung violently to the floor, cursing in a voice like the squall of an angry seagull.

Barry was as energetic as ever in the execution of his duties. Soon after his arrival in Montreal he made a series of recommendations for improving the soldier's rations, currently one pound of meat and one pound of bread. Observing that "nothing contributes more to general health than change of diet," Barry advised the deputy quartermaster general in Montreal of "the necessity of varying the Diet of the Troops in this Command." In addition to making recommendations on the rations that should be supplied, Barry also further suggested the innovation of installing ovens in all the barracks cookhouses. Such a measure would, he observed, make available to the troops "the cheering change of a roast instead of eternal boiled beef and soup."

Harking back to his lifelong campaigning on this issue, Barry drew attention to the widespread problems with sanitation at the Quebec barracks, "and indeed generally through the Command the Drainage and Sewerage might be improved which would be beneficial in a sanitary point of view." Barry was also disgusted by the conditions in which the troops were quartered, and in August 1858 wrote a letter specifically on the subject of bedding provision for the troops, demanding:

> that Hair Mattresses and Hair or feather pillows be substituted for the palliasses and straw pillows now issued to the various hospitals in this Command. As it must be evident the great comfort it would be to a poor sufferer to rest his emaciated and feverish limbs on something more genial than hard straw.

Aside from the almost demonic execution of his duties, Barry still had time to socialize. It was a measure of his standing in the community of colonial gentlemen that he was one of the first invited to take up membership in the newly opened gentleman's club in Montreal, named, suitably enough, the St. James Club. The food was good and the atmosphere inviolate. Servants and waiters were trained to talk only in lowered tones. Here Barry rubbed shoulders with the venture capitalists and financiers building the new nation's wealth. Or perhaps he simply

dozed in the warmth reading the papers from London while convalescing from yet another bout of the bronchitis to which he had become
prone. As the attacks became worse, Barry sought the medical opinion
of a fellow surgeon—never something he enjoyed doing when it came
to his own health. Dr. G. W. Campbell treated him throughout his stay
in Canada, and later became dean of McGill University.

Barry strained to present himself as energetic, and indeed, for his age
and experience, he was sprightly. Infuriated by his deteriorating health
and the cold weather, Barry nevertheless forged ahead with his reforms
of the Canada command. In December 1858, his persistence was rewarded by a promotion to inspector general. Barry must have felt finally
rewarded by this promotion to the most senior rank his profession offered.

Perhaps one of Barry's profoundest personal victories in Canada was
his campaign to reform the arrangements of married quarters in the
barracks. His thoughts on this were of a piece with his contemplations
of the causes of drunkenness among soldiers, a problem he had tackled
throughout his career. The report that Barry issued on this subject was
his last. It demonstrates clearly that his reforming passion stayed with
him until the end of his life. One of the chief causes of drunkenness,
Barry argued, was

> the absence of separate accommodation for married persons, as
> however limited, still a room for each family would indeed be not
> only a great boon to the soldier but diminish intemperance,
> which is the chief cause of crime, punishment, sickness and
> death. This I have annually iterated and re-iterated.
>
> For example, a woman humbly born, but modestly and reli-
> giously educated, becomes the wife of a soldier, is suddenly placed
> in a Barrack room with 10 or 20 men, perhaps some married, she
> becomes frightened and disgusted, next becomes habituated, or in
> despair has recourse to drunkenness, and not infrequently the
> husband, a good man, joins with his wife and he becomes the oc-

cupant of a cell in a military prison, which, had a similar room been told off for each married person, they might live with decency and bring up their children in the fear of God, without being tainted with the awful and disgusting language of a barrack room.

This report reflects Barry's lifelong concerns with conditions for the soldiers, and emphasizes the particular plight of the women who shared their lives. Yet there is a tone of yearning in Barry's vivid illustration of the obstacles presented to the soldier and his wife wishing to sustain a decent relationship and bring up a family in the army. Is this a regretful fantasy about married life and a family from a man who has long known he will never have either? Or is it not about family at all, but an echo of Barry's exaggerated horror of social situations that disallowed for the possibility of sexual privacy?

Barry could not have been more correct when he said that he was being sent to Canada to cool himself. Two years living in the icy climes chilled his tropical blood. Recurrent bouts of yellow fever during his island-hopping years combined with chest infections during the long northern winters finally took their toll. During the winter of 1858 he was beset by what he owned was "a serious attack" of bronchitis. By April, he was too weak even to visit the St. James Club and wrote a letter withdrawing his name from the list of members, "being unable, from ill-health, to enjoy the privileges of the Club." A founding member, he was courteously placed on the list of supernumerary members.

In May 1859, Barry returned to England. His condition was worsened by seasickness during the voyage. Barry was so weakened by the time he arrived at Liverpool that he was forced to remain there for a few days recovering his strength for the journey to London, where he arrived on July 1.

He described how "immediately on my arrival in London scarcely recovered and in addition labouring under the effects of Sea Sickness during a rough and tempestuous voyage I was ordered before a Medical

Board." He waited anxiously for the outcome, and on July 19 he received the verdict. Declared unfit for further service, Barry was devastated by the outcome:

> Of the proceedings of this Board which consisted of three Junior Officers perfect strangers to me and to my peculiar habits, I know nothing, but the result was my being placed on Half Pay without having completed my period of service in the Rank I had attained which I deemed hard considering my faithful and active service extending over a period of more than 40 years.

He refused to accept that he was being retired. It was unthinkable to him that his long career as an army medical doctor could be so suddenly over. He prepared a detailed memorandum to the secretary of state for war, documenting his career and laying out his argument for his reinstatement.

As well as insisting on the resilience of his health, Barry was terrified by having to finally confront the fact that he had not made adequate financial provision for his old age. He querulously harked back to his old theme of the expenses and debt he had accumulated in the execution of his duties: "On each change of Station I was put to an immense personal outlay the climates of each being of such different temperatures. Each move entailed a sacrifice of property then in my possession and an outlay to procure that required for the service in prospect."

Barry begged the service to order him back to Canada, "praying to be restored to full pay." According to his calculations he needed to serve another twenty months, "by which means your Memorialist will be saved from great pecuniary loss." His constant money worries evident in this final appeal confirmed that he had never stabilized his financial position and now faced a retirement in sadly diminished circumstances. Yet perhaps as equally worrying as his impecunious state was the prospect of a sedentary future. Since 1816 he had not spent more than sixteen months continuously in London. Moreover, having reached the most senior rank of his profession, he clearly had entertained hopes of receiving a public honor:

> I am now prepared to serve Her Majesty in any quarter of the Globe to which I may be sent and am loath to close a career which impartially may be deemed to have been a useful and faithful one without some special mark of Her Majesty's gracious favour.

No call came to any quarter of the globe. Canada was Barry's last post. Nor did he ever receive the royal honors he so guilelessly regarded as being due to him. His career was over.

Despite the fact that he had nowhere of his own to live and needed to budget carefully to provide for himself, Barry made one last journey during his retirement before he finally came to rest in London. Some time between late 1860 and 1861, he made an extended trip to Jamaica, accompanied of course by his manservant and the devoted Psyche.

Barry's final voyage into the sun was not only to warm his bones but also to bid farewell to his great friend Josias Cloete, now a major general in command of the Windward and Leeward forces. With Cloete, Barry shared his happiest memories of his heyday at the Cape and his beloved Lord Charles. He found Kingston much changed, but it still held some of its old pleasures. As well as reminiscing with old friends he enjoyed the company of professional acquaintances, in particular the druggist and chemist Mr. McCrindle, who managed Mitchell's Old Drug Store. Mrs. McCrindle told how Barry would have "his hair cut in their drawing room," adding the domestic detail that "all the floors were polished, so it was not difficult tidying up after he left." Barry was a close enough friend to playfully suggest to the McCrindles that he might adopt their young baby daughter, for whom he showed great affection, doting on her with gifts. According to her brother John McCrindle, Barry said "he would send her to his cousin in Scotland—I think a Lady Jane Gray of Gordon. He gave my sister many presents, among them a solid silver drinking mug and silver knife, fork, spoon, and engraved on them 'Presented by James Barry.'"

John McCrindle was himself an old man when he wrote up his family's recollections of Barry. The relationship to a "Lady Jane Gray" seems to have been an embellishment of fancy, as there is no evidence of such a relationship. Or perhaps the fancy came from Barry himself?

The McCrindles were the recipients of other unexplained mementos of Barry's past. "One piece he gave to my father was a signet ring with a crest on it; to my mother he gave a memorial ring with 'Sacred to the Memory of Marion' engraved inside it." With such gifts Barry reflected his old generous style—except that now pride prompted him to give away his most treasured possessions. Such things might be regarded as properly gifts to family. But Barry, it seemed, had not a single living soul alive to whom he could lay claim as family.

While in Jamaica, Barry also gave a photograph of himself to his friend surgeon-general C. B. Mosse. To have a portrait photograph taken was then a novel and unfamiliar event, and very much an occasion in its own right. The only photograph of Barry known to exist, the picture was produced by Adolphe Duperly & Son, the first and in the early 1860s still the only lithographer-photographer in the West Indies. Duperly's shop was situated at 85 King Street, and, judging by the studio arrangement of the image, we can assume it was here that Barry arrived with his entourage.

The subjects of the photograph are Barry, Psyche, and an unidentified black man. Dressed in civilian clothes in a frock coat, his high starched collar trimmed with a necktie, Barry stands in a pose of masculine self-assurance. His left arm is set akimbo, hand resting smartly on his hip. Psyche sits obediently next to him on a plump cushion in a wicker chair. His right hand rests firmly on top of her head, a gesture distinctly evocative of Hamlet grasping Yorick's skull. For all his air of certainty and self-confidence, Barry looks frail. This photograph of Barry when he was elderly and ill has led to his depiction as frail in stature throughout his life—but the fact is that by this time old age and the ravages of yellow fever and bronchitis had diminished him. His jaw is set in firm resolve beneath his unsmiling mouth, his gaze averted to an invisible point beyond the camera frame. His expression is stern, pugnacious—and inscrutable. Notwithstanding the ravages of time, Barry is every inch the white Victorian gentleman. Standing beside him, taller, more robust, and also in civilian clothing, is a sprucely dressed and broad-chested man. He wears a large cravat, and a watch chain is prominently attached to his waistcoat button. Dressed for the photograph, like Barry, in what is probably his best set of clothes, he is not identifiable merely by what he is wearing. His hair is grizzled. He is not a young man. He is black. Beyond this his identity remains an enigma.

Is this man a friend from Barry's earlier days in Jamaica—perhaps someone Barry knew from his involvement in antislavery circles? He might be a former soldier from the West India regiment, which had black troops. Some said that Barry had a black batman assigned to him from this regiment when he first arrived in Jamaica. If he was, the military record of this assignment is lost. Is it possible to speculate that this man was Dantzen, who accompanied Barry on his departure from the Cape in 1828? If so, then Dantzen, along with the serial Psyches, was the only constant companion with whom Barry shared his life after the death of Somerset. Following Barry's death, the media gave his manservant the invented name of "Black John." In the absence of certain evidence, we can only conjecture as to the real identity of the unnamed, unknown man standing beside Barry. However, he was significant enough in Barry's life to be a prominent subject in the only photographic portrait of him known to exist.

Barry's trip to Jamaica was his last journey beyond the shores of Britain. He spent the final years of his life in London, visiting friends when his health allowed, such as Lady Mary Fitzroy Somerset, the widow of Lord Raglan. In the autumn of 1864, he was again a guest of the earl of Lonsdale at Lowther Castle. He took "morning drives in company with Miss Lowther of Distington" and "attended by a black servant" was a familiar sight on the streets of Whitehaven. By the summer of 1865, Barry was back in London, where he rented rooms in a dentist's house at 14 Margaret Street, Cavendish Square. Barry hated being in London during the summer and it is unlikely he remained in the stuffy and unhealthy city by choice.

London blistered under a heat wave in the summer of 1865. The hot weather and inadequate sanitation incubated an outbreak of chronic diarrhea that spread throughout the fetid metropolis. During the first week of July alone, three hundred people died. Only a few days later, staff surgeon William McKinnon was called to attend on James Barry, who had succumbed to the epidemic. McKinnon, who described himself as having been "intimately acquainted" with Barry "for a good many years," had first met him in Jamaica where they had both been posted. McKinnon did what he could to make Barry comfortable and alleviate his pain, but it was clear that Barry was dying and there was little that he could do. It is not known whether Barry had any visitors other than McKinnon during the final weeks of his life. Solicitously attended by his manservant, Barry had only one other constant companion, Psyche.

At 4 A.M. on July 25, 1865, James Barry died. His manservant called one of the household's maidservants to confirm that he was dead. On the same day, six thousand miles away in Cape Town, his godson, James Barry Munnik, whom he had delivered by cesarean section, celebrated his thirty-ninth birthday. The same week Barry's name appeared among the registrar general's list of fatalities from the epidemic—261 for the returns of July 29. Barry had died of a disease caused by poor social planning, sanitation, and inadequate scientific knowledge.

On the following day, Henry Durham, registrar of the stricken district of Marylebone, issued a death certificate recording that the previous day "James Barry Inspector General of Military Hospitals," a "male about 70 years," had died of "diarrhoea." The certificate was witnessed and confirmed by "the mark of Sophia Bishop present at the death." Unable to write her name, Sophia Bishop signed the document with a cross, and confirmed her address as 14 Margaret Street.

Hart's Army List for 1865 ranked Dr. James Barry as the most senior of Her Majesty's inspectors general of hospitals. Pressed by the contagion of the disease, the military authorities swiftly arranged for the military funeral due to his senior rank, without first requesting a postmortem. Barry was buried at Kensal Green cemetery in a three-guinea plot, where he lies surrounded by dissenting artists, politicians, and poets. He left no instructions for his memorial. His headstone merely records his name, rank, date of death, and age. These last two are incorrect. The headstone states that he died on July 15, 1865, aged 71. Even so shortly after his death the facts of his life were being inaccurately recorded. As Barry, ever attentive to the facts in the reporting of things might have said—as he so often did when proved right in a dispute—"no comment."

Chapter 10

BEYOND A DOUBT

When that day comes a few doctors will make a little stir around my corpse; they will shatter all the extinct mechanisms of its impulses, will draw new information from it, will analyse all the mysterious sufferings that were heaped upon a single human being. Oh princes of science, enlightened chemists, whose names resound throughout the world, anlayze then, if that is possible, all the sorrows that have burned, devoured this heart down to its last fibres; all the scalding tears that have drowned it, squeezed it dry in their savage grasp!

Herculine Barbin, *Memoirs*

ON A STIFLING DAY EARLY IN AUGUST 1865, SOPHIA BISHOP, MAID-servant, presented herself at the offices of Sir Charles McGrigor, Bart. & Co., army agents, and demanded to see the person who was handling the affairs of the late Dr. James Barry. The bemused clerk she accosted retreated to refer the matter to his senior. Asked to explain the nature of her enquiry, Sophia Bishop said she was owed money for having at-tended to the laying out of Dr. James Barry for burial. Her mistress, to whom she had applied for payment, was withholding what was due to her. The army agents, she reasoned, must compensate her from Barry's estate. Dr. William McKinnon, she said, would vouch for her atten-dance at the death of the "General."

Flushed with heat and anger, Sophia Bishop waited for several hours brooding over the events of the day while Dr. McKinnon was sent for. She had argued with her employer, the wife of the dentist who rented out rooms at 14 Margaret Street, stormed out of the house, and undoubtedly lost her job. By the time McKinnon arrived, Bishop's ire and anxiety were at their peak and she was ready for another fight.

Some weeks later, McKinnon described the interview that ensued between the two of them in an official letter to the registrar-general, G. Graham. He explained how he had been called to come immediately to the army agents, "and there the woman, who performed the last offices for Dr Barry was waiting to speak to me." The agitated Sophia Bishop told him "she wished to obtain some prerequisites of her employment which the Lady who kept the lodging house in which Dr Barry died had refused to give her." Here, then, was the source of the dispute between servant and mistress that had driven the resourceful Bishop to find her way to the offices of Charles McGrigor, the accredited agents who had taken possession of Barry's effects. Barry died intestate and penniless, the personal possessions about him in his rented lodgings at his death all he had left in the world. No longer able to afford to buy presents for his friends and hosts, he had proudly given away his few valuable items of jewelry—such as the memorial ring that he gave to Mrs. McCrindle. There is, however, no record of what became of one of Barry's most expensive possessions, a gift from a Hapsburg emperor that he recorded in one of his service memoranda: "I received also at Corfu through the British Government a magnificent Diamond Ring from the Archduke Maximilian for services to one of his Imperial Highnesses Crew."

It is possible that Sophia Bishop was advised to go to McGrigor's by Barry's manservant before he left 14 Margaret Street, perhaps with Barry's pining little dog. Where he went, no one knew. Nor is it known whether Barry had settled him for his retirement before he died, as some claimed he had. The story published in Dickens's *All the Year Round* two years after Barry's death provided the romantic speculation that "a nobleman's valet came for the animal; settled accounts with

'Black John', even to giving him the return passage money to the island whence he came." As the years progressed and the events surrounding Barry's death turned into myth, the return of Barry's servant "whence he came" was stated as a matter of fact, but there is no evidence to support this rather dubious narrative of repatriation.

It may have been that Sophia Bishop was peremptorily dispatched directly to McGrigor's to claim her fee by her angry employer. The dentist's wife was keeping Barry's money to cover his rental and the annoyance of a lodger dying in residence. Most probably, she did not regard herself as responsible for settling her dead lodger's laying-out fees.

It now fell to McKinnon to report on the extraordinary assertion that Sophia Bishop had dramatically made that hot afternoon in the confines of McGrigor's offices. Dr. Barry's doctor repeated Bishop's amazing claim: "Amongst other things she said Dr Barry was a female and that I was a pretty doctor not to know this and that she would not like to be attended by me."

It was as if McKinnon were trying to play down the revelation. To suggest that the most senior medical military officer in the British army was, in fact, a woman can hardly be represented as a fact "amongst other things." This was not all. The agents waited expectantly for McKinnon to deny this apparently ludicrous assertion. But McKinnon made an unexpected response: he chose not to deny Bishop's declaration that James Barry was not what he seemed.

As McKinnon later reminded Registrar General Graham, he had established credentials of friendship with Barry. Unlike Sophia Bishop, McKinnon had known Barry during his life, while she had only encountered him at his death. He was seemingly in a good position to comment on the departed doctor:

I had been intimately acquainted with that gentleman for a good many years, both in the West Indies and in England, and I had never had any suspicion that Dr Barry was a female. I attended him during his last illness, and for some months previously for

bronchitis, and the affection causing his death was diarrhoea produced apparently by errors in diet.

While denying that Barry was a woman, McKinnon did not counter
Bishop's claim by saying that Barry was incontrovertibly a man. Instead
McKinnon gave a response that fanned the flames of a dispute that has
raged unresolved to this very day. He, a fully qualified medical man, admitted to doubt over the status of Barry's body: "I informed her that it
was none of my business whether Dr Barry was a male or a female, and
that I thought that he might be neither, viz. an imperfectly developed
man."

McKinnon's statement that Barry's sex was none of his business was
extraordinary. The notion that Dr. James Barry, inspector general of
hospitals, a senior military man, may in fact have been a woman was
potentially a national scandal. Women were barred from studying medicine and prevented from entering the military. Perhaps it was precisely
for these reasons that McKinnon prevaricated, sensing that the matter
was best left alone rather than exposing an internationally renowned
institution, of which he was a member, to a sensational outrage. In the
same year that Barry died, Elizabeth Garrett Anderson was in the thick
of her battle with the British medical establishment over her ambition
to study medicine and qualify as a surgeon and doctor. A lead editorial,
responding to Garrett Anderson's campaigning, that had been published in the *Lancet* sums up the climate of opinion in the 1860s on
women entering the medical profession:

> The apple of discord is to be cast into our hospitals. A lady has
> penetrated to the core of our hospital system and is determined to
> effect a permanent lodgement. The advanced guard of the Ama-
> zonian army which has so often threatened our ranks on paper has
> already carried the outposts and entered the camp.
>   A lady of admirable purpose and highly respected for her ex-
> cellent bearing, has advanced so far as to have taken courses of

Materia Medica and Chemistry at the School of the Middlesex Hospital. This lady has also applied for admission to courses of anatomy and physiology.

How should this fair intruder have been received? Is she to be welcome as on all other occasions we should welcome a lady, or should we resist the charge of parasols, and run the risk of "taking our quietus with a bare bodkin?"

When all that has been said in favour has been heard, there will remain the unalterable sense of impropriety in mingling young women with young men in classes destined to hear and see daily—sights, descriptions and explanations which cannot be tolerated by men in the presence of women. . . .

While the *Lancet* rolled out its militia against the charge of the Amazonian parasols, the *British Medical Journal* added its own uncompromising view on the issue of women wishing to become doctors:

It is high time that this unnatural and preposterous attempt on the part of one or two highly strongly minded women, to establish a race of feminine doctors should be exploded. How is it possible in accordance with any of the notions of propriety or sentiment which we feel towards the female sex in this country, for any man of proper feeling to sit by the side of a lady at a dissecting table or in an anatomical lecture-room?

These contemporary male views on women trying to study medicine and become qualified practitioners are but a small sample from a bitter fight that persisted for decades. Ten years after Barry's death, in 1875, a mob of male medical students chased a small group of women down a London street, crushing them against the railings and pelting them with rotten vegetables, eggs, and mud. The women wanted to study medicine and become doctors. No charges were brought against the men who participated in the "Riot of Surgeon's Hall." In 1876, the

Royal College of Surgeons of England found itself confronted with new legislation requiring they examine women. Rather than concede to this apparent outrage, the entire board of examiners resigned and was not replaced for a decade, thus preventing any exams from taking place.

In this context, Sophia Bishop's assertion that the inspector general of hospitals had in fact been a woman had serious ramifications. McKinnon's attempt to underplay the significance of her statement was both political and personal—politically, he knew the revelation was problematic; personally, he had known Barry for ten years and as his physician was technically bound to silence by the professional oath of Hippocrates.

But it was too late. By admitting to a margin of doubt, McKinnon had given Sophia the ambiguous inch she needed to seize the floor. Alert to the vulnerable position of the men questioning her, she grabbed the opportunity provided by McKinnon's uncertainty to persist with stating her case:

> She then said she had examined the body, and that it was a perfect female and farther that there were marks of her having had a child when very young. I then enquired how have you formed that conclusion. The woman, pointing to the lower part of her stomach, said, "From the marks here [i.e. striae gravidarum]. I am a married woman, and the mother of nine children and I ought to know."
>
> The woman seemed to think that she had become acquainted with a great secret and wished to be paid for keeping it. I informed her that all Dr Barry's relatives were dead, and that it was no secret of mine, and that my own impression was that Dr Barry was a Hermaphrodite.
>
> But whether Dr Barry was male, female or hermaphrodite I do not know, nor had I any purpose in making the discovery as I could positively swear to the identity of the body as being that of a person whom I had been acquainted with as Inspector-General of Hospitals for a period of eight or nine years.

McKinnon revealed these startling events only when pressed to do so nearly a month later. It is unclear whether or not Sophia Bishop left McGrigor's with payment for the laying out in her pocket. Certainly her attempt to blackmail the doctor and the army agents weakened her case, but they might have thought it judicious to acknowledge that she was due her "prerequisites" for laying out the body. McKinnon said nothing further about the matter—at least not in public. Contrary to later claims, neither *The Times* nor any other London newspaper published an obituary of Barry. Given his senior status and groundbreaking career, this omission seems odd.

On August 14, four weeks after his death, a sensational story regarding Dr. James Barry was published in Dublin. It appeared unattributed in *Saunders' News Letter and Daily Advertiser,* "From our own correspondent." How the story was leaked to the press and why it was released first in Ireland is unknown. Had McKinnon discussed the story in his gentleman's club or with his medical cronies? Did the story seep through the corridors of gentlemanly gossip to Fleet Street and into the ears of *Saunders*'s London correspondent? Or did an employee at McGrigor's who was privy to the remarkable interview between Barry's doctor and the maidservant who prepared him for burial whisper the story to the press? It is also possible that the evidently resourceful Sophia Bishop sold her story. Whatever its source, it was picked up with alacrity by the English press and republished in an abridged form by the *Manchester Guardian* on August 21:

A STRANGE STORY

An incident is just now being discussed in military circles so extraordinary that, were not the truth capable of being vouched for by official authority, the narration would certainly be deemed absolutely incredible. Our officers quartered at the Cape between 15 and 20 years ago may remember a certain Dr Barry attached to the medical staff there, and enjoying a reputation for considerable skill in his profession, especially for firmness, decision and rapidity in difficult operations. The gentleman had entered the army in 1813, had passed, of course, through the grades of assistant surgeon and surgeon in various regiments, and had served as such in various quarters of the globe. His professional acquirements had procured for him promotion to the staff at the Cape. About 1840 he became promoted to be medical inspector, and was transferred to Malta. He proceeded from Malta to Corfu where he was quartered for many years. . . . He there died about a month ago, and upon his death was discovered to be a woman. The motives that occasioned, and the time when commenced this singular deception are both shrouded in mystery. But thus it stands as an indubitable fact, that a woman was for 40 years an officer in the British service, and fought one duel and had sought many more, had pursued a legitimate medical education, and received a regular diploma, and had acquired almost a celebrity for skill as a surgical operator! There is no doubt whatever about the "fact," but I doubt whether even Miss Braddon herself would have ventured to make use of it in fiction.

Filled with factual errors, this was the first published account of Barry's career. The story was reprinted also by Cumbria's *Whitehaven News*, which ran it in their August 24 issue, correctly assuming that it would be of great interest to the inhabitants of a town where so recently Barry had been a familiar figure. Yet while the regional newspapers rushed to print the scoop that the recently deceased inspector general of hospitals had actually been a woman, the London press remained entirely and uncannily silent on the matter. The reticence of the metropolitan press did nothing to stem the tidal wave of gossip that swept through the corridors of power, flooding every quarter of fashionable London with speculation.

The rumors must have proved irresistible to the many people who had encountered Barry during his career. "The mystery was discussed for weeks in every regimental mess in the British Army." It was passed with the port around the dinner tables of military barracks, and carried back with the empty plates to kitchens by servants who listened in impassive fascination as their masters guffawed over the scandal. Wives and daughters, always sympathetic to Barry for the courtesy and attentiveness he showed to them, gently pressed their men to tell them more and compared notes at sequestered female tea parties or while strolling in Hyde Park.

All the while, the Horse Guards and the army medical department remained publicly silent on the matter. This was not just a tale of swashbuckling cross-dressing and derring-do; James Barry was a surgeon and scientist, renowned for his skills at cutting up dead bodies and performing operations on live ones. Barry had trained in morbid anatomy and anatomical dissection. In the 1860s, English doctors found the idea of women receiving instruction in anatomy entirely "undesirable in every respect and highly unbecoming." The dissection room and anatomical theater was no place for a woman; "It is not necessary that fair ladies should be brought into contact with such foul scenes." Barry had spent his career as witness to foul scenes and the stench and squalor of nineteenth-century medicine. He had filled the files of the War Office and army medical department with reports on venereal diseases, syphilis, and drunkenness—none of them a suitable subject for a woman. He had researched and published an innovative cure for syphilis and gonorrhea. This was the surgeon credited with performing the first successful cesarean section known to British medicine.

And then there was that other matter remembered by the older ranking members of the exclusively male military and medical community. What new light did this rumor throw on that embarrassing business about the relationship between Lord Charles Somerset and James Barry? The sodomy libel took on an entirely new aspect in the face of this revelation.

There was also a practical problem that potentially amounted to an administrative embarrassment. No postmortem had been carried out on Barry's corpse. It was claimed that one of Barry's last requests was that no examination of his body should be made. It was an understandable request from someone with a physical secret to hide.

As Barry had died of epidemic dysentery, burying him as soon as possible was a measure borne of necessity. It did, however, leave the military and medical establishments with no anatomical description of the subject whose life was being so obsessively—and inaccurately—disgorged in the national press. In the absence of any physical evidence, the only option was to seek the opinion of the doctor who had attended his death.

When the pressure finally got too much, Registrar-General Graham, responsible for the registration of births, marriages, and deaths, wrote from Somerset House to Dr. McKinnon:

> Sir
>
> It has been stated to me that Inspector-General Dr James Barry, who died at 14 Margaret St. on 25th July, 1865, was after his death found to be a female. As you furnished the Certificate as to the cause of his death, I take the liberty of asking you whether what I have heard is true, and whether you yourself ascertained that he was a woman and apparently had been a mother?
>
> Perhaps you will decline answering these questions: but I ask them not for publication but for my own information.

It was understandable that Graham, in the interest of wanting to keep his records straight, would wish to verify whether or not the death certificate was correct in its statement that Dr. James Barry was a "male." Graham's diplomacy in acknowledging that McKinnon may "decline answering these questions" implies respect of McKinnon's Hippocratic confidentiality, but there is unquestionably a hint of prurient curiosity in the letter.

Did McKinnon, bound by his professional code of confidentiality, hesitate before divulging what he understood of Dr. Barry's secrets? "Whatever I see or hear, professionally or privately, which ought not to be divulged, I will keep secret and tell no one," runs the oath of Hippocrates. Although not required to answer Graham's queries, McKinnon did reveal what he knew. His letter of reply of August 24, in which he gave in detail his dramatic encounter with Sophia Bishop, reached Graham the following day. Whatever Graham's personal conclusions about the argument between the doctor and the servant over Barry's body, he chose to leave the death certificate unaltered. Officially, Barry's sex remained as male.

From this point, the story passed into the realm of speculation. No fresh proof was produced to corroborate Sophia Bishop's story or to confirm McKinnon's uncertainty about Barry's sex. The question was never raised of disinterring Barry's body to enact the postmortem eluded by his ambiguous corpse. McKinnon's letter remained the sole source for the secondhand testimony of Sophia Bishop. Her statement that Barry was a "perfect female" is contravened in the only other official document where her name appears. This, of course, is Barry's death certificate, on which Bishop placed her signatory cross to confirm Barry's sex as male. Why did she do this if she knew the facts to be otherwise? Perhaps she, an illiterate serving woman, felt pressured by the patrician high-handedness of the registrar, Henry Durham, and Dr. McKinnon, who merely pushed the indecipherable document toward her and asked her to "mark it here" without bothering to explain its contents. Of course, it cannot be ignored that the discrepancy between Bishop's confirmation of the death certificate and her later story—which she told only when she did not receive the remuneration she expected—may cast doubt upon the reliability of her tale. Yet she had little to gain from inventing such a fantasy. Although she had some sense of his importance as a professional gentleman, the dying Barry was no longer an imposing figure. His celebrity as a medical innovator was probably unknown to her. She just wanted payment for the services she had performed, and perhaps a little more for keeping her mouth shut. On balance, it seems fair to assume that Sophia Bishop believed that what she had seen was a woman's body.

In a matter of a few weeks, Bishop's reported story had been embellished almost beyond recognition. McKinnon's own opinion, however, "that Dr Barry was a Hermaphrodite," was not reported as part of the leaked story. It seemed that from the point of view of the press, the story of Barry as a woman was the more romantic version and, crucially, easier to understand, there being a long tradition of women cross-dressing to join the military.

The original breaking story in *Saunders' News Letter* contained several passages left out of the *Manchester Guardian* that demonstrate the degree to which the story was very quickly overlaid with distortion. In this version the maidservant, Sophia Bishop, who laid claim to the discovery of Barry's femaleness, has become "two nurses who attended him":

> Very probably this discovery was elicited during the natural preparation for interment, but there seems to be an idea prevalent that either verbally, during the last illness, or by some writing perused immediately after his (for I must still use the "masculine") death, he had begged to be buried without any post-mortem examination of any sort. This, most likely, only aroused the curiosity of the two nurses who attended him, for it was to them, it appears, that the disclosure of this mystery is owing. Under the circumstances the fact was deemed so important that medical testimony was called in to report upon and record its truth. By this investigation not only was the assertion placed beyond a doubt, but it was equally beyond a doubt brought to light that the individual in question had, at some time or another, been a mother.

In fact nothing was placed "beyond a doubt." The "investigation" that was claimed to substantiate the truth had, needless to say, never happened. The truth was that the entire story hung on the reported testimony of Sophia Bishop, who had immediately been written out of the account and replaced by "two nurses."

And what of Sophia Bishop's claim that Barry bore the "marks of her having had a child when very young"? Bishop, a mother of nine, had sound experience on which to base her observation that Barry's stretch marks revealed the birth of a child. Barry, in his midseventies, died, effectively, of dysentery. He was chronically emaciated from a disease that had overlaid itself on a body ravaged by remittent yellow fever, from which he had suffered since the early 1850s. The objective fact that Barry's body had been subject to nearly two decades of a degenerative tropical disease that never leaves the body once it enters it cannot be ignored. Sophia Bishop's claim was that she could read the marks of childbirth on a body already inscribed with the effects of yellow fever and dysentery.

If Barry did have a child, who was the father, how was the pregnancy concealed, and what had become of the baby? The obvious way to address this is to look for unaccounted time in Barry's career. There are two periods over which hang some ambiguity. The first is his mysterious youth, before he appeared at Edinburgh as a medical student. The second was at the end of 1819, when Barry briefly left the Cape and went to Mauritius. "During the choleras at the Mauritius" is how this was written up in Barry's army record. But according to June Rose, Barry left for Mauritius before the news of the cholera epidemic had reached Cape Town. He left also, strangely, before Somerset sailed back to England to find a new wife and marry, missing the grand ball thrown in tribute to his departure. If we are to look for evidence of Barry having given birth, this would be the only viable period in a long career that might have presented the opportunity. Barry returned from Mauritius alone; if the child survived, we must assume it was either adopted or absorbed into a shadow life of Barry's of which there is absolutely no trace remaining. If Barry was a "perfect female" the claim that she had a child remains an unsolved mystery.

The *Saunders'* correspondent who stopped to explain his use of pronouns by saying "for I must still use the 'masculine' " in reporting Barry's story had stumbled over the problem of pronouns raised by Barry's uncertain gender. This very first publication on Barry's strange life admitted that the mystery surrounding him made the pronouns through which he was described a problem for all posterity. As will be shown, in the immediate aftermath of his death Barry was still swathed in the mantle of masculine pronouns. But as time progressed and the tale of his cross-dressed disguise gained popular currency, the man who had lived all his life as a man, and insistently referred to himself as an officer and a gentleman, was progressively described by the feminine gender. Commentators gave up struggling with the ambiguity, and subtly but surely Barry was wrapped in the petticoats of feminine pronouns that he had never worn during his professional lifetime.

Florence Nightingale's letter to her sister is a classic example of someone who knew Barry as "him" struggling with how to handle pronouns when discussing this person who now appeared to have been a "her." It is significant that Nightingale makes no claim to have suspected Barry's secret when they met. Given Nightingale's own unique position in relation to the army, medicine, and nursing, her remarks on Barry are particularly intriguing. Nightingale concedes not an inch of sisterhood to Barry, whose ambitions were apparently so similar to her own. Her concern is far more that Barry behaved badly:

> I never had such a blackguard rating in all my life—I who have had more than any woman—than from this Barry sitting on (her) horse, while I was crossing the Hospital Square with only my cap on, in the sun. (He) kept me standing in the midst of quite a crowd of soldiers, commissariat, servants, camp followers, etc., etc., every one of whom behaved like a gentleman during the scolding I received, while (she) behaved like a brute.
>
> After (she) was dead I was told (he) was a woman.
>
> PS I would say (she) was the most hardened creature I ever met.

Although the regular newspapers in London appeared uninterested in the story, or perhaps were discouraged from circulating it, the medical journals adopted the revelation with a fascination that was to last for 150 years. The *Medical Times and Gazette* and the *British Medical Journal* reprinted the copy that had appeared in *Saunders'* and the *Manchester Guardian* with their own commentary. The *Medical Times* observed that Barry's story "has been the subject of not a little 'club tattle' ":

> The author has fallen into many inaccuracies but he is correct in the main point—the sex of the deceased. . . . the physique, the absence of hair, the voice, all pointed one way and the petulance of temper, the unreasoning impulsiveness, the fondness for pets were all in the same direction.

It is entertaining to read that in the absence of a postmortem report, the "evidence" of hairlessness, bad temper, irrationality, and a fondness for animals were the set of verifiable physical criteria used by this august medical journal to prove that Barry was a smooth-faced, bad-tempered, irrational, pet-loving female.

For its part, the *British Medical Journal* reproduced the story and assured readers that it was clear that Barry was a woman because people who had met him said so: "The gentleman alluded to was well known to many members of the profession. It was always suspected by those who knew him well in the army that he was a she." But this confident assertion does not square with the reports of those who did know Barry at first hand, and who admitted to having had no suspicions at all that "he was a she." John McCrindle, who described the time Barry spent with his parents in Kingston during his retirement, confirmed, "They never at any time suspected his sex." Dr. McKinnon, of course, stating that he had known and attended on Barry for nearly a decade, conceded candidly, "I never had any suspicion that Dr Barry was a female." McKinnon was not the only personal doctor who confessed his ignorance of Barry's secret. Dr. G. W. Campbell, who attended Barry in

Canada for the bronchitis that ended his military career, freely admitted that despite treating Barry, he never suspected "her" sex. Dr. Campbell became dean of McGill University, and used to tell his all-male medical students the story of his attendance on Barry as a cautionary tale:

> Gentleman, if I had not stood in some awe of Inspector General Barry's rank and medical attainments I would have examined him—that is her—far more thoroughly. Because I did not, and because his—confound it, her—bedroom was always in almost total darkness when I paid my calls, this, ah, crucial point, escaped me. Which shows you should never let yourself be too impressed by any colleague to treat him just like any other patient.

One of Campbell's students was William Osler, who became later Sir William Osler, Regius Professor of Medicine at Oxford University and much preoccupied with the identity of James Barry. It was he who finally established beyond a doubt that there were no postmortem records and that no autopsy had been carried out on Barry. John Jobson, Barry's university friend who so unsuccessfully tried to teach him to box, was "astonished as anybody" when told of the revelations about his old friend, and "could not shed light on why" Barry had chosen this disguise.

The wives and daughters of military men who had met Barry during his career had also formed their opinions of Dr. Barry. Although forcibly struck by Barry's appearance, Sarah Esther Horniman was like several women who had met Barry but were unprepared to assert that they had suspected Barry was female. Horniman gave equal weight in her recollections to Barry's skill as a surgeon and charm as a suitor:

> There was a Dr B——, an Army Doctor, whose appearance and voice used to strike my childish wonder. He was very short and spare, a smooth not very prepossessing face, scanty carrity [*sic*] locks and a high thin voice which might have been termed

squeaky, but he was considered very clever and a skilful surgeon and much respected. He seemed to seek the society of nice young girls and I have heard my eldest sister joked about his intentions to her. I was reading a newspaper not many years ago and my attention was drawn to a paragraph headed "wonderful discovery". It gave Dr B's name, or perhaps the name assumed, and said it was found that it was a woman but had personated a man to pursue the calling he had chosen after a love disappointment.

Horniman's suggestion that Barry had cross-dressed because of disappointment in love was to become a familiar theme of the cluster of legends that attached themselves to the figure of James Barry within weeks of his death.

Edward Bradford, inspector general of hospitals, was particularly riled by the manner in which the Barry story was reported in the *Medical Times* and *British Medical Journal*. He issued a letter of response that appeared on August 26 in the *Medical Times,* claiming loftily: "The stories which have circulated since his death are too absurd to require serious refutation." It was the first time in the whole public furor that a senior military medical officer had committed himself in print on the affair, and his intention of "contradicting and playing down" the revelations coupled with the seniority of his rank may suggest that the hitherto silent military had deputized him to make an unofficial response to the scandal. While Bradford condemned the "absurd" nature of the stories circulating around Barry, he gamely went on to adumbrate a number of absurdities of his own about Barry's personality. Without providing any substantiating evidence, Bradford described Barry as a prematurely born orphan who qualified as a medic at a very young age:

I met him for the first time in 1832 in Jamaica. His appearance and manner were most singular. He was scarcely five feet tall. He was completely devoid of all the outward signs of manly virility.

His voice was that of an old woman. He tried in every respect to make himself conspicuous and wore the longest sword and longest spurs that it was possible to find. He was often to be found in the company of all sorts of animals, dogs, monkeys, parrots. His diet at this time was composed exclusively of milk and fruit, but afterwards he made use of solid nutritious food.

He was delighted to be at the centre of scandal and gossiping, and he used to say that at the Cape he had had many duels "and that in one encounter he had killed his rival." Called upon to do something which he did not like, he would go quickly to bed, and cry like a child until the crisis was past, then he would turn against his tormentors, as he called them, and would pose before the authorities of the station as the unhappy victim of his immediate superiors. When he fell ill he would never forget to make his doctor promise that if he died, the doctor would make quite sure that no examination of his body was made.

Subtly undermining Barry's professional behavior, Bradford damned Barry with patronizing praise. Barry was "endowed with a lively mind and an excellent memory." Treated with deference he "kept his good humour and remained smiling and happy," but his "anger was unbounded" if anyone questioned his status or powers. He "flouted all authority" and his "irritable and impatient nature put him in opposition with authority all his life." Childish, wilful and uncontrollable, Barry was "nevertheless susceptible to generous sentiments and was well disposed towards those who showed him good will." But in spite of this feminization of Barry's personality, Bradford did not conclude that Barry was a woman:

There could not have been any doubt among the people who knew him on the subject of his physical constitution, which was really that he was a male in whom the development of the organs of sex had been arrested from the sixth month of pregnancy. It is sad that no qualified persons took the opportunity of his death to examine closely the physical condition of the deceased.

This was the first time in the public domain that someone claimed that Barry was neither man nor woman, but something else. It was to be far from the last.

Bradford correctly raised the issue of the absence of an anatomical report on Barry's body. He might have quoted Barry himself: "In the natural sciences, the truth of principles must be confirmed by observations." Although Sophia Bishop was the only person to say publicly that she had seen Barry unclothed after his death, there were a few who claimed that they had observed Barry's naked body during the doctor's lifetime and discovered "her" secret. The most persistent among these was Lieutenant Colonel Edward Rogers, who maintained: "Col. de Montmorency and General Lowry are two of four gentlemen who discovered Barry's sex and are still alive." Rogers's story was published in the *Lancet* in 1882. These men, he said, had confessed to discovering Barry's femaleness in the following way. One of them, a doctor, was summoned to treat Barry in Trinidad while he was sick. The doctor turned up at Barry's lodgings with three fellow officers in tow and entered the bedroom where Barry lay in feverish delirium:

> The assistant surgeon of the station [Trinidad] discovered what Col. de Montmorency reported to me—namely that on throwing back the sheets from off the unconscious "Doctor" it was seen that she was a woman—and upon recovery of her senses she made those present swear that her secret would not be disclosed until after her death.

Despite Rogers's insistence on the truth of this tale, at least one of the people he cited as a firsthand observer was unwilling to corroborate the story. Colonel de Montmorency wrote to Rogers qualifying his part in the alleged incident:

I was not actually in the room when Dr James Barry's sex was discovered in 1841; the matter was confidentially told me immediately after the discovery by one of the party present, so I would not wish that his name, nor mine, to be brought before the public in the matter.

Rogers continued doggedly undeterred to assert the truth of the tale. As author of the three-volume bodice-ripper *The Modern Sphinx,* a thinly veiled and highly romanticized account of the life of "Dr Fitzroy," Rogers was motivated to feed the Barry myth in order to sell more copies of his books.

Another account by someone who had apparently observed Barry in a state of undress appeared in the journal of Mrs. Fenton, whom Barry had spent time with when stationed on Mauritius. In 1829, Mrs. Fenton and her husband had interrupted their journey from India to New South Wales at Mauritius in order for her to give birth to a baby daughter, Flora. Barry had assisted Mrs. Fenton during the last stages of her pregnancy, and complained when two other doctors were called in to attend to Mrs. Fenton's labor. The incident did not prevent the two from continuing their acquaintance, and Mrs. Fenton spent time with Barry while recuperating from the birth, as recorded in her diary: "Just put Flora in her basket and set off on a pedestrian tour through the island with my friend Dr Barry." Mrs Fenton recalled that she had been told a story about Barry in India, little expecting she was to encounter him shortly in Mauritius:

I remember one night in India, I was sitting in the room of a friend assisting to watch her, along with a nurse tender much in esteem in Calcutta, who to pass the hours began to recount some "passages" in her former life. She said she had been driven from the Cape by Dr Barry, over whom there hung some extraordinary mystery. She was in high repute there, and often engaged when Barry attended. One night when she supposed a lady she was with to be in want of immediate aid, she sent for him—he slept in the house—but not being so expeditious as she wished, she ran herself and made an unceremonious entrance into his room.

Thereon he flew into a most violent passion. She declares and steadily maintains, that the nominal Dr Barry *was and is a woman.* From this time he displayed the most implacable dislike to her, even to making it a condition not to attend in any family where she was employed. The truth of this strange tale I cannot pledge myself to uphold, but well I remember listening to it one tedious night, when I very little expected to come into contact with the individual concerned.

Mrs. Fenton's remark upon meeting him "that there is certainly something extraordinary about this same Dr Barry" is surprisingly evasive. Careful to say that she "cannot pledge" herself to "uphold" the "truth of this strange tale," she permits herself to comment on Barry's ambiguity, but refrains from stating positively that Barry was a woman. Fenton died in 1875 and her journals were first published in 1901. Aside from her prevarication, there is the question, as is so consistently the case, of whether these enticing accounts are rendered dubious by their appearing only after Barry's death.

There were others who, though they did not claim to have observed Barry undressed, in a general way maintained that Barry's disguise was a matter of "common repute" during his lifetime. An anonymous contributor to the *Lancet* wrote: "I lived in the same neighbourhood at that time [the early 1850s] and knew her perfectly well by sight, and it was a matter of common repute that she belonged to a different sex than the one indicated by her clothes." Yet people who knew Barry far better than just "by sight" were in fact far less willing to declare with such certainty their awareness of Barry's gender deception. George Thomas Keppel, Lord Albemarle, whose memoirs were published in 1876, spent time with Lord Charles Somerset at the Cape in 1819, when Barry was at the height of his powers and living at the governor's residence:

I had heard so much of this capricious, yet privileged gentleman, that I had a great curiosity to see him. I shortly afterwards sat next to him at dinner at one of the regimental messes. In this learned Pundit I beheld a beardless lad, apparently of my own age, with an unmistakably Scotch type of countenance—reddish hair, high cheek bones. There was a certain effeminacy in his manner, which he seemed to be always striving to overcome. His style of conversation was greatly superior to that one usually heard at a mess-table.

Commenting on the revelation that Barry was a woman, Albemarle observes, "It is singular that neither the landlady of her lodging, nor the black servant who had lived with her for years, had the slightest suspicion of her sex." For his own part, although commenting on the "effeminacy" of Barry's manner, Albemarle avoids positively stating that it was his impression when meeting Barry that "he" was a woman.

A more intriguing example is provided in the memoirs of Vice Admiral Sir William Henry Dillon. Dillon visited the Cape in 1816 on his way back from an Admiralty commission in China. Taken ill when the ship was at anchor, he summoned medical assistance:

The ship had not long been at anchor when I was attacked by a violent inflammation in both eyes, the result of a cold caught in the late gales. The Surgeon attended me constantly, and inflicted upon me some painful trials. Both the lower eyelids were scarified, my right temple opened, which only produced temporary relief. As I suffered so much, I applied to the family physician of the Governor, Lord H [*sic*] Somerset. This gentleman was in the Army, and considered extremely clever. Many surmises were in circulation relating to him; from the awkwardness of his gait and the shape of his person it was the prevailing opinion that he was a female. He was extremely assiduous, but did not approve the remedies resorted to, plainly telling me that a milder treatment would have sufficed. Having written down his instructions, and explained fully the system I was to follow, he took his leave.

The vice admiral died in September 1857, eight years before Barry. The Navy Records Society published his professional adventures first in 1956, and—if they can be relied upon to have been published a century later without editorial amendment—they constitute a remarkable testimony. Remarkable not the least for the fact that Dillon was able to so attentively observe the "awkwardness" of Barry's gait and the "shape of his person" while suffering from "a violent inflammation in both eyes" for which "both the lower eyelids were scarified."

There was in fact one person only who had described Barry in print as having the form of a woman during his lifetime, and that was Las Casas, who all those years ago in the Cape had experienced confusion when meeting Somerset's precocious young protégé: "The poor Dr who was presented to me was a boy of 18—with the form—the manners and the voice of a woman. But Mr Barry (such was his name) was described to me to be an absolute phenomenon!"

Las Casas, as we know, went on to form a high opinion of Barry, and to be grateful to him for his care of his son Emmanuel. Indeed, Barry was one of the only people Las Casas met at the Cape who came off unscathed from the otherwise vituperative insults launched against the British administration in Las Casas's Napoleonic journal.

Lord Albemarle's reflection that it was singular "that neither the landlady of her lodging, nor the black servant who had lived with her for years, had the slightest suspicion of her sex" raises the question of Barry's relationship with servants, who had particular intimacy in regard to the domestic habits of their masters—or mistresses. People were curious about what Barry's servants might have known and regarded his black manservant in particular with a mixture of anxiety and titillation. The *Whitehaven News,* for example, made a great play of directing the attention of its readers toward the fact that the white, female Barry's relationship with her black servant might be questionable in the light of these new revelations:

Many of our readers will have a distinct recollection of the person referred to. It will be remembered that upon her last visit she was attended by a black servant, of singular acuteness. The complexion of Sambo contrasted in a remarkable degree with the pale, sallow look of his mistress, and still more remarkable was the contrast between the lady and her servant in point of stature as well as in other minor respects. Their appearance in public naturally excited considerable attention. The attenuated form of the lady was generally understood to be due to a vegetarian diet, and many were the jokes that were passed at the "Doctor's" expense during her ladyship's sojourn at the Castle.

The revelation that Barry might have been a woman, stated as fact by the newspaper, produced popular unease about what might have been the relationship between white mistress and black servant who had traveled so long and far together.

The story that appeared in Dickens's journal *All the Year Round* in 1867 highlighted the role played by servants at Barry's death:

John drew the sheet over the face, and descended to the kitchen for a charwoman, who he knew would be there at that hour. He summoned her to assist at the last toilet of the dead "general." As she closed the door of the room, he retreated to his own, and lay down, tired out. He was closing his eyes, when the charwoman hurried in. "What do you mean," she said, "by calling me to lay out a general, and the corpse is a woman's?"

One Lieutenant Colonel R. C. Francis, writing to *Guy's Hospital Gazette* in a "factual" article in the twentieth century, actually asserted that the name of the "nurse" who laid out Barry's body was Mrs. Gamp—the name of a character in *Martin Chuzzlewit.* That an invented character from a Dickens novel was now claimed to have been actually present at the scene of Barry's death is a significant measure of how much fiction had entangled the legends that accumulated around Barry's life in death.

Some who knew Barry were angered by the claim that his servants had been privy to his secret. C. B. Mosse impatiently underlined Captain Dadson's assertion that "No doubt his servant was in his confidence" and noted in the margin, "No he wasant!" [*sic*]. It was to Mosse that Barry had given the photograph taken in Kingston. Dadson recalled that Barry was "a great friend" of his father and that as a boy he had "often shaken hands with him":

> He was rather short, with red face, close shaven, and always wore the blue frock coat and a high black silk sock of that period. Many years afterwards when I was stationed at the Stony Hill Barracks in Jamaica I was asked by Mrs Magnus, an old coloured lady who lived in the village, whether I ever heard that Dr Barry was at his death found to be a woman. She then told me that he lived for some time in the colonel's quarters in the Barracks (then occupied by me) and was very peculiar in his habits, never allowing a woman to attend on him or even to enter his quarters. . . . She especially noticed the delicacy of his hands and smallness of his feet.

The recollections of Mrs. Magnus, another servant ventriloquized in print by a speculative male, place her within the group of people who were keen to report that they had indeed thought Barry unusual when they encountered him, even though they had for reasons of their own chosen not to remark on it during his lifetime.

Barry's story, first published in the British press, went international. Not surprisingly, it found its way quickly to the Cape, appearing in the *South African Advertiser and Mail* on October 11, 1865. The paper published some correspondence it had received in response to its story, one from an unnamed source in Cape Town stating:

> Your paragraph in last evening's issue relative to the late Dr Barry was no secret to many of the inhabitants of this city, as, at the time of his, or rather her, residence here, it was currently talked of, and

she was well known to many by the name of the "Kapok Doc-tortje."

A week later, a Mr. J. M. Howell sent his own memories for publication to the paper, refuting this claim that Barry was well known to have been a woman:

> I recollect him, or rather her, well, some thirty-five years ago. The doctor was a staff assistant surgeon, attached first to Lord Charles Somerset's household, and afterwards to Sir Rufane Shaw Donkin's. . . . He was designated the "kapok doctor," from being supposed to be a seven months' child, brought to light under the Caesarean operation, and swaddled in cotton. The doctor was effeminate in appearance and voice. The general impression was that he was a hermaphrodite. He was very much attached to another supposed hermaphrodite of the name of Sannah, a servant of the late Fiscal Denyssen. . . . Dr Barry was esteemed a very learned man by the savants of Cape Town, and a great advocate for the free press; and during the reign of terror in Cape Town . . . Dr Barry exerted all his influence with Lord Charles to obtain a reversal of his order, but without effect. I remember well his or her having expressed himself very indignantly on the occasion.

Of course, Barry was known to have performed one of the first cesarean sections, rather than having been born by this method himself. One wonders what his godson, James Barry Munnik, by now a prominent Cape Town merchant, made of Howell's account. Barry was known as the "kapok doctor" from his habit of stuffing his jacket with cotton wadding, a fashionable and common practice among dandified officers of the time. It is also possible that the epithet was a reference to his wrangle with the authorities in 1836 over the mass destruction of his linen at the Cape on his way to St. Helena.

Within ten weeks of James Barry's death, the story that he was in fact a cross-dressing woman had been published and discussed on at least three continents. "Nobody knows when or why he began her masquerade," wrote James Bannerman in the now-familiar cocktail of pronouns deployed when discussing Barry's life. The motivation most commonly attributed to Barry's deception was that she had fallen in love with an army surgeon and cross-dressed in order to follow him throughout the pathways of his career. "Motive alleged for disguise— love for an army surgeon," as Olga Racster and Jessica Grove, who freely admitted themselves much enamored of the "adorable" James Barry, so succinctly summarized the explanation in the 1930s.

The other motivation ascribed to Barry was that she was a young woman who cross-dressed in order to enter a male profession from which she was barred. In fact, Barry's case breached the barricades of not just one but two professions: medicine *and* the military. Rose Weigall, the daughter to the Viennese ambassador who had met Barry as a child, was certainly of the opinion that Barry had cross-dressed for the love of medicine, and not a medical man, when she wrote to *The Spectator* in 1919:

> The explanation undoubtedly was that an adventurous, strong-willed girl, consumed with a passion for surgery and medicine, could find in those days no possible training, in what was her ruling passion, and so adopted this extreme course, and probably found it easier to maintain the deception in the roving life of an Army doctor than if settled anywhere. Nowadays she would, of course, have been a distinguished lady doctor, and it is rather pathetic that one whose life was certainly devoted to the relief of suffering, and who in her assumed character, and in spite of so much that was ridiculous, had earned the respect and esteem of her colleagues and superiors, should be made the peg on which to hang so distorted a story regarding her strange career.

The manifold accounts that Barry cross-dressed either for love of a man or in order to pursue a medical career conformed to what cross-dressing expert Julie Wheelwright has identified as the accepted story of why women cross-dressed. In stories that prevailed from the middle of the eighteenth century up to the 1920s, "A woman, seeking a lost lover or hoping to support herself or her children through honest labour, swaps petticoats for trousers and takes to the road." Looking back in a broad sweep over the varied histories of women who cross-dressed as men in pursuit of "life, liberty and happiness," Wheelwright, however, cautions of "the danger in generalizing about women's motives for living as men."

These were some of the theories given for why "he began her masquerade," but Sophia Bishop's revelation and the proliferation of speculation that followed in its scandalous wake raised another, more profound question. Who, exactly, was James Barry?

There were many romantic theories about Barry's parentage. Whoever he or she was, James Barry was born before the compulsory registration of births, probably somewhere in the British Isles, between 1790 and 1795. Among the most far-fetched were claims that she was the bastard child of the duke of York, Lord "Hellgate" Barrymore, or, most unlikely, the Prince Regent himself. Others averred that Barry was an orphan "adopted and reared by persons of high rank" who for reasons unexplained maintained an enduring interest in him and protected him throughout his career. More obvious candidates were people Barry actually knew in his younger life. Lord Albemarle inferred that Barry was "the legitimate grand-daughter of a Scotch Earl," presumably Lord Buchan, while others wondered if his putative uncle, the artist James Barry, might in fact have been his father. Francisco de Miranda has been suggested as another possibility, although Miranda had his own illegitimate children, Leandro and Francisco, whose paternity he cheerfully admitted. Miranda, never one to keep his multifarious sexual conquests a secret, was devoted to their mother, Sarah Andrews, and the four lived together as a family in Miranda's house in London. Given these circumstances, is it likely that Miranda would have concealed the birth of another illegitimate child? Barry's intimacy with Lord Charles Somerset had led one politician to assert that Barry was his son during the sodomy libel in 1824.

There is more romance than realism in these claims. They also signally fail to explain why Barry's parentage was kept a secret. The prejudice against illegitimacy as something socially deviant or risqué bespeaks the values of a later age. To those who peeped at Barry's story retrospectively from behind the stiff skirts of Victorianism, there was something scandalous about uncertain origin and illegitimacy. But Barry was a child of the Romantic age, to whose progressive artists, liberal thinkers, and aristocrats illegitimacy was as common as street whores, smallpox, and men in stockings and heels. Indeed, illegitimacy was rather fashionable among the demimonde. The dissenting artists and aristocrats who populated Barry's milieu were more likely to flaunt than hide a child born the other side of the sheets. The truth—or as close as we ever come to it where James Barry is involved—is perhaps even more curious and dramatic.

The first documented appearance of James Barry, the medical student who became inspector general of hospitals, is in 1809, when he enrolled at the University of Edinburgh as a literary and medical student. James Barry arrived in Edinburgh accompanied by his "guardian," Mrs. Mary Anne Bulkley, who stayed with him until 1810, when she abruptly disappears from Barry's story. Mary Anne was the sister of the irascible James Barry, R.A., whom the young James Barry had referred to as "my late uncle" in his curious letter to Francisco de Miranda in 1810. In this letter Barry had been at great pains to underline that he was "Barry's nephew" and that Mrs. Bulkley was his "Aunt." The only woman to appear in Barry's life at an early age, this indomitable and wily woman occupies a uniquely important position in Barry's story. The Bulkley-Barry connection provides the most enduring clue to Barry's ancestry, suggesting that James Barry's parents were not blue-blooded aristocrats, but greengrocers.

From his arrival at the university, James Barry possessed some very influential and powerful mentors who continued to help him establish his career. His acquaintance with all of these mentors leads back to his namesake, the history painter James Barry. For nearly forty years Mary Anne had been wholly estranged from her brother, but in the six years before James Barry turned up at Edinburgh as a medical student the brother and sister had been uneasily reunited.

In their youth, while her brother pursued his artistic ambitions, Mary Anne stayed in Ireland and married one Jeremiah Bulkley. For a while, life went well for the Bulkleys. They had a son and two daughters, and a prosperous grocery business. But their indigent son proved their undoing. Lavished with the attentions accorded to an elder son, John Bulkley was apprenticed to an attorney in Dublin. He preferred the pursuit of Dublin debutantes to the pursuit of his legal studies. Having fallen in love with a Miss Ward, "a young lady of genteel connections," he begged his parents to settle him with a large farm and pay for an expensive wedding. The Bulkleys conceded, both laying out their capital and mortgaging their future business to meet their son's desires. John Bulkley, however, was no more suited to the land than the law, and repaid the generosity of his doting parents by failing utterly as a farmer, leaving his parents destitute and hounded by creditors.

While her husband made plans to go to the West Indies in an attempt to restore their fortune, Mary Anne decided to throw herself upon the sympathy of her brother for assistance in deflecting her husband's creditors. After forty years, on April 14, 1804, Mary Anne decided to make contact:

My dear brother,

I have always been always [*sic*] very unwilling to trouble you, knowing the multiplicity of your avocations, or you should have often heard from me, while things were going prosperously with me. I thought it sufficient if you heard of me and mine, thro my much esteemed friend Mr Penrose, who I knew corresponded with you. I must say he has been ever kind and attentive to me and mine, but I must now trouble you.

With the bailiffs knocking at the door, Mary Anne's letter explains in detail the series of disasters that had transformed her family's fortunes from prosperity to penury. A note of indignation enters her tone as she shows how their ruin has resulted from her husband's desire to assist their ungrateful son, "whom we strained every point to forward in the World." Her letter ends by revealing the purpose of her appeal to her brother. Her husband, she says, bound over his family's remaining security to the goodwill of his son when meeting his demands:

> He [Jeremiah Bulkley] was ever partial to John (as being an only Son) and wished to make him as respectable as possible. I fear very much he will not act up to the tenor of his, or my expectations, as the property settled upon him was intentionally for the purpose of assisting me, and my two Daughters if occasion required his doing so. I received a letter from him from Dublin a few days ago which gave me great pain, and which I imputed to his youth and want of experience. I also fear he is badly advised, I can not immediately form any opinion respecting himself or his letter, as my Husband is in the Country until he comes home. If he cannot bring his creditors to a settlement and give him time to pay them he purposes to go to the West Indies until something can be done (*a very great fall indeed in the space of about three years from a comfortable situation*) and remit his earning.
>
> With the greatest deference I remain most truly and sincerely, your most affectionate sister,
>
> Mary Anne Bulkley

James Barry read this as a begging letter, and ignored it. Perhaps, understandably, after an intermission of four decades, he was suspicious of his sister's motives and the truth of her tale. Such skepticism might be forgiven coming from the most generous of brothers, but James Barry was not a generous man. Nor was he easy. Temperamental and quarrelsome, he was little predisposed to answer this cry for help from a sister from whom he had long been alienated. There was a painful broken bond between the brother and sister. As a small child, James had begged to sit up late practicing his drawing. His parents had agreed on condition that Mary Anne stayed up watching over him to ensure that his candles did not set fire to the house. He remembered this care with affection, and in the first decade after leaving Ireland had even promised to try and offer financial support to his sister should she need it. It seems, however, that the provincial, mercantile family was unsure how to respond to the budding metropolitan artist, and failed to offer him the news and contact he sought. Affronted, he turned for solace to his new city friends. Nearly half a century later, the soft bruise of emotional injury had hardened into a deep emotional scar. Barry was slow in reaching back across the years to the younger sister for whom he had once cared so much.

Desperate and determined, Mary Anne Bulkley was not to be deflected. Having received no reply, she set out for London two months later with her eldest daughter, Margaret, at her side. Once in London, Mary Anne used her daughter as a go-between. Mary Anne sent the young Margaret with messages to her brother's house, hoping that he would soften toward his niece, whose prospects were now so diminished. There is no record of how Barry received his importunate niece. However, as far as Margaret's mother was concerned, the trip proved unsuccessful, and her attempts to further petition her stubborn brother failed. How much time Barry spent with his niece, and whether or not he introduced her to any of his patrons or friends, chief among them Lord Buchan, Francisco de Miranda, Edward Fryer, and Astley Cooper, remains a matter of speculation.

The fate of Mary Anne Bulkley and her daughters worsened. Unsuccessful in London, they returned to Ireland. By January 1805, they were homeless and on the verge of destitution. Jeremiah Bulkley had joined forces with their son, and the pair had thrown Mary Anne and her two daughters out of their home. With no other quarter to turn to, Mary Anne threw herself once again upon the compassion of her brother. The strain in the relations between brother and sister becomes clear in Mary Anne's formal address:

London, 14 January 1805

Sir

From the message you sent today by Margaret, saying that you would not sign a settlement of the House . . . I have been induced to write to you to explain my reasons for soliciting you for the Deed.

At the Death of my dear father (and only true friend) he left that house and the houses in Crones, and portneys lands (now fallen to the ground) to my Mother, for the term of 31 years, that being the longest lease that could then be given to a Roman Catholic, and the reversion to you, whom he thought would act as his son and my brother, by giving it to me, my *OTHER* brothers being wild, he left me with one hundred pounds, £40 of which was paid after my marriage to my Mother for her Interest of the House. . . . Now as Bulkley has made over that House and my all on my good Son, what proceeding? . . . nothing but a Deed of Settlement drawn on a Stamp in favour of Margaret will do, as Bulkley's Creditors could fall on it if given to me, his debts being over £600—Now Sir Margaret being but 15 years old and of course not of Age, it would be requisite to have a person to take it in trust for her during her Minority, a friend of mine has offered to draw the Deed and take it on Trust for her (Mr Reardon Atty) if you will be so kind as to sign it, if not it will remain with my son for Ever.—You ask why I came to London, sure Sir you could not have deceived yourself so much as to think *I came to BEG from you.*

If indeed you did think so I am convinced this will alter your opinion. Give me leave to propose a single question to you— *WHAT* did you give my Child when she was here last June. Did you ask her to Dinner, in short did you act as an Uncle or as

Christian to a poor unprotected, unprovided for Girl who had not been brought up to think of Labor. And, alas, whose Education is not finished to put her in a way to get decent Bread for herself and whose share has been given to a brother.

I must indeed have lost my reason if I came to you for support. No Sir, I left Ireland because I have been ill-treated there. Thrown out of house and home by a Husband and Son. Good God what could I do if I was to Induster there, the fruits of my Labor would be seized on by Bulkley's Creditors even he would have given them up himself to them. I had no choice left but to starve or come here to try and see you but I would not—nor would I come here now if I knew any other Country. I forget I am speaking to a disinterested person, but I have not said this much for any Interest. No Sir, but as you are a Well Bred Man who knows the World, let you know my reason for coming to London.

I shall no longer intrude on your time but just tell you why I called to you, it was to see you after a period of more than 30 years to see if there was one relation of mine of whom I may ask advice in the World—but Disappointment has attended that and many others of the undertakings of Sir.

Yours &c., Mary Anne Bulkley

PS You will greatly oblige the Daughter of John and Julia Barry if you will sign the deed, it is my last request. Adieu.

Following her previous rejection, Mary Anne harbored no illusions that her brother would offer a warm welcome. Desperate to secure the future of her daughter, she put a clear proposal to her recalcitrant brother. If he would sign over the deed securing Margaret's entitlement to her portion of the Barry inheritance, her future could be guaranteed. This letter reveals the further disasters that had enveloped the already importunate Mary Anne and her two daughters since the previous year.

Dispossessed by both husband and son, transient in an unfamiliar and inhospitable city, she was frantic about the security of her eldest daughter. In the first decade of the nineteenth century a fifteen-year-old daughter of reasonable upbringing was potentially a source of security. Yet Mary Anne Bulkley makes no mention of the marriageability of her eldest daughter. This would have been the obvious solution, yet the protective Mary Anne regards her daughter's future as unavoidably precarious. Is it possible that this obsessive protectiveness betrays a mother's intimate knowledge that there was some defect in her daughter that made marriage an impossibility? Had Mary Anne's own marriage foundered on a troubling family secret about their daughter that, as the marriage came under increasing financial pressure, had become an irresolvable point of contestation between herself and Jeremiah Bulkley?

A possible answer to the question of James Barry's parentage, however, lies not in this letter, but in the missive written the previous year, when Mary Anne had first applied to her brother for assistance. A startling clue to the mystery lies in the postscript to the letter of 1804, which advises James Barry that the letter is written in the hand of his niece Margaret Bulkley:

> PS My Mother is not able to write legible on account of a tremour in her hand, desired me to write for her, my inexperience and so much unaccustomed to letter writing I hope will be accepted by you as an Apology the length, the many faults and errors in this letter.
>
> > By yours Most Affectionately & C,
> > Margaret Bulkley

On a further note of desperation, Margaret Bulkley appends a further postscript, "I am concerned for not being able to ascertain your address with exactness." Beset with anxieties, Mary Anne Bulkley's feeble hand could not steady itself to write this momentous letter to her brother, of whose address even she was uncertain. So she asked her eldest daughter, Margaret, to write it for her. By this act of dictation we have fair copy of the hand of the fifteen-year-old Margaret Bulkley. The writing is studied, laboriously careful—the hand of a teenager preparing a letter in her best script while her anxious mother stands looking critically over her shoulder. What went through Margaret's mind while she transcribed the woes that had befallen her mother, sister, and self—the key subject of this awkward, beseeching letter? The formal tone of the postscript strives for maturity and approval: "my inexperience and so much unaccustomed to letter writing I hope will be accepted by you as an Apology the length, the many faults and errors in this letter."

As one might suspect, there is a clear match between the handwriting of Margaret Bulkley in 1804 and that of James Barry, medical student, who signs the register of Names of Dresser Pupils at Guy's and St. Thomas's in 1812. The capital "B" in "Bulkley" and "Barry," although rendered in a more confident hand in the later version, are identical. The capital "M" in "Margaret" and "M.D." are perfect matches in style. Barry's script and signature on his early reports and correspondence at the Cape retain this consistency with the style of Margaret Bulkley. The carefully drafted *Memorandum of Services,* submitted in a determined attempt to prevent his retirement in 1859, still bears unmistakable resemblance to the younger hand of Margaret Bulkley. The evidence of handwriting is not conclusive. Handwriting can be peculiar to a time, nation, or manner of education as well as an individual person. Nevertheless, the circumstances of the letter form a compelling link between the disappearance of Mary Anne Bulkley's eldest daughter, Margaret, after 1805 and the appearance of the young James Barry at Mary Anne Bulkley's side in 1809.

Mary Anne Bulkley knew that if her portion of the Barry inheritance was signed over to her, her husband's creditors could fall upon it and deny her the final possibility of security for her beloved, strange changeling daughter. Terrified of this outcome, she urgently needed James Barry to sign the deed securing Margaret's inheritance to be held in trust until she reached majority. History is as taciturn as James Barry toward his unfortunate sister when it comes to eliciting a record of the cantankerous artist's response. There is no evidence that James Barry, R.A., met his sister's "last request," but history—his own favorite subject—held a reprimand in store for the painter's lack of compassion. Incompetent at managing his own affairs, Barry died intestate in 1806. As next of kin, Mary Anne Bulkley inherited his estate. It was these funds that perhaps secured an education at Edinburgh for Mary Anne's daughter "to put her in a way to get decent Bread"—disguised as a boy. As it was probably James Barry's money that furnished the young Margaret's legs with the breeches that suited her so much better than petticoats, mother and daughter showed a practical irony in renaming the diminutive but dashing young man after his temperamental uncle. More practically, the calculated adoption of "his" famous relative's name was a passport into a world of patronage and professional progression.

Much has been made of the assistance the young Barry received from august male patrons. The significance of their explicit but mysterious influence in fashioning the fortunes of the young male medical student is beyond a doubt. But Mary Anne Bulkley's maternal persistence and determination were equally important. Abused by her husband and son, rejected by her brother, sheltering a perhaps strangely sexed child on the cusp of puberty, Mary Anne Bulkley well understood the uncertain state of women and social outsiders. It is likely that her buffeting at the rough hands of men played a significant role in the metamorphosis of the rejected, uprooted, and perplexed Margaret Bulkley into the brilliant, dashing James Barry. Margaret Bulkley's body was changing as fast as her family circumstances. There had to be a way to secure both her secret and her future. The solution was logical—one just as likely to be chosen by a mother who could think of only one way to enable her child to survive, as by a group of aristocrats in search of the amusing diversion of an unlikely social experiment.

As we know, Lord Buchan played a crucial role in furthering Barry's prospects, allowing him access to study in his private library during his university vacations. In October 1811, Buchan had also sought to smooth the way over the problem of Barry's unusually youthful appearance, assuring his mentors at Edinburgh: "tho' he is much younger than is usual to take his Degree in Medicine and Surgery yet from what I have observed likely to entitle himself to them by his attainments." Clearly, Barry's immature and rather androgynous appearance was already raising eyebrows as he practiced and developed the role that became his life's part.

Buchan remarks on Barry's youth as an obvious fact, although his exact age remains uncertain. Prior to the compulsory registration of births, ordinary people were used to approximating their own and their family's ages. It is possible that even Barry was himself unsure of his exact birth date. Sadly, there is no note anywhere in his career of his having ever celebrated or marked his own birthday, although it was often remarked about him that he was very fond of attending other people's birthdays and christenings. Equally possible is that he deliberately obscured this information in order to protect the secrecy of his origins, concealing the disappearance from history of Margaret Bulkley. If this was his intention he succeeded. His birth date has been estimated as being sometime during the 1790s. "About 1799" is the only partially legible date scrawled on his statement of service, but even this is an overwritten date, and followed by blotted and scratched-out marks and numbers. Given that Barry became increasingly anxious that his age counted against him as he approached retirement, it has to be admitted that much later in his career he had good reason to try to pass himself off as younger than he actually was. Nevertheless, some have gone with this claim that he was born in 1799, even though this would have made him a rather unlikely eleven years old when he went to Edinburgh. Moreover, 1799 clearly gives the lie to his own statement that he was eighteen when he took his military exams. Mrs. Bulkley claimed that her daughter Margaret was fifteen in 1805, dating her birth to 1790. If Mrs. Bulkley's letter of 1805 can be relied upon, James Barry was in fact nineteen when he arrived at Edinburgh and twenty-one when he graduated.

Certainly Buchan regarded Barry as youthful for his achievements, but this alone does not clarify the degree to which the aging aristocrat was aware of Barry's peculiarities. Buchan himself was predisposed to step across the barricades of sexual difference. In June 1791, he sent the first of his famous "Sophia" letters to the editor of *The Bee,* "a periodical designed for the edification and entertainment of young ladies." In this series of pseudonymous essays, Buchan assumed the persona of a mother expressing her views on female education and the "barbarous" situation of women in contemporary society. The imaginary Sophia offers educational advice to her three daughters and to other mothers. It may be too late for mothers to do anything to remedy the misfortunes of their own "preposterous education," Sophia advises, but they might yet save their daughters. In this persona, Buchan claims:

> Dean Swift's famous letter to a young lady on her marriage, though it is by far the most capital thing I ever saw upon the subject, yet it proceeds upon what I hope I shall be able to prove is a false position; that women are incapable of becoming truly and logically learned, or of applying the fruits of study to useful purposes of society. . . . The whole code of female education must be changed, before Dean Swift's assertion can be verified, or that it can be proved that it would not be infinitely better, that women, in the present state of society, should have . . . an as truly learned institution as men. . . . The rights of men begin now to be everywhere felt, understood and vindicated; by and by, I would fain hope, the rights of our sex will be equally understood, and established on the basis of a new code of education suited to the dignity and importance of our situation in society.

With considerable wit, "Sophia" points out that the faults attributed to ill-educated women are "equally incident to well educated men," while opining that "the education of boys by women is more favorable for the growth of great men." Indeed, she argues, "all the great men of the world have been indebted to this circumstance for their superiority." Sophia regards it as essential that women should "receive every instruction in the sciences and fine arts," as well as in philosophy and literature.

Foreshadowing a metaphor used by feminists, in these essays Buchan speaks of the constraints placed on women of his time as analogous to the practice of Chinese foot-binding:

> As well might the philosophers of China hold the women in that Empire, who are of better condition, cheap, because they cannot walk without difficulty or awkwardness. The men of Europe have crushed the heads of women in their infancy, and then laugh at them because their brains are not so well ordered as they would desire.

If James Barry was indeed Margaret Bulkley, then she was a young girl who exchanged the bondage and trappings of petticoats for the stuffing of masculinity in order to refashion herself into the boy of her dreams. A boy entitled to education, the self-sufficiency of a profession, and liberty of the mind. Whatever the ambiguities of James Barry's origin and body, the fact of his education remains. Barry would free himself from the constraints placed on his physical incarnation by learning all he could about the body and its potential for transformation. Brought up as a girl who was disinherited by her own brother and father, Barry had a deep empathy for the plight of women. The study of medicine would enable him to better understand how to assist them. James Barry, R.A., had been a Romantic artist who studied anatomy to better represent the elements of his figurative art. James Barry, M.D., child prodigy of a raft of heretical Romantic mentors, studied anatomy in order to become an artist of the flesh.

James Barry died in 1865, but Margaret Bulkley had disappeared more than half a century earlier, the last mention of her existence appearing in her mother's letter of 1805. If James Barry was born Margaret Bulkley, it was a fact that he chose utterly to conceal for the duration of his life. He spent the latter years of his life lonely and in penury. He could have chosen—as did many celebrated nineteenth-century cross-dressers—to reveal his deception and make money from the celebrity that would have entailed. But revelation was not the point, nor was it Barry's style. By that act he would have undone the one thing he held most dear above all else—his professional reputation as a surgeon, soldier, and scientist. To reveal himself during his lifetime would have also caused acute embarrassment to the Beaufort family and to the memory of his beloved Somerset.

Standing unprotected in the dock, reliant on his own ingenuity to determine his fate, Barry had once declared: "When I was a boy, I was told that when I began a story, to begin at the beginning and continue to the end." It was a paradox of Barry's life that his beginnings became questionable only after his end. Even if it could be proven beyond a shadow of a doubt that Margaret Bulkley was the girl who became the male medical student James Barry, it does not follow, and this point is crucial, that because Margaret Bulkley was apparently born a girl she was unproblematically female.

Since Barry's death there have been those who have speculated that the doctor might have been something other than a woman or a man plain and simple. In the light of modern medical knowledge about the human body, it is no longer possible to dismiss these claims simply on the grounds that they are a sexist diversion and misogynist detraction from her unprecedented achievements.

Barry is not known to have left any personal diary, memoir, or correspondence commenting on his identity. But the person who was James Barry did, after all, leave some other circumstantial written evidence, and it is beyond a doubt that he—as he preferred to call himself—would disapprove of the fact that for 150 years the possible truth contained in this evidence has not been "confirmed by observations."

Chapter 11

HABEAS CORPUS

We do not even in the least know the final cause of sexuality.
The whole subject is hidden in darkness.

Charles Darwin, "On the Various Contrivances by Which
British and Foreign Orchids Are Fertilised by Insects, and on the
Good Effects of Intercrossing"

Thus, when in fast embrace their limbs were knit,
They two were two no more, nor man, nor woman—
One body then that neither seemed and both.

Ovid, *Metamorphoses*

"I RECEIVED A DIPLOMA DATED IN 1812 AS DOCTOR OF MEDICINE
from the University of Edinburgh," James Barry wrote in his record of
service. This unadorned statement disguised a historic achievement
whose significance does not lie only in the fact that a person born a female had become a qualified surgeon at a time when women were dis-
barred from both medicine and universities. For, if we go by the
evidence of one of the only documents of his early life to which he
would confirm authorship, Barry did not study only to become someone else; he studied medicine to learn more about himself.

To acquire his degree from Edinburgh, Barry had to present an original thesis examined by leading scientific teachers and thinkers of the

day. Between terms, he made use of the legendary libraries of his progressive patrons Francisco de Miranda and Lord Buchan. He worked hard on this forty-page dissertation, his diligence noted approvingly by Lord Buchan, who observed how earnestly Barry was concentrating on the project while he was at Dryburgh Abbey in the summer of 1811. For nearly two hundred years, Barry's thesis has laid gathering dust in the Edinburgh archives. Yet its content is probably the single most significant clue to his identity that Barry knowingly left to posterity.

We will never know all we want to about James Barry, for the simple reason that he did not wish us to know. Barry was probably born and brought up as a female. He entered adolescence as a girl, and emerged from it metamorphosed into a young man. His fantastic transformation is not, in fact, so very unusual. Today, medical science proceeds on the basis that most mixed-sex babies can be identified at birth, although it is still not uncommon for intersexual subjects to experience the manifestation of their difference at puberty, or even later in life. Modern scientists are increasingly willing to admit that human sex is a process of dynamic development. In short, we are not born with a sex, we develop into it. In some intersexual people, the unusual reproductive or genital organization is manifestly visible on the surface of the body, in others it is not. Modern technologies that enable medicine to peer inside the human body to detect unexpected variation have, in some cases, made possible the detection of intersexuality earlier in life. To Barry, born toward the end of the eighteenth century, no such scrutiny was available. Western cultures have become rigidly organized around the unquestioned belief in two sexes. Yet history throngs with people who, apparently born into one sex, developed into another either during puberty or sometimes later in their adult lives. In the majority of recorded cases of the discovery of intersexuality, hernia plays a key role in the drama of revelation.

Hernia was the subject on which Barry chose to write his thesis and be examined:

Few diseases are more important than Hernia, whether we consider the frequency of its occurrence, or the distressing and often fatal symptons which accompany it: and there is none which calls for more anatomical science, more care and more experience and judgment in applying the skills necessary to remove or alleviate it.

Barry's thesis was centrally concerned with the instance of hernia in *females*. An uncommon coincidence presents itself. Barry, whose life turned out to be so ambiguous after his death, chose to write on the one condition that led most consistently to the discovery of an error of sexual definition. As Alice Dreger explains, "Supposed hernias in supposed women which turned out to be recently descended testicles more frequently than any other condition led to the discovery of an error of sex." Suspected hernias and real hermaphrodites go together.

This common twinning of hernias and hermaphrodites can be illustrated through just a handful of some of the most well-known cases. On February 9, 1886, a forty-two-year-old Belgian domestic servant, Sophie, presented herself at her local clinic, seeking help for a sexual problem. She explained her predicament to Professor Michaux, on duty at the clinic that day. She had been married for two months to her first husband and, try as he might, Sophie's husband could not sufficiently penetrate her vagina to his satisfaction. Did the doctor know what was wrong with her, and could he help resolve the problem? On close inspection of Sophie's genital region, Michaux discovered that she had an uncommonly large clitoris, ending—like a penis—in a glans. Her labia contained "at least one" testicle. In terms reminiscent of Florence Nightingale's tangled syntax on hearing the news of Barry's "revelation" as a woman after death, Michaux announced to the stunned Sophie, "But my good woman, you are a man!" Inquiring into Sophie's past, Michaux discovered that her parents had some doubts about her sex when she was born and had taken her to a doctor who confessed that he could not yet determine Sophie's sex, and that they should return when the child was a little older. Fearing their child might be damaged by his further investigations, Sophie's parents did not return. Formulating the opinion that she must be female because her genitals looked feminine, they raised her as a girl. Early in her twenties Sophie developed what she thought to be a hernia, and from that time onward had worn supportive bandages. According to Michaux, what Sophie thought was a hernia was in fact a descended testicle. Satisfied with her otherwise happy marriage and life as a woman, Sophie ignored Michaux's admonitions and decided to continue her life as a woman. Was the young Margaret Bulkley at some point confronted with a Michaux figure declaring her to be other than she thought? Or was her secret known only to her family?

In the late nineteenth century, the Polish gynecologist Franciszek Neugebauer told a similar story of a German woman who presented herself to a Professor Berthold with an inguinal hernia. When Berthold informed her of his discovery that she was in fact a hermaphrodite, she "blushed to her forehead and in outraged modesty would not believe the Professor's statement." Jean Samuel Pozzi, one of France's most famous nineteenth-century hermaphrodite experts, reported a case of mistaken sex where the error was discovered only during a hernia operation: "If the appearance of the internal organs in a painful double hernia had not necessitated an operation, one would never have been able to suppose that this woman carried testicles, and consequently was a man."

In 1892, a Frenchwoman, Louise-Julia-Anna, presented herself to a Dr. Reumeaux requesting treatment for an inguinal hernia. His examination revealed testicles and what he decided looked like a small penis. Thinking of herself as a woman, Louise-Julia-Anna insisted on her femininity. Reumeaux asked her to accept a referral to his colleague Dr. François Guermonprez for a second opinion. Guermonprez endorsed Rumeaux's findings, and insisted that Louise-Julia-Anna must give up her pretense of being a woman. Troubled as she was by the confusing revelations, her clinician revealed that Louise-Julia-Anna shed "not a tear, not a sigh, not the least vestige of an attack of nerves! There was nothing of that profound distress of a true woman found in the presence of an event which reverses her life all at once." In fact, Guermonprez concluded, she took the news with "a firmness thoroughly virile," proving, in his view, that his diagnosis was right and she was in fact a "true male"!

Another French doctor, Debout, took an entirely different course of action. Presented with "as it first appeared" a young girl complaining of an aching hernia, Debout diagnosed that the girl was in fact a boy, unaware of his true state. Debout decided not to inform the patient of his discovery, and instead made the patient "a custom bandage to relieve her pain so that she could return to her occupation of weaver."

An earlier example of an error of sex discovered through the complaint of hernia arose in the famous case of Gottlieb Göttlich, who turned his intersexuality into a lucrative career in the 1830s. Born in 1798, christened Marie Rosine Göttlich, and raised a girl in the Saxon village of her birth, Marie Rosine's sex was exposed to doubt when at the age of thirty-three she sought help for an "apparent double hernia." Medics concluded "that the supposedly herniated organs were in fact descended testicles." Göttlich was ordered to dress in men's clothes and rename himself Gottlieb. Equipped with his new legal status as male, Gottlieb Göttlich launched himself into a career traveling around Europe in the early 1830s, offering himself to medical schools and eminent physicians for examination. Alice Dreger records:

> At medical schools he stripped and was examined by dozens—and perhaps ultimately hundreds—of men of science and medicine who came to see this curious case and render their often-conflicting opinions as to Göttlich's "true sex." His customers included such luminaries as Blumenbach, P. D. Handyside, Sergeant-Surgeon to the Queen Sir Astley Cooper, Robert Knox and Robert Grant.

Astley Cooper was Britain's leading expert on the treatment of hernia. Göttlich's hermaphroditism was of great interest to him. The publication of his *Anatomy and Surgical Treatise of Inguinal and Congenital Hernia* between 1804 and 1810 was the culmination of tireless dissection and experimental operations. In the borrowed words of William McKinnon, Cooper was interested in men, women, and hermaphrodites. In 1829 he published a *Treatise on the Diseases of the Breast,* the first of its kind. Ahead of his time, Cooper continued to advocate radical mastectomy throughout his career. Turning his attention to the testicles, Cooper published his *Observations on the Structure and Diseases of the Testis* in 1830, and in 1845 a cutting-edge work, *On the Anatomy of the Breast.*

But above all, Cooper revolutionized the treatment of and surgery for hernia, and was legendary for the dexterity with which he performed this most tricky of procedures without asepsis or anesthetic. Prior to Cooper, many types of hernia were classified as potentially fatal. In his lecture on hernia delivered to the medical students of Guy's and St. Thomas's, Cooper explained the arousal of his interest in the subject:

> When I was sixteen or seventeen years of age, on hearing a lecture in this theatre, I discovered that I was myself the subject of this complaint. As soon as I felt satisfied of this fact, I could attend no more to the lecture. I went home, threw myself on the bed with my legs elevated against the bedpost and remained in this position until Mr Cline [his lecturer and landlord] returned. I requested to see him the moment he entered. I then told him that I had a swelling for some time, and after hearing his lecture I was sure that it was a hernia. Mr Cline laughed and gave me a common truss. I wore it continuously for three years, at the end of which time there was no appearance of the hernia. I would not leave it off, but wore it for two years more, and from that time to this I have never had the least appearance of the complaint. The truss should be worn night and day, if not it cannot produce adhesions of the walls of the sac.

Despite Henry Cline's amusement at his student's seeming hypochondria, Cooper's self-diagnosis of the condition that he was to become so famous for treating was many years later proved correct. Cooper left a detailed request for the conduct of his own postmortem, in which he "directed that special attention be paid to four points: a cured oblique inguinal hernia; a cured umbilical hernia; some suspected phthisis in his youth; and an inability to sleep on his left side." The postmortem report states that Cooper wore a truss from the age of nineteen to twenty-five and confirms "the evidence is definite that Astley Cooper carried the remains of a true congenital hernia."

As a student at Guy's and St. Thomas's apprenticed as pupil dresser to Astley Cooper, Barry, of course, heard this famous lecture. Having written his own qualifying thesis on hernia, Barry had a burning ambition to work with Cooper, whose research he had gamely questioned in his university research. Cooper and James Barry, R.A., had been great friends to the end of the latter's life. We can never know whether Barry introduced his nephew—or niece—to Cooper prior to 1809. At the very least Cooper recognized the young James Barry's name as a mark of his progressive credentials. Given the friendship between the two adult men, if Cooper had never previously met the younger James Barry, what did he make of the fact that this brilliant and brash student was a previously unmentioned nephew of his old friend? Or is it possible that Astley Cooper knew exactly who James Barry the younger was?

Whatever truth may or may not be buried in this conjecture, mutual fascination with hernia and a shared relation to James Barry, R.A., formed a connection between the young Dr. James Barry and one of nineteenth-century Britain's greatest—and most dandified and urbane—surgeons. Barry embarked on his project on hernia before he worked with Cooper, which raises the question of what sparked his own interest in the complaint. Cooper had been motivated to develop the study of hernia as a result of suffering himself from the condition. Research from self-experimentation is a long-established tradition in medicine. Cooper's own venerated teacher, John Hunter, was widely reputed to have deliberately infected himself with pus from a patient suffering from gonorrhea in order to advance his groundbreaking work on venereal diseases. Who, apart from the corpses he learned at Edinburgh to dissect, was the subject of Barry's study of hernia? Was Barry's own thesis "confirmed by observations" of which he was the self-diagnosed subject?

The circumstantial evidence suggesting that Barry knew that he was on the boundaries of the explicable lies in his pursuit of a career in medicine. Both as a student and a qualified professional, he worked obsessively on anatomy, dissection, surgery, gynecology, obstetrics, midwifery, and sexually related diseases. Many of these obsessions can be seen in embryonic form in his thesis on hernia.

Defined as the protruding of an organ or a part of an organ through the wall that normally contains it, hernias can occur in several different parts of the body. The *Edinburgh Medical and Physical Dictionary,* published four years before he began working on his thesis, offers this definition of Barry's object of study:

> Hernia Cruralis; the crural or femoral hernia. There is no difference between an inguinal and crural hernia, but what arises from the places where they are formed. Men are most subject to inguinal, and women to crural hernia, proceeding from the figure of the pelvis which is largest in women.

This question of the formation and dimensions of the female pelvis was, as will be seen, a matter with which Barry's thesis was much preoccupied. The anatomical regions most affected by hernia were also those commonly taken to determine sex itself:

> The parts of the human body in which herniae usually appear are the groin, scrotum, labia pudenda, the upper and fore part of the thigh, the umbilicus, and different points between the intestines of the abdominal muscles. . . . From these circumstances of situation and contents, all the different appellations are derived by which herniae are distinguished. Thus they are termed inguinal, femoral, umbilical, and ventral; from their appearing in the groin, scrotum, thigh, naval, or belly.

Like every conscientious student, Barry set out on his journey through the crural hernia by establishing the existing body of work in the field. He named Verheyen's 1693 anatomy, Giovanni Battista Morgagni, the Spanish surgeon Gimbernatus, and Bernhard Siegfried Albinus as pioneers in the field. Albinus, who also republished Vesalius's anatomical works, was known in particular for his lavishly illustrated work on the bones, muscles, and *gravid uterus*. Barry, of course, also paid proper homage to contemporary experts in the field, among them some of his own tutors, Monro, Hey, and Lawrence, acknowledging their contributions to the study of hernia and then swiftly—and gamely—moving on to illustrate and question the shortcomings in their work with his own unique observations. Central to his thesis was the argument that crural hernia, which affected mostly women, was an inadequately studied subject.

The elements of the body that concerned Barry in his thesis are anatomically described as the deep crural arch, intercrural fibers, intercrural fascia, and crural muscles. These are situated over a large area of the body, from the ankles, up the legs, to the thigh where the femur pierces into the lower abdomen. The femoral and abdominal regions intimately connected to the reproductive organs were the focus of Barry's attention. Femoral, or crural, hernias occur near the groin area, in or near the leg crease, and are much more common in females. As Barry correctly observed,

> This species occurs more often in women than men on account of the greater size of the crural arch and the breadth of the adjacent internal pubic edge. Morgagnus who carried out anatomical investigations says that he never encountered crural hernia except in women.

Barry repeated the view established by his sources that the femoral defect is very similar anatomically to that found in inguinal hernias, and as femoral hernias can occur simultaneously with inguinal hernia it can be difficult to differentiate clinically between them.

The problem of differentiation was a central aspect of Barry's argument. At the heart of his thesis is a close comparative anatomy of the reproductive zones in men and women. Barry observes in careful detail the thick and strong texture of the crural arch and the way it stretches between spinal base and pelvic bone, noting, "It is accepted that because of the greater width of the pelvis, this part is longer and slacker in woman than man." Sliding inexorably toward the places where these crural structures interface with the reproductive components of the body, Barry describes "the entrance to the reproductive passage which is a spermatic funnel in a man and the ligaments of the rounded uterine enclosure in woman." He examines the "tendonous segments" of the "crural vagina" or sheath containing the "large receptacle" (uterus) of female reproduction and explores the physical connections between this, the pelvic floor and the large muscles of the upper femur. All this interarticulation of reproductive body parts leads him to the triangular pubic area, and an internal exploration of the vagina:

> Exploring the vagina there seem to be tendonous segments that pass between the receptacle itself and the invisible sexual parts which together are attached to the crural arch and the adjacent bones.

Having offered up the results of his anatomical inquiry, Barry analyzes the causes, types, and recommended treatments for crural hernia occurring in women. Following the precedent established for inguinal hernia, Barry argues that "the causes of crural hernia are divided into predispositions and those produced by stimulation." In other words, congenital crural hernia and those caused by the accidents of life:

> Amongst the former are counted:—
> everything which increases the pressure on the abdominal
> organs,
> the particular structure of the female pelvis,
> the resistance of the crural arch to the strains of child-birth,

physical weakness however induced,

the relaxing effects of warm regions, in which Hernia seems to
  occur seriously

and more often and to reach greater size than in Northern
  regions.

Turning to the "induced causes" of crural hernia, Barry counts "all that
occur suddenly," the consequence of violent coughing, vomiting, or
"anything at all which gives rise to strong or sudden action of the di-
aphragm or the abdominal muscles." Indeed, he laconically remarks, "it
is amazing what tiny causes produce a Hernia." Barry is most critical
of women's fashions when discussing the social triggers of hernia: "The
other cause of crural hernia above all in women is the custom, now fortunately rarely used, of tightly lacing the waist which displaces the internal organs of the abdomen, restructuring its cavity and thereby
adding force to the existing causes."

Those who ride a lot, Barry argues, are more prone to this painful condition: "The inhabitants of South America, spending a great part of their
time on horseback, with legs stretched out, are greatly liable to Hernia."
This, Barry argues, proves Livy's view that those who gallop around on
horseback have a higher likelihood of suffering from hernia. Barry himself was, of course, a keen equestrian all his life, riding everywhere and
over great distances for both work and pleasure. On this topic, he describes the following story regarding Marcus Servilius and his hernia:

In Livy an opinion is expressed which shows that horseriding was
considered by the Romans to be a cause of Hernia, indicating with
what contempt that warlike people looked on someone unskilled
in warfare. Marcus Servilius, while proclaiming his just deserts in
public, is said to have taken off his clothes and explained in what
war he had received each of his wounds. While he was showing
openly what perhaps should have been covered up, a swelling in
his groin provoked laughter in those near him. He then said,
"What you are laughing at I acquired from sitting on a horse day

and night; and I am no more ashamed of it, nor do I regret it, any more than these scars, since it never hampered me from serving the state at home or as a soldier."

Here, then, is the young Barry citing a story about a public servant and warrior exposing himself and his hernia to the crowd and, when laughed at, defending himself in true Roman style.

Having condemned corsets and warned against the hazards of child-birth and the effects of horseriding, Barry advises that treatment is divided between the options of medicinal remedies and radical surgery. Among recommended medications he includes a prescription of a magnesium sulphate compound, opium, and a regular course of tobacco enemas. He points out that the patient should be advised that the side effects of large doses of opium and the tobacco douches will include "nausea, spasms, vertigo, vomiting," and, in the case of the opium, "ample sedation."

As described by Cooper, the treatment of these kinds of hernia most commonly involved also the use of trusses, supports, and bandaging. This raises an interesting question about the "three pillows of a particular description" about whose loss Barry was so frantic as he passed through the Cape on his way to St. Helena. Do these "pillows" provide some clue to Barry's ambiguous reference to "the peculiar circumstances which severe Accidents have placed me"?

Barry's thesis is unerringly preoccupied with distinguishing and naming body parts. In particular, he scrutinizes, contemplates, and obsesses over the significance of the size, dimensions, and peculiarities of that ubiquitous signifier of sexual difference, the female pelvis. The thesis is also deeply concerned with the dangers presented by childbirth to those either suffering from, or susceptible to, crural hernia. Barry writes of the agonizing tearing caused by childbirth that can leave women with a range of herniated conditions. For those already suffering from the problem, giving birth was to risk the almost certainly fatal danger of rupture to the hernia. Barry's thesis, the culmination of his extensive extracurricular study of midwifery, gynecology, and obstetrics, provides evidence of his passionate desire to become the champion of reproductive women. Barry's detailed disquisition on the question of female reproduction carries with it a sense of medical urgency—women are misdiagnosed by doctors, and consequently placed in peril at childbirth. Placed in this context, it can be seen that the successful cesarean performed by Barry in 1826 was far from an accident of necessity. Barry had been thinking about the possibility of achieving childbirth without passage through the birth canal for a long time.

There are many clues in this thesis to Barry's awareness of the problem of conclusively establishing sexual difference. These are shown in the extended contemplation of comparative anatomy offered by the essay and by the fact that it was not possible to study the classical texts on sexual difference without reading extensive theorization on the question of hermaphroditism or indeterminate sex. Such concepts were an integral part of the very possibility of being able to discuss the definition of sex in the first place.

Barry's education made him aware of the classical debate over how sex was determined and how many sexes there were. Early scientific texts laid a great deal of emphasis on the influence of temperature in the determination of sex. Men were hot. Women were cool. Masculine women or feminine men were warm. Sexual difference was imagined as a continuum of variation, not a matter of a few distinct categories. Aristotle argued that it was the heat of the heart, not the genitalia, that determined masculinity and femininity. The significance of heat in producing the different sexes continued on into medieval thought. Inheriting the classical model, medieval manuscripts argued that the heat on the right side of the uterus engendered males, while the fetus developing in the cooler left side of the womb would become a female. Fetuses developing toward the middle would grow into womanly men or manly women. This theory of the "continuum of heat" was conjoined with the notion that the uterus contained seven discrete chambers: the three on the right were assigned to males, the three on the left to females, and the central chamber produced hermaphrodites. Although many of these notions of classical theory were progressively challenged, some of their basic assumptions could—surprisingly—still be seen in theories of sexuality constructed in the late-twentieth-century age of biomedicine. There are numerous contemporary examples of august theories of sexuality that claim that there are seven degrees of separation between the truly manly man and the womanly woman, still guided by this classical model of conceptualizing sexual variation.

The influence of these classical notions of the construction of sexuality can still be clearly detected in Barry's thesis, which is a curious interlacing of his own practical experience of dissection with classical theories and textbook notions of sexual difference. Morbid anatomy was a subject in which Barry was utterly absorbed. There is also an implied third party of his study: the unidentified subject prodded, poked, and squeezed to explore the genital and reproductive conformation of the living body: "Exploring the vagina there seem to be tendonous segments that pass between the receptacle itself and the invisible sexual parts which together are attached to the crural arch and the adjacent bones."

Galen, the single most influential force on the birth of Western medicine, disputed the Aristotelian belief that, whatever their manifold forms of physical variation, all humans were composed of relative quantities of two principles: femaleness and maleness. For Galen, hermaphrodites belonged to an intermediate sex of their own. It is not clear from his thesis what James Barry believed. But it is clear that he was familiar with these competing theories of sex, cited throughout his thesis.

There is nothing new about intersexuality. It reaches back into the earliest founding myths of many global cultures and has long preoccupied religious, legal, and medical systems. European concepts of intersexuality derived from the Greek myths that encompassed the form of Hermaphroditus, child of Hermes and Aphrodite; early biblical interpretations of the creation myth that understood Adam to have been a hermaphrodite who divided into male and female only after his fall from paradise; and Plato's sexual schema, in which humanity is actually missing its third sex. His belief was that there were originally three sexes but the third gradually disappeared over time.

The word *hermaphrodite* comes from the Greek myths of Hermes and Aphrodite, who gave birth to a child who was so completely a replica of both of them in every way that being unable to determine the sex of the child for sure, they named it Hermaphroditus. In another version of the myth—adopted famously by Ovid—Hermes and Aphrodite gave birth to a son so exquisitely beautiful a water nymph fell passionately in love with him and interwove her body into his so that they became one. Today it is still possible even for an obstetrician equipped with the artillery of modern technology to be uncertain of the sex of an infant when it is born. Consequently, such a child is reared as a girl or a boy depending on the diagnosis of the sex at birth, or the decision of the parents. Unlike their classical antecedents, Hermes and Aphrodite, modern parents are advised to secure their ambiguous children with one sex—male or female. When James Barry successfully delivered Wilhelmina Munnik of a baby by cesarean section, it fell to Barry to announce that Mrs. Munnik had given birth to a son. In the case of James Barry himself, who determined the sex of the child whose origins became so shrouded in mystery—a midwife, a doctor, or his parents? However the decision was made at this stage, it was later radically reversed.

Yet if it was a unique set of physical differences Barry had to confront and learn to live with, it set him apart from his contemporaries. From the point that Barry became aware that his body was a strangely sexed anomaly, he would have understood that he must hide himself in order to live a normal life, and not be turned into a medical freak. Safer by far to become a medic himself and hide behind the guise and growing professional authority of the scholar-gentleman-surgeon than run the risk of becoming a specimen himself, exposed to the curiosity of medical science. It was the perfect disguise.

Moreover, Barry could study himself unimpeded. The budding surgeon was required to develop a sharp observant eye, exacting and acute to the activities and behavior of the human body. Such skills of observation and capacity for understanding imitation were essential to the role of the actor and surgeon alike. For Barry, the realms of medicine and myth were intertwined by his studies of philosophy and classical literature that ran parallel to his scientific courses. He was exposed to a classical realm teeming with tales of metamorphosis, morphology, and parthenogenesis that was very close to the contemporary scientific and artistic preoccupations of the age. Enlightenment medicine was obsessed with strange bodies, aberrant growths, physiological changes, monstrosity, and grotesquerie. The textbooks from which Barry learned were peopled by detailed illustrations of hermaphrodites, strangely stylized flowering pregnancies, people uncommonly tall, and people strangely small. Such was the stuff of myth and modern medicine. The surgeon was a modern Ulysses, offered the possibility of exploring the interior wonders of a hitherto unknown world.

Human beings have not always been required to have only one true sex. For centuries it was agreed that hermaphrodites had two. There is evidence that they were tortured and persecuted in classical and premodern societies. However, there is also a long history of court and religious records dating from the early modern period onward that tell a different story. In cases where the two sexes were juxtaposed, in whatever variable proportions, both canon and civil law decreed that it was the duty of the father or godfather to decide when the child was baptized which sex should be retained. Once adults, hermaphrodites who wished to marry were free to decide for themselves whether they wished to continue in the sex consigned to them or switch to the other. The most important requirement was that once they had avowed which sex they preferred, it must be kept until the end of their lives. Those who changed their decision would be declared and punished as sodomites. It was those who changed their mind about their sex who were subjected to the legal and social condemnation associated with the history of hermaphroditism.

Sometimes the courts accommodated a compromise. In 1629, an American court in Virginia declared Thomas Hall's claim that he was both female and male as valid: "it shall be published," announced the court, "that all inhabitants around shall take notice thereof and that he shall go clothed in man's apparel, only his head will be attired in a coiffe with an apron before him." One of the most celebrated cases of cross-dressing in Britain during Barry's youth was the Chevalier D'Eon, a French diplomat in London who was the subject of frequent betting among Regency fops as to "his" true sex. Most suspected that D'Eon was a woman who periodically dressed as a man, but when he died the opposite was found to be the case. So fascinated were people by the Chevalier's sex that one of his testicles was removed and later purchased at auction by the Royal College of Surgeons for the sum of ten shillings and sixpence.

The possibility that a girl might turn into a boy was in fact more easily accommodated by earlier models of sexuality still influential in Barry's day. In the early nineteenth century, sexuality was still largely understood as being a state of inherent doubleness within one body rather than division between two. Social notions of the difference between the sexes have not been always as they are today. The key difference in attitudes to sexual difference between the genders in the early nineteenth century was that women were seen as inferior copies of men, rather than their diametrical sexual opposites. Prevailing notions of sexual difference were still heavily shaped by the belief that women were imperfect, inferior versions of men. In the Renaissance, human life was seen not in sets of binaries but as part of a continuum in which men were the incarnation of physical perfection and women inferior copies; humanity was a sliding scale of perfection on which women slid pretty much to the bottom.

Since Galen, the prevailing belief had been that female genitals were merely an inverted version of the male genitals. "Turn outward the woman's, turn inward, so to speak, and fold double the man's, and you find them the same in both in every respect," he wrote. Woman and man were perfectly comparable mirror images of each other. Even though Fallopius published a challenging account of the female genitalia in the 1560s, and the discovery of ovaries in the late seventeenth century challenged the common belief in female testicles, it was not until the nineteenth century that the specific function of the ovaries was properly understood.

In this different sexual reality where the uterus was analogous to the scrotum and the vagina to the penis, stories of friction and ambiguity between the boundaries of the sexes abounded. Montaigne's travel journals, Shakespeare's plays, folktales, and songs are full of shadow stories in which women successfully pass themselves off as men. These proliferating stories make sense in the context of a culture where it was generally believed that women literally carried within them the equipment of masculinity, inverted and concealed. Given the right motivation of desire or circumstance, this mirror-image masculinity might just slip out. It was the role of society and the law to intervene and repress its all too likely physical expression.

The notion that women were defective men prevailed through the eighteenth century. But this natural order of human bodies that was utterly unlike our own was challenged by the advent of modern medicine.

When surgery and anatomy began to obsessively probe the shape and workings of the pregnant body, the belief that women were merely physically inverted versions of men was challenged fundamentally. The reproductive body was discovered to be the area in which female and male bodies, otherwise so alike, most diverged. Attention focused more and more on this reproductive difference, until it became *the* difference. It is fascinating to remember just how very novel these ideas were as Barry embarked on his journey through the human body. The view of men and women as divided by an uncrossable binary division is a very twentieth-century conceit, inherited from the Victorians, who were great lovers of organizing their culture—and other people—around binary divisions and rigid classifications.

In relation to the career of Dr. James Barry, it is strange to consider that it was medicine that had the biggest influence on drawing a firm dividing line between the sexes. People were generally vague about their bodies and knew little about the inner functioning of what lay beneath their outward appearance. And they knew less about what those internal organs looked like. As the anatomists persisted with opening up and revealing the insides of humanity—what Hunter, the father of modern surgery, called "the animal economy"—they focused more and more on the creation of life itself, on the reproductive woman and the process of gestation and childbirth. Anatomical samples of female, male, intersexual, and hermaphroditic genitalia removed from bodies dissected and operated on were preserved and turned into medical preparations for scientific observation and study. These uncanny specimens were central to the training of the scientist and medic. Barry was part of this process: all surgeons were looking for clues about themselves as humans, but he had a particular quest to understand the odd conformation of his body. In an age where there was no sex education and the information passed on by mothers like Mary Anne Bulkley to daughters like Margaret would have been rudimentary at best, he would have had little notion of how very different his own body was until he had the unique opportunity to study others. Or unless someone else told him, as happened to other intersexuals, whose condition had been identified when they presented themselves with a supposed hernia.

As the emotional landscape of Barry's thesis on hernia so eloquently demonstrates, the facts that Barry was born and raised as a girl and that she was intersexual are not mutually exclusive. Barry's thesis is written from the position of someone who identifies with both the physical complexities and social plight of being a woman in a male medical world. Barry's questing and contumacious thesis tackles the key medical authorities of the day. If James Barry himself was indeed the unnamed subject of this startling document of the problems of sexual differentiation, then he speaks in the voice of one who believes he has been wrongly diagnosed. Barry, now dressed and living as man, still felt like a woman. Although over time she grew into her new persona, she could not instantly unlearn the childhood lessons of femininity. A child of indeterminate sex, Barry was a person who grew up as a girl, and was forever driven by the brutal reality of what that meant to an ambitious female yearning to study and travel in the early nineteenth century. Her guise was born equally of economic necessity. Along with her mother and sister she had been disowned by her family and thrown out of her home, and due to her physical condition seemed unmarriageable.

Barry set up his own self-diagnosis in opposition to established medical opinion. Believing himself to be wrongly diagnosed, he made himself the vehement champion of everyone like him—the marginalized, dispossessed, and disempowered. Cloaking himself in the garments of institutional power, Barry stepped into the position of the male doctor with the authority to be a hero to women, children, slaves, prostitutes, prisoners, the insane, and the poverty-stricken. Beneath all the legendary swagger and disguises of Barry's identity these things hold true: he was a scientist and humanitarian who advocated the rights of the people most downtrodden by the advance of nineteenth-century British imperialism and the social inequality and injustice it drew in its wake. Most particularly—and irrespective of whether he was ultimately one himself or not—Barry advanced the medical and professional needs of women.

Doctors would still argue that even with the evidence of his physical body, it would not be possible to conclusively determine the exact nature of Barry's sex from the scanty particulars of his physical remains. But what does remain in the archives of the history of sexuality is the body of a curious text researched and written by one of the most remarkable military surgeons of the nineteenth century. Barry's thesis, like his life, was an intellectual body of his own creation. Taken together with the evidence of his fulsome career and his curious preoccupations, it seems that, after all, James Barry was willing to leave a document that spoke to the future.

EPILOGUE

I began with the desire to speak with the dead.

Stephen Greenblatt, *Shakespearean Negotiations*

I do earnestly wish to see the distinctions of sex confounded in society.

Mary Wollstonecraft, *Vindication of the Rights of Women*

*I*N MY PURSUIT OF JAMES BARRY, I WONDERED OFTEN WHETHER OR not he wished ever to be discovered. The traces of his origins were silted over by the death of his mentors. For the remainder of his life, Barry deflected any inquiry into his family background. As to the secrets of his body, he above all knew well the boundaries of medical knowledge. Social attitudes towards the ambiguity of his sex were not something that would change radically in his lifetime. But did James Barry hope that he might be understood better by a future age?

I began my search for James Barry in search of a postmortem. What I very quickly discovered was that Barry himself did not seem to think that his sex was the most important thing about his own life. James Barry was much more than just the sum of his physical parts. His body conditioned his experiences, but it did not finally determine who he was or what he achieved. This is what makes James Barry a hero.

Curiosity and the desire to witness Barry's resurrection drove me forward. Despite my uneasy feeling of plundering Barry's grave—and at times some of my friends worried seriously that they would find me digging in the dirt at Kensal Green cemetery—it was Barry's own dictum that the truth of principles must be confirmed by observations that led me closer to the end of the threads from which it seemed his life could be unraveled. I followed Jean-Martin Charcot's advice to Sigmund Freud to look at the same things again and again until they themselves begin to speak, and went back to the corpus of Barry's own texts. Barry left plenty of clues for us to find if we look hard enough. They were the practical clues of a scientist and reformer. James Barry was not a poet. He had neither the time nor the predisposition to keep a reflective memoir or write confessional letters. Barry spent more time improving and saving lives than he did cogitating on his own.

It seems likely that Margaret Bulkley considered herself, or was considered by her mother, to be unmarriageable. A teenager brought up in a middle-class mercantile family, she was suddenly thrown out of her home with her mother and her sister by a father who perhaps would not acknowledge her as his own. Margaret Bulkley's options were either menial employment in a role of feminized servitude, or self-display as a medical wonder and a life of sensationalized freakery. James Barry, however, became a university student. The doors of expansive private libraries were thrown open to him. He was encouraged to become an intellectual, to argue, and to equip himself as a sportsman. He was indulged as he played the role of the rake, the dandy, and the smart officer. He could travel unaccompanied wherever he wished. He was utterly self-sufficient and economically independent, and he had complete freedom of movement.

James Barry was never married and he never, it seems, had children. But he was not lonely, penniless, or bored. Although by predisposition an individualistic, idiosyncratic loner, Barry had many friends—some of whom shaped the age in the fields of politics, medicine, and the military. He reached the height of his profession, and performed one of the most famous operations of the nineteenth century. In an age in which women were barred from a proper education or entry to any serious profession, disenfranchised, unable to own their own property in marriage, and legally classified as goods and chattels, Barry stood at the fork in the road that was his body and chose the path that enabled him to determine his own life.

In 1812, Lord Buchan wrote that anxious note to Robert Anderson, Barry's tutor and landlord, requesting him to "look to the Latinity of [Barry's] thesis." Had history only taken more careful note of Buchan's request, the enigma of James Barry might have been debated a little differently. The dedication to Barry's thesis, "Do not consider whether what I say is a young man speaking, but whether my discussion with you is that of a man of understanding," is of course a tantalizing tease, but it is also a warning to look to the work of the student and not just to his appearance. It is Barry's thesis written as a young man that finally reveals his intersexual identity.

Barry, who took up his guise at an early age, understood that gender impersonation was not a matter of false hair and accoutrements of disguise, which would be noticed. Woman-manly and man-womanly in his physical make-up, he accentuated his characteristics that suited a masculine role. From his time at Edinburgh, Barry occupied the mood and temperament of a young, ambitious medical student, eager to pursue his profession and develop scientific knowledge. He identified himself fully with the medical and military institutions he worked in, and whether as a London dandy in the first decades of the nineteenth century or a Victorian gentleman photographed in Jamaica in the early 1860s, he dressed strictly in accordance with the male fashions of the time.

The secret of Barry's success in presenting himself to the world as a man lay in his knowledge that gender was a matter of entitlement: Barry acted this entitlement with every gesture, alone or in company. As he grew older, he grew into this set of habits. Assertiveness, authoritativeness, speaking in contradiction to those who assumed power, were all improper in a nineteenth-century woman. But they were expected of an intellectual, scientific, colonial gentleman.

Sharing the road with Dr. Barry illustrated to me in a very practical way that language is far more of a constraint than the possible pluralities of the physical human body. The telling of James Barry's story is a struggle with pronouns, just as Barry's life was a struggle with pronouns. How limited English seems in allowing us only a male "he," a female "she," or a dehumanizing, debasing "it." From the time that James Barry bid adieu to Margaret Bulkley and entered the university, until his death in 1865, he chose to be identified as a man. Throughout his life Barry fought for his reputation and status as a gentleman, a man of honor, and an Englishman. It was how he wished to be known, and his choice of identity should be respected.

As Barry's biographer, I was overwhelmed by the frequency with which the same question was asked of me: Was Barry, in fact, a man or a woman? I felt like a midwife confronted by expectant parents who wanted the clear, incontrovertible answer to the question that accompanies the birth of all lives: is it a boy or a girl? The desire behind this question was to make Barry's life knowable. Establishing Barry's sex would, the question supposed, confirm both the inner and outer truth of his life. I was fascinated by the fact that my ambivalent responses drew responses of frustration, anger, or disbelief. My both and neither, betwixt-and-between answers were received as if I were, somehow, obstructing the real truth of Barry's identity. In pursuit of Barry's life, I discovered that at the end of the twentieth century it was still necessary for a person—living or dead—to have a "true" sex that lined up with the available categories of human sex around which culture is still organized: all two of them. It seemed that there was no place for uncertainty, and that uncertainty was not a truth.

This desire to reveal Barry, resting on the belief that at the bottom of sex lies the truth about a person, is part of the same impulse that drove those who encountered Barry in his lifetime to rush to reconstruct their memories of him after he died. In so doing, many constructed a persona for him that was draped with telltale signs of what was in fact his well-kept secret. All of these embellished recollections of Barry were driven by the same desire to make the secret truth of his sex *visi-*

ble. The fact is that Barry passed successfully for a lifetime. He got away with it, and those who failed to detect him were unsettled by their misapprehension. From reading these animated recollections of Barry, one gets the sense that everybody knew about his imposture but nobody said anything. While this could easily be construed as a quite believably British response, I am not convinced that the world actively colluded with Barry merely out of politeness. Rather, the ringing tones of those who insisted that Barry's secret was legible betrayed the same anxiety over and again: why was it not immediately evident that he was not what he seemed?

Returning to the observation of objects, I have dwelt on the legend described by Barry's carefully staged photograph, the only image of real similitude left to us. It is a portrait of man, servant, and dog that is made elusive by its very conventionality. Barry's constant companion, his nameless black servant, about whom we know so little, might have been able to tell us something more about the truth of Barry's identity. It is a salutary reminder of the dynamics of race in the nineteenth century that we know so much more about Barry than about the life of his servant, who appears to have traveled around the world with him for three decades. I have wondered, and still do, what was the nature of the relationship between them. In this singular photograph, flanked by his servant arrayed in dress so similar to his own, Barry stands with his hand placed firmly on the head of Psyche. Did the first Psyche, and all who followed her with the same moniker, earn the name as a punning reference to the myth of the beautiful princess who made herself a willing sacrifice to the consummately sexually adept Cupid, who would receive her only in darkness? Psyche first appears in Barry's story at the high point of his relationship with Lord Charles Somerset. Indeed, Psyche may even have been a gift from Somerset. In the myth of their tumultuous path to love, Psyche one night lit an illicit lamp in Cupid's usually darkened bedchamber. So doing, she revealed "the most soft and sweet of monsters," the beautiful god Cupid. Whether a knowing, witty gift from Somerset or Barry's own wry comment on the secrets of his own strangely sexed body, the reference to sex, desire, and beautiful monstrosity is unmistakable. As ever, Barry leaves a tantalizing trail of revelation, partially gratified, always deferred.

Barry was unusual in his physical make-up, and his life was uniquely idiosyncratic and mysterious. Yet in another sense Barry's story of transformation from girl to boy throws into relief a certain ordinary truth about sex that we know yet do not always sufficiently acknowledge. Sex is not altogether something we are born with. Human sexual development is a dynamic developmental system that continues for many years after the birth of a child. As they grow into puberty, adolescence, adulthood, and old age, all boys and girls become progressively sexed. Bodies change and develop. Human beings are not born reproductive; they become so through the evolution of an organic, changing body. Our sex, just like our sexuality, evolves and changes. Normal sex, then, is a developmental, shifting, transitional process. Medical science, that branch of human endeavor to which Barry was so passionately wedded, has progressively normalized the human body in the Western world. The pluralistic diversity of bodies ravaged by untreatable diseases, deformity, and difference have been modified into conformity by inoculation, biomedicine, and greater understanding of nutrition.

Our classical ancestors regarded hermaphrodites as people who confirmed the existence of sexes beyond the binary of male or female. The nineteenth century dwelt in fascination on the body of the hermaphrodite as the exception that could be used to define the rule of what was a normal man or a normal woman. Now, in our modern age, intersexual people claim the right of self-determination of their own sex. Nearly two hundred years ago, James Barry seized this right as his own and lived his life in obdurate contravention of the conventional laws of sex and gender. Whether we identify with Barry through his difference from us or his sameness to us, his life leaves those same laws of sex, gender, and human desire deeply unsettled and disturbed. Barry's life is one among many that tell us it is time to change the ground of our thinking about sex and human difference. James Barry made the rules, he did not follow them. His example encourages us to do the same.

Setting out on the journey through a remarkable life, James Barry bid adieu to Margaret Bulkley. Who can imagine the emotions of this young person as she, now he, consigned the childhood of Margaret Bulkley to a past that was to remain hidden for nearly two centuries? I sit writing the end of Barry's story at the southernmost tip of the world—from which Europe looks turned upside down. A winter wind is blowing across this distended peninsula appended to the bottom of Africa, stirring up a storm where two oceans meet and mingle indistinguishably. It blows through the windswept Cape flats, and through the hopes and dreams of millions of people whose lives are still rocked by the legacy of colonialism the effects of which Barry strove so ardently to ameliorate. Barry never truly belonged anywhere, but it was in his progressive desire to struggle against injustice and inequality that Barry finally can claim his belonging.

Dr. James Barry has haunted me, but will continue to wander the pathways of our imaginations, in search of the spirit of an age, now or in the future, that can accommodate his difference. The world will continue to disagree on the phenomenon of James Barry, but then, as Barry observed, "In fact, the world in general disagrees."

Cape Town, May 2001

ACKNOWLEDGMENTS

This book has been a decade in the making, and along the way I have accrued enormous debts of gratitude to numerous individuals and institutions. Librarians and archivists have generously given of their time and expertise. In particular, I have benefited from the help provided by the staff at the University of Edinburgh Library, the National Library of Scotland, the British Library, the Wellcome History of Medicine Library, the Tate Gallery Library, the London Library, the Guy's and St. Thomas's Hospital Library, the Public Records Office in London, the National Library of Jamaica in Kingston, the Lewis Walpole Library, Yale University, and the National Library of South Africa. I am eternally grateful to Erika Le Roux, who did her utmost to help me with my research at the Cape Archives Repository, and to whose persistence and skill I owe the discovery of new materials on Barry's period at the Cape. Mark Anstee proved himself an able researcher, and I want to thank him for his thoroughness and patience.

I wish to express my immense admiration and thanks to Margaret Reynolds, Midi Achmat, Theresa Raizenberg, Kenneth Parker, Cheryl Gillwald, and Charles Cousins, whose valuable intellectual insights, generous friendship, and unstinting encouragement have helped to make this a better book. Rob Nixon and Anne McClintock have offered unique inspiration and unfailingly wise counsel both on the subject matter of this book and on how to complete it. Neville Hoad has understood and supported its every lateral twist and turn with his usual panache, as well as providing a great research companion in Jamaica. Thanks to Tanya Hudson, Christina Smedley, Chris Woods, Hugh McLean, Pete Wheeldon, and Jordana Moskowitz for fun and for keeping me going. My interest in Barry emerged in the context of an explosion of interest in the history and politics of sexuality and gender in the academy in the 1990s; my thanks here to Alan Sinfield, Jonathan Dollimore, Vicki Lebeau, and Mandy Merck, who—often without knowing it—made rigorous theoretical and analytical contributions to this project and have always challenged me to rethink the basis of my intellectual assumptions. It has also been a pleasure to share a passion for James Barry with Patricia Duncker, whose recent novel *James Miranda Barry* paints a compelling imaginative portrait of Barry's childhood and inner life. For generously sharing their Barry expertise and correcting my mistakes, my thanks also to Professor John Barrell, John Forbes, and Edward Myers. I am very grateful to Nigel Coulton, to whose expert translation of Barry's thesis and keen eye for telling reference I am greatly indebted. Any errors of interpretation, however, remain entirely my own.

This book would not have been possible without Lisa Jardine. She has followed me on my journey with Barry from the very beginning, and the value of her insights and mentoring are beyond measure. He unique Latin scholarship enabled me to crack the code of Barry's life, and her advice and suggestions throughout the highs and the lows have been infallible. My admiration for her is without reserve, and I owe her a debt of gratitude I can never repay.

I also wish to thank all my parents—Karin, Don, Sarah, and Helmut—for their unconditional support for me throughout the process of writing *Scanty Particulars*, and for the education that made it possible.

It is a daunting prospect for any writer to hand over her manuscript to another writer whose work she greatly admires. This is the situation I found myself in with David Ebershoff, my brilliant editor at Random House. His experience and finesse have made this a far better book, and I have learned a great deal from working with him. I am very grateful to my agent, Maggie Pearlstine, who had proved herself Dr. Barry's most indefatigable champion. My thanks also to the team at Random House: Judy Sternlight, Benjamin Dreyer, Evan Camfield, Kate Norris, J. K. Lambert, Molly Lyons, and Gaby Bordwin, whose efficiency and professionalism have made working on a transatlantic project as easy as if we lived in the same city.

For the last ten years, Jerry Brotton, Zackie Achmat, and Jack Lewis have lived Barry's life with me. I wish to thank them for their support and unending intellectual insights and for putting up with my endless ramblings about Barry. Jack Lewis and Zackie Achmat have been the best of friends and most fearsome of critics. Their unceasing questioning and demands for elucidation have constantly forced me back to the search for truth and greater clarity. They goaded me just when I needed it most, and were always willing to give me their precious time to argue over the minutiae of the Barry phenomenon. Finally, I would like to thank my partner and soulmate, Jerry Brotton, without whom *Scanty Particulars* would never have been completed. He has read and commented on every page of this book, offered unending help and advice, and willingly shared his life with Dr. Barry. Always my greatest champion and the guardian of my better self, his love and unflagging support have guided this book every step of the way. My love and admiration for these three people is without reserve, and it is to this fair triumvirate of wits—Jack Lewis, Zackie Achmat, and Jerry Brotton—that this book is dedicated.

SELECT BIBLIOGRAPHY

I am indebted to the authors of the following books:

Apuleius. *The Golden Ass* or *Metamorphoses*. London: Penguin, 1998.

Baker, Rachel. *The First Woman Doctor: The Story of Elizabeth Blackwell MD*. London: Harrap & Co, 1946.

Barthes, Roland. *S/Z*. New York: Hill & Wang, 1974.

Bird, Wilberforce. *State of the Cape of Good Hope in 1822*. London: John Murray, 1823.

Blackburn, Robin. *The Overthrow of Colonial Slavery 1776–1834*. New York: Verso, 1988.

Brock, R. C. *The Life and Work of Astley Cooper*. Edinburgh: E. & S. Livingston, 1952.

Burrows, Edmund. *A History of Medicine in South Africa*. Cape Town/Amsterdam: A. A. Balkema, 1958.

Davila, Vincente, ed. *Archivo del General Miranda*. 24 vols. Caracas: Academia Nacional de la Historia, 1929–50.

Dillon, Sir William Henry. *A Narrative of My Professional Adventures*. London: Navy Records Society, 1955–56.

Dreger, Alice Domurat. *Hermaphrodites and the Medical Invention of Sex*. Cambridge, Mass.: Harvard University Press, 1998.

Dunker, Patricia. *James Miranda Barry*. London: Serpent's Tail, 1999.

Ebershoff, David. *The Danish Girl*. London: Weidenfeld & Nicolson, 2000.

Elkins, James. *Pictures of the Body: Pain & Metamorphosis*. Stanford, Calif.: Stanford University Press, 1999.

Fausto-Sterling, Anne. *Sexing the Body: Gender Politics and the Construction of Sexuality*. New York: Basic Books, 2000.

Feinberg, Leslie. *Transgender Warriors*. Boston: Beacon Press, 1996.

Fenton, Mrs. *The Journal of Mrs Fenton 1826–1830*. London: Edward Arnold, 1901.

Foucault, Michel, ed. *Herculine Barbin*. New York: Pantheon Books, 1980.

Fryer, Edward. *The Works of James Barry, Esq., Historical Painter*. London: 1809.

Gray, Henry. *Gray's Anatomy*. New York: Gramercy, 1977.

Gutsche, Thelma. *The History and Social Significance of Motion Pictures in South Africa, 1895–1940*. Cape Town: Howard Timmins, 1972.

Havelock Ellis, Henry, and John Addington Symonds. *Studies in the Psychology of Sex*. Vol. 1, *Sexual Inversion*. London: Wilson & Macmillan, 1897.

Holt, Thomas. *The Problem of Freedom: Race, Labor, and Politics in Jamaica and Britain, 1832–1938*. Baltimore: Johns Hopkins University Press, 1992.

Juta, Réné. *Cape Currey*. New York: Henry Holt, 1920.

Kendal Millar, Anthony. *Plantaganet in South Africa: Lord Charles Somerset*. Cape Town, London, New York: Oxford University Press, 1965.

Keppel, George Thomas, Earl of Albemarle. *Fifty Years of My Life*. Vol. 2. London: Macmillan, 1876.

Laidler, P. W. *The Annals of the Cape Stage*. Edinburgh: William Bryce, 1926.

Laidler, Percy, and Michael Gelfland. *South Africa: Its Medical History 1652–1898*. Cape Town: Struik, 1971.

Las Casas, Count Emmanuel de. *Mémorial de Sainte Helene: Journal of the Private Life and Conversations of the Emperor Napoleon at Saint Helena*. Vol. 4. London: Henry Colburn & Co., 1823.

Mostert, Noël. *Frontiers: The Epic of South Africa's Creation and the Tragedy of the Xhosa People*. London: Jonathan Cape, 1992.

Newman, Karen. *Fetal Positions: Individualism, Science, Visuality*. Stanford, Calif.: Stanford University Press, 1996.

Nightingale, Florence. *Notes on Nursing: What It Is and What It Is Not*. London: Harrison, 1860.

Packenham, Thomas. *The Scramble for Africa*. London: Weidenfeld & Nicholson, 1991.

Parry, J. H., and A. Maingot. *A Short History of the West Indies*. London: Macmillan Caribbean, 1987.

Peterson, Gulielmus. *M. Tulli Ciceronis, Orationes*. Oxford: Clarendon, 1960.

Petherbridge, Deanna, and Ludmilla Jordanova. *The Quick and the Dead: Artists and Anatomy*. Berkeley: University of California Press, 1997.

Porter, Roy. *The Greatest Benefit to Mankind: A Medical History of Humanity from Antiquity to the Present*. London: Fontana, 1999.

Pressly, William. *The Life and Art of James Barry.* New Haven, Conn.: Yale University Press, 1981.

————. *James Barry: The Artist as Hero.* London: Tate Gallery, 1983.

Prosser, Jay. *Second Skins: The Body Narratives of Transsexuality.* New York: Columbia University Press, 1998.

Racster, Olga. *Curtain Up! The Story of Cape Theatre.* Cape Town: Juta & Co., 1961.

Racster, Olga, and Jessica Grove. *The Journal of Dr James Barry.* London: Bodley Head, 1932.

Rae, Isobel. *The Strange Story of Dr James Barry.* London: Longmans, 1958.

Rogers, Edward. *The Modern Sphinx.* London: J. & R. Maxwell, 1881.

Rosario, Vernon A., ed. *Science and Homosexualities.* London: Routledge, 1997.

Rose, June. *The Perfect Gentleman: The Remarkable Life of Dr James Miranda Barry.* London: Hutchinson, 1977.

Searle, Charlotte. *The History and Development of Nursing in South Africa 1652–1960.* Cape Town: Struik, 1965.

Swaine Taylor, Alfred. *Medical Jurisprudence.* Vol. 2. London: John Churchill and Sons, 1879.

Thackeray, William Makepeace. *Notes of a Journey from Cornhill to Grand Cairo.* London: Chapman and Hall, 1846.

Twain, Mark. *More Tramps Abroad.* London: Chatto & Windus, 1897.

Wheelwright, Julie. *Amazons and Military Maids.* London: Pandora, 1989.

Williams, Eric. *From Columbus to Castro: The History of the Caribbean 1492–1969.* New York: Harper and Row, 1970.

Wollstonecraft, Mary. *A Vindication of the Rights of Woman.* New York: W. W. Norton & Co., 1975.

Ziggi, Alexander, and Audrey Dewjee, eds. *The Wonderful Adventures of Mrs Seacole.* Bristol: Falling Wall Press, 1984.

NOTES

CHAPTER 1: BETWIXT-AND-BETWEEN

5. **"necessary inhumanity"** See Roy Porter, *The Greatest Benefit to Mankind: A Medical History of Humanity from Antiquity to the Present* (London: Fontana, 1999).

7. **"a great horse godmother"** Ibid.

8. **Edinburgh teaching system** For Edinburgh's preeminence in medicine, see R. D. Lobban, *Edinburgh and the Medical Revolution* (Cambridge, Eng.: Cambridge University Press, 1980), and Anand Chitis, "Medical Education in Edinburgh, 1790–1826, and Some Victorian Social Consequences," *Medical History* 17 (1973).

10. **"Barclay and Murray's"** See *Return of the Services and Professional Education of James Barry MD from 5 July 1813 to 7 April 1824,* Public Records Office, London, WO 25/3190.

10. **art and science** This relationship is typified in the 1772 painting by Johann Zoffany of surgeon William Hunter lecturing in anatomy to young painters at the Royal Academy.

12. **"ought to bear"** Thomas Chevalier, "Observations in Defence of a Bill Brought Lately into Parliament for Erecting the Corporation of Surgeons of London into a College," 1797.

12. **the provision of bodies** See Ruth Richardson, *Death, Dissection and the Destitute* (London: RKP, 1988), and Jonathan Sawday, *The Body Emblazoned: Dissection and the Body in Renaissance Culture* (London: RKP, 1995).

13. **"Birthing had essentially been"** See Porter, *The Greatest Benefit to Mankind.*

14. **aspired to be gentlemen**   For the definitive argument of the period, see Mary Wollstonecraft, *A Vindication of the Rights of Woman* (London, 1792), and also Buchan, *The Anonymous and Fugitive Essays of the Earl of Buchan* (Edinburgh: J. Ruthven, 1812).

15. **"roaring beer parties"**   Janet Carphin, letter to *Lancet* (October 14, 1895).

15. **"these scanty particulars"**   Ibid.

15. **James Barry, R.A.**   See James Barry, R.A., *Papers and Letters,* Horace Walpole Collection, Lewis Walpole Library, Yale University. For evaluations of Barry's life and works, see Edward Fryer, *The Works of James Barry, Esq., Historical Painter* (London: 1809); William Pressly, *James Barry: The Artist as Hero* (London: Tate Gallery, 1983); and Francisco de Miranda, "Posthumous Works of James Barry," *Archivo del General Miranda* 22 (Caracas: 1929–1950).

16. **"the cause of"**   James Barry, lecture to the Royal Academy, cited in *The Diary of Joseph Farington* 3:964 (January 8, 1798).

16. **"found the idea"**   William L. Pressly, *The Life and Art of James Barry* (New Haven: Yale University Press, 1981).

18. **Francisco de Miranda**   Miranda's papers and correspondence can be consulted in the *Archivo del General Miranda* (Caracas: 1929–1950). For his life and career, see William Robertson, *The Life of Miranda* (London: 1929); William Atkinson, *Miranda: His Life and Times* (London: 1950); and Robert Harvey, *Liberators: Latin America's Struggle for Independence, 1810–1830* (London: John Murray, 2000). An intriguing fictional portrait of Miranda as father and lover can be found in Patricia Duncker, *James Miranda Barry* (London: Serpent's Tail, 1999).

19. **"a Don Quixote"**   See Harvey, *Liberators.*

20. **"an indefatigable"**   Ibid.

21. **"I love freedom"**   *Archivo del General Miranda.*

23. **a letter from James Barry**   Ibid.

25. **"Known by Lord"**   See University of Edinburgh Register of Pupils, 1810.

CHAPTER 2: "AN EAGLE'S EYE, A LADY'S HAND,
AND A LION'S HEART"

30. **"De merocele"**   James Barry, "Disputatio medica inauguralis de merocele vel hernia crurali," M.D. dissertation (Edinburgh: C. Stewart, 1812). Barry's thesis can be consulted in the University of Edinburgh Library.

30. **Sir Astley Paston Cooper**   See Bransby B. Cooper, *The Life of Astley Cooper* (London: 1843), and R. C. Brock, *The Life and Work of Astley Cooper* (London: 1952).

30. **"an eagle's eye"**   See Brock, *The Life and Work of Astley Cooper.*

34. **"Do not consider whether what I say is a young man speaking, but whether my discussion with you is that of a man of understanding"**   In Latin, "Ne hoc consideres, si junior loquar, Sed si viri prudentis sermones apud te habeo."

34. *Return of the Services and Professional Education of James Barry MD*   Public Records Office, London. WO 25/3910.

34. **Guy's and St. Thomas's**   See Register of Pupils, 1799–1883, and Pupils and Dressers Cash Book 1812, Guy's and St. Thomas's Hospital Library. For background on the hospitals, see F. G. Parsons, *The History of St. Thomas's Hospital* 3 (London: 1936).

35. **"I have to observe"**   See Parsons, *The History of St. Thomas's Hospital.*

36. **"My long esteemed and ingenious friend"**   See Edward Fryer, *The Works of James Barry, Esq., Historical Painter* (London: 1809).

36. **"voluminous studies"**   Ibid.

38. **"The Dressers possess"** and **"He has the absolute"**   Parsons, *The History of St. Thomas's Hospital.*

41. **"You are anxious"**   Ibid.

44. **"young gentlemen who smoke"**   Dickens, *The Pickwick Papers* (London: 1836).

44. **"unique in appearance"**   Dickens, "A Mystery Still," *All the Year Round* 17 (May 18, 1867).

44. **"rage for fashion"** and **"on their mounts"** and **"appear more manly"** and further references on this subject, see Christopher Breward, *The Culture of Fashion* (Manchester: 1995); J. Anderson Black, *A History of Fashion* (London: 1975); and Miles Ogborn, *Spaces of Modernity* (London: 1998).

45. **the term** *dandy*   Believed to have been coined by the eccentric dresser Beau Brummell, the term *dandy* entered the English language in 1813.

46. **"If the Dr orders"**   See Parsons, *The History of St. Thomas's Hospital.*

46. **"short, brushed forward"**   See various, Mytchett Collection, Barry Papers, Royal Army Medical Corps archive (RAMC), Wellcome Library, London; and Isobel Rae, *The Strange Story of Dr James Barry* (London: 1958).

46. **"with elbows *in* instead of outward"**   See Edward Rogers, Barry Papers, RAMC 238, Wellcome Library, London.

47. **"had not a hair"**   See, for example, William Cattell, "Memoirs of William Cattell" (1829–1919), Mytchett Collection, Barry Papers, RAMC, Wellcome Library, London; and Alfred Swaine Taylor, *Medical Jurisprudence* 2 (London: 1873).

48. **"dandified top boots"**   Olga Racster, *Curtain Up! The Story of Cape Theatre* (Cape Town: Juta & Co., 1961), and see various, Barry Papers, RAMC, Wellcome Library, London.

49. **"it was not desirable"**   See Rae, *The Strange Story of Dr James Barry.*

49. **"I send you"**   Mytchett Collection, Barry Papers, RAMC, Wellcome Library, London.

50. **"long Ciceronian nose"**   Lieutenant Edward Rogers, letter to Jamaican newspaper, unidentified, Barry Papers, RAMC, Wellcome Library, London.

CHAPTER 3: AN ABSOLUTE PHENOMENON

54. **"He was an eighteenth-century viceroy"**   See Anthony Kendal Millar, *Plantagenet in South Africa: Lord Charles Somerset* (Cape Town, London, New York: Oxford University Press, 1965).

59. **Reports of Barry's voice**   For a few of many examples of this, see Edward Bradford, General Correspondence, *Medical Times and Gazette,* September 9, 1865; *South African Advertiser and Mail,* November 18, 1865; and George Thomas Keppel, Earl of Albemarle, *Fifty Years of My Life* 2 (London: Macmillan, 1876).

59. **redness**   See various, Mytchett Collection, Barry Papers, RAMC, Wellcome Library, London.

59. **dyed his hair red**   For a refutation of the claims about Barry's own hair—rather than his wig—being red, see Rose Weigall, letter to the *Spectator,* August 2, 1919. Weigall met Barry as a child in 1853. Edward Rogers, who met Barry in the late 1850s, reports that Barry's "hair was light, of a reddish hue—perhaps dyed—but very thin, and cut close." Letter printed in Jamaican newspaper, unidentified, ca. July 7, 1898, Barry Papers, RAMC 238, Wellcome Library, London.

60. **some speculation about a romantic relationship**   See Réné Juta, *Cape Currey* (New York: Henry Holt, 1920), and Olga Racster and Jessica Grove, *The Journal of Dr James Barry* (London: Bodley Head, 1932). Both are fictional works.

60. **"as long as the army"**   Wilberforce Bird, *State of the Cape of Good Hope in 1822* (London: John Murray, 1823).

61. **"Of late there has been"**   Ibid.

61. **" 'inexpressibles' "**   See Dickens, "A Mystery Still."

61. **"It was also"**   See various, Mytchett Collection, Barry Papers, RAMC, Wellcome Library, London.

62. **"a perfect dancer"**   See June Rose, *The Perfect Gentleman: The Remarkable Life of Dr James Miranda Barry* (London: Hutchinson, 1977).

62. **"in appearance a beardless lad"**   See Keppel, *Fifty Years of My Life* 2.

62. **"Whilst the public and private balls"**   See Bird, *State of the Cape of Good Hope.*

64. **"Knowing the state"**   See Las Casas, "My Residence at the Cape," in *Mémorial de Sainte Hélène: Journal of the Private Life and Conversations of the Emperor Napoleon at Saint Helena* 4 (London: Henry Colburn & Co, 1823). All quotes from Las Casas are from the *Mémorial.*

65. **"the celebrated Dr O'Meara"**   See J. M. Howell, *South African Advertiser and Mail,* November 18, 1865.

67. **Newlands**   For the history and significance of Newlands House, see Joyce Newton Thomson, *The Story of a House* (Cape Town: Howard Timmins, 1968), and *South African Heritage: From Van Riebeeck to Nineteenth-Century Times* (Cape Town and Pretoria: Human and Rousseau, 1965).

67. **"I furnish him"**   On Somerset's correspondence and historical background, see G. M. Theal, ed., *Records of the Cape Colony* 1–36 (London: 1903).

68. **"the sacred fire"**   See Harvey, *Liberators.*

68. **a sensitive mission**   For a detailed account of this mission and its historical significance, see Noël Mostert, *Frontiers: The Epic of South Africa's Creation and the Tragedy of the Xhosa People* (London: Jonathan Cape, 1992). Also see George E. Cory, *The Rise of South Africa* 1 (London: 1913–1930), and S. A. Rochlin, "Thomas Sheridan," *Africana Notes and News* 7, no. 2 (March 1950).

68. **"fully responsible"**   Mostert, *Frontiers.*

69. **George Rex**   See S. Metelerkamp, *George Rex of Knysna* (Cape Town: 1955).

69. **"the largest"**   Mostert, *Frontiers.*

69. **"Lord Charles Somerset's"**   Miller, *Plantagenet in South Africa.*

70. **"100 dragoons"**   This and following quotes are from Mostert, *Frontiers.*

72. **"We continued gazing"** Thomas Pringle, *Narrative of a Residence in South Africa* (London: 1835).

73. **"to entreat that"** and **"I have besides"** See Theal, *Records of the Cape Colony.*

73. **"The ship had not been"** See Sir William Henry Dillon, *A Narrative of My Professional Adventures* (Naval Records Society, 1955–56).

74. **"a state of"** and **"typhus with dysentery"** See Miller, *Plantagenet in South Africa.*

74. **"There appears to have been"** See Theal, *Records of the Cape Colony.*

75. **"When I was young"** See Barry to Captain Packenham, ADC, October 13, 1848, Public Records Office, London, CO 158/143.

75. **"The event justified"** Ibid.

78. **"most wayward of men"** Keppel, Earl of Albemarle, *Fifty Years of My Life.*

78. **"plucky and fearless"** Ibid.

78. **"Honi soit"** Barry to Brink, March 2, 1824, State Archives, Cape Town, CO 204.

78. **"immensely interested"** Cattell, "Memoirs," Mytchett Collection, Barry Papers, RAMC, Wellcome Library, London.

78. **"made love to a handsome"** Ibid.

79. **"When I was ADC"** Letter from R. C. Bellenger on the personal papers of Gen. Sir A. J. Cloete, Barry Papers, RAMC, Wellcome Library.

80. **"of his feeling"** See Réné Juta, *Cape Currey.*

83. **one biographer** See Rose, *The Perfect Gentleman.*

83. **"during the lengthened period"** "Memorandum of the Services of Dr James Barry, Inspector General of Hospitals," ca. May 26, 1859–July 18, 1859, Barry Papers, RAMC 373, Wellcome Library, London.

CHAPTER 4: SIEKETROOST

86. **"Sir: Dr Robb"** See Theal, *Records of the Cape Colony,* and Barry, *Return of the Services and Professional Education,* WO 25/3910.

88. **Barry's "Report"** James Barry, M.D., "Report upon the *Arctopus echinatus* or Plat Doorn of the Cape of Good Hope," *Materia Medica* (February 17, 1827).

88. **In scientia** "In the natural sciences, the truth of principles must be confirmed by observations."

89. **"Sir, to learn"** See Brock, *The Life and Work of Astley Cooper.*

89. **"It is scarcely necessary"** Barry to Brink, State Archives, Cape Town, CO 226.

91. **"for the reception"** See Edmund H. Burrows, *A History of Medicine in South Africa* (Cape Town/Amsterdam: A. A. Balkema, 1958), and Percy Ward Laidler and Michael Gelfland, *South Africa: Its Medical History, 1652–1898* (Cape Town: Struik, 1971).

92. **"the whole establishment"** Barry to Brink, March 8, 1824, State Archives, Cape Town, CO 204.

92. **Its report was detailed and damning** See Public Records Office, London, CO 48/61.

95. **"To my certain knowledge"** This and subsequent correspondence and reports on patent medicines and medical licensing at the Cape are to be found in the State Archives, Cape Town, CO 204, and Public Records Office, London, CO 48/97.

99. **"No merchant"** *The Cape Town Gazette and African Advertiser,* September 27, 1823.

101. **"Rightly it has"** See George Schmidt, Moravian missionary, *The Cape Odyssey,* no. 1 (February/March, 2001).

101. **"seem a living death"** See Porter, *The Greatest Benefit to Mankind.*

102. **"As an impression obtains"** *The Cape Town Gazette and African Advertiser,* February 22, 1817.

103. **"Nothing . . . could exceed the misery"** This and subsequent correspondence and reports on Hemel-en-Aarde and Barry's treatment of leprosy are to be found in the State Archives, Cape Town, CO 180, and Public Records Office, London, CO 48/97.

113. **"differences of a private nature"** This and subsequent correspondence and reports on the Barry-Liesching dispute are to be found in the State Archives, Cape Town, CO 204/235.

CHAPTER 5: SACRIFICED TO INFAMY

119. **African Theatre** For the history of the theater, see P. W. Laidler, *The Annals of the Cape Stage* (Edinburgh: William Bryce, 1926).

119. **"His Lordship and Lady Charles"** Samuel Eusebius Hudson, *Journal,* State Archives, Cape Town, A 602, vol. 3, 1824.

121. **"saw a libel"** This and all subsequent cited documentation relating to the sodomy libel, investigation, and trial are to be found in the Records of the Court of Justice, State Archives, Cape Town, CJ 3352.

124. **"With courteous devotion"**   See *South African Advertiser and Mail,* October 21, 1865.

124. **"proceed to the residence"**   See *South African Advertiser and Mail,* November 1, 1865.

125. **a proclamation**   Records of the Court of Justice, State Archives, Cape Town, CJ 3352. The proclamation was published in *The Cape Town Gazette and African Advertiser,* on Saturday, June 5, 1824.

126. **"Being this afternoon"**   William Edwards, in Records of the Court of Justice.

129. **"Every corner of the streets"**   Hudson, *Journal.*

134. **"Mr Bigge seemed"**   Millar, *Plantagenet in South Africa.*

134. **"Lord Charles ought not"**   *Hansard,* ZHC 2/54, Col. 1166, Thursday, June 16, 1825.

135. **"His house was invaded"**   Ibid.

136. **commission of enquiry**   "The Case of Dr Barry," *Report of the Royal Commission of Enquiry,* 1825–26, Public Records Office, London, CO 48/97.

136. **"Permit me to entreat you"**   Somerset-Bigge correspondence, Rhodes House, Oxford.

138. **"I am decidedly of the opinion"**   Barry to Sir Richard Plaskett, September 12, 1825, State Archives, Cape Town, CO 226.

139. **"partially deranged"**   Ibid.

139. **"threatened to cut off"**   See Plaskett correspondence in "The Case of Dr Barry." Public Records Office, London, CO 48197.

140. **"In consequence of"**   Barry to Lord Charles Somerset, October 13, 1825, State Archives, Cape Town, CO 226.

141. **"His Excellency desires"**   See Plaskett correspondence in "The Case of Dr Barry." Public Records Office, London, CO 48/97.

142. **"On more than one"**   Lord Charles Somerset in "The Case of Dr Barry." Public Records Office, London, CO 48/97.

143. **"The contents of"**   Plaskett to Barry, October 4, 1825, "The Case of Dr Barry." Public Records Office, London, CO 48/97.

144. **"Having been informed"**   For this and subsequent correspondence of James Barry and Lord Charles Somerset, see "The Case of Dr Barry." Public Records Office, London, CO 48/97.

146. **"Thus, in the midst"**   Barry to Earl Bathurst, December 6, 1825, Public Records Office, London, CO 48/97.

150. **"His Excellency, Lady Charles"**   See Millar, *Plantagenet in South Africa.*

150. **"Quite theatrical"**   Dudley Percival, "Letters, 1825–28," South African Library.

CHAPTER 6: "MY GOOD NAME"

153. **"It was a portrait"** Mark Twain, *More Tramps Abroad* (London: Chatto and Windus, 1897).

153. **"The abdomen, the chest"** See Porter, *The Greatest Benefit to Mankind.*

154. **"unequalled"** Senator G. G. Munnik, in E. M. Sandler, "The First Caesarean Section at the Cape of Good Hope," *South African Journal of Obstetrics and Gynaecology* (June 17, 1967).

154. **"bemoaning their tendency"** See Porter, *The Greatest Benefit to Mankind,* and Elizabeth Nihell, *A Treatise on the Art of Midwifery,* 1760.

154. **female midwives** See Harriet J. Deacon, "Cape Town and Country Doctors in the Cape Colony During the First Half of the Nineteenth Century," *Journal of African History* 39 (1998), and Charlotte Searle, *The History of the Development of Nursing in South Africa, 1652–1960* (Cape Town: Struik, 1965).

155. **"until 1800 only"** See Dyre Trolle, *The History of the Caesarean Section* (Copenhagen: 1982).

155. **"if the woman is strong"** William Smellie, *A Set of Anatomical Tables, with Explanations, and an Abridgment of the Practice of Midwifery* (1754).

156. **"turn pale as ashes"** Laurence Sterne, *Tristram Shandy* (London: 1760).

156. **"a matter of good luck"** See Porter, *The Greatest Benefit to Mankind.*

156. **"compressing the nerves"** Benjamin Bell, *System of Surgery* (1783).

157. **"the reduction of"** Victor Robinson, *Victory Over Pain* (London: 1947).

157. **"How often, when operating"** Valentine Mott, "Pain and Anaesthetics," in William Hammond, ed., *Military, Medical and Surgical Essays* (Philadelphia: Lippincott, 1864).

157. **Dr. James Hamilton** See Guenther Risse, *Hospital Life in Enlightenment Scotland* (Cambridge: Cambridge University Press, 1986).

158. **"As for the Caesarean section"** See Phillip Rhodes, *A Short History of Clinical Midwifery: The Development of Ideas in the Professional Management of Childbirth* (Cheshire: Books for Midwives Press, 1995).

159. **at the child's baptism** James Barry Munnik's baptismal certificate can be found in the Evangelical Lutheran Church, Cape Town.

159. **"which was a riotous affair"** See Rose, *The Perfect Gentleman.*

160. **"a fine, tall"** Senator G. G. Munnik, cited in Sandler, "The First Caesarean Section at the Cape of Good Hope."

161. **General J.B.M. Hertzog**   See C. M. Van den Heever, *Generaal JBM Hertzog* (Johannesburg: A. P. Boekhandel, 1943).

161. **medical treatises**   See Astley Cooper, *Treatise on Diseases of the Breast* (1829), *Observations on the Structure and Diseases of the Testes* (1830), and *On the Anatomy of the Breast* (1845).

163. **"flourishes abundantly"**   Barry, "Report upon the *Arctopus echinatus.*"

163. **"With reference to"**   Ibid.

164. **"trusting that when"**   For this and subsequent correspondence with Earl Bathurst, see Dr. Barry's correspondence in "The Case of Dr Barry."

166. **"Black John"**   The sobriquet was created by Dickens in "A Mystery Still."

167. **"The evening passed harmoniously"**   *The Cape Town Gazette and African Advertiser,* September 25, 1828.

167. **"Occasionally the wind"**   See Racster, *Curtain Up!*

167. **Frank Lascelles**   See Thelma Gutsche, *The History and Social Significance of Motion Pictures in South Africa, 1895–1940* (Cape Town: Howard Timmins, 1972).

CHAPTER 7: DOCTOR JAMAICA

170. **subsequent publication**   John Hunter, *Observations on the Diseases of the Army in Jamaica; and on the Best Means of Preserving the Health of Europeans in That Climate* (London: 1788).

170. **"I . . . was recalled"**   "Memorandum of the Services of Dr James Barry, Inspector General of Hospitals," Barry Papers, RAMC 373, Wellcome Library, London.

171. **"He would chuckle"**   Dickens, "A Mystery Still."

172. **"There is indeed a melancholy satisfaction"**   See Erik Olaf Eriksen, "A Letter by Dr James Barry Concerning the Death of Lord Charles Somerset," *Africana Notes and News* 28 (September 7, 1989).

174. **"peculiar habits"**   "Memorandum of the Services of Dr James Barry," Barry Papers, RAMC 373, Wellcome Library, London.

174. **"in a harsh"**   Lieutenant Edward Rogers, letter to Jamaican newspaper, unidentified, Barry Papers, RAMC, Wellcome Library, London.

175. **Couba Cornwallis**   See Mary Seacole, *Wonderful Adventures of Mrs. Seacole in Many Lands* (Bristol: Falling Wall Press, 1984).

175. **Piracy had a tradition of cross-dressing**   See Julie Wheelwright, *Amazons and Military Maids: Women Who Dressed as Men in Pursuit of Life, Liberty, and Happiness* (London: Pandora, 1989).

175. **"feathered hats, wigs"** See Marjorie Garber, *Vested Interests: Cross-Dressing and Cultural Anxiety* (London: 1992), and Wheelwright, *Amazons and Military Maids.*

175. **Daniel Defoe** *A General History of the Pyrates* (London: 1724). Published originally under the name of Captain Charles Johnson; authorship historically attributed to Defoe.

175. **reported the arrival** *The Watchman and Jamaica Free Press,* June 12, 1831, National Library of Jamaica, Kingston.

176. **Jamaica in the 1830s** For general introductions, see Thomas C. Holt, *The Problem of Freedom: Race, Labor, and Politics in Jamaica and Britain, 1832–1938* (Baltimore: Johns Hopkins University Press, 1992); Eric Williams, *From Columbus to Castro: The History of the Caribbean 1492–1969* (London: Andre Deutch Ltd, 1970); J. H. Parry, Philip Sherlock, and Anthony Maingot, *A Short History of the West Indies* (London: Macmillan, 1987); Clinton Black, *History of Jamaica* (London: Longman Caribbean, 1983); Richard Sheridan, *Doctors and Slaves* (Cambridge, Eng.: Cambridge University Press, 1985). For political conditions on Barry's arrival, see also *Jamaica Courant and Public Advertiser,* August–Oct. 1831, and *Watchman and Jamaica Free Press,* 1831–32, British Library (Collingdale Newspaper Library), London, CO 142/1 and 142/2.

178. **"requisite in a long voyage"** Barry to His Excellency the Governor Sir B. D'Urban, August 21, 1836, State Archives, Cape Town, CO 4372 (5).

179. **"sickness and mortality"** Sir George Muray to J. Stewart, July 1830, Public Records Office, London, CO 142/33. See also Alexander Tulloch and Henry Marshall, "Statistical Report on the Sickness, Mortality and Invaliding Among the Troops in the West Indies," prepared from surgeon's reports to Sir J. McGrigor, 1838, Public Records Office, London.

180. **"I need not say here"** John Watson to James Anderton, November 16, 1852, Wellcome Library, London, MSS 6233.

180. **"This is a superb country"** Dr. Cynric R. Williams, "A Tour Through the Island of Jamaica from the West to the East End, in the Year 1823" (London: 1827).

180. **outbreak of yellow fever** See Public Records Office, London, WO 334/5, and *Monthly Returns for Jamaica,* Public Records Office, London, WO 17/2023.

181. **"very peculiar in his habits"** See Captain Dadson to Jamaican newspaper, unidentified, Barry Papers, RAMC, Wellcome Library, London.

181. **Mary Seacole** See Seacole, *Wonderful Adventures of Mrs. Seacole.*

183. **marquis of Sligo**   Marquis of Sligo, "A Letter to the Marquis of Normandy Relative to the Present State of Jamaica," 1839, British Library, London.

184. **"There were only"**   Parry, et al., *A Short History of the West Indies.*

185. **"Phantasmagoria"**   *Jamaican Courant and Public Advertiser,* March 15, 1832.

186. **"most singular"**   See Edward Bradford, *Medical Times and Gazette,* September 9, 1865.

187. **"crowded with the fashionables"**   *Jamaican Courant and Public Advertiser,* February 27, 1832.

190. **"Sir Willoughby's firmness"**   *Jamaican Courant and Public Advertiser,* January 6, 1832.

191. **"a domestic correction"**   For a detailed account of this episode, see Laidler and Gelfland, *South Africa: Its Medical History 1652–1898.*

192. **"I beg to assure you"**   James Barry to P. G. Brink, February 10, 1824, State Archives, Cape Town, CO 204.

193. **"He remains halfway between"**   Alexis de Tocqueville, *Democracy in America* (1835).

CHAPTER 8: INSULAR OBSESSIONS

195. **"has continuously served"**   *The Humble Memorial of Dr James Barry, Inspector General of Hospitals,* c. 1856–58, Barry Papers, RAMC, Wellcome Library, London.

196. **"cool off"**   Barry to J. Bell, Deputy Inspector General, August 3, 1857, Barry Papers, RAMC, Wellcome Library, London.

197. **"a gloomy little island"**   See Keppel, *Fifty Years of My Life.*

197. **McGrigor**   Public Records Office, London, CO 247/52. See also McGrigor, *Autobiography of Sir James McGrigor* (1861).

199. **"I am sure"**   See Barry to D'Urban, August 21, 1836, and official correspondence, State Archives, Cape Town, CO 4372.

200. **"However, on the subject"**   See Barry to James McGrigor, October 29, 1836, Public Records Office, London, CO 247/52.

201. **"correct accounts"**   See Public Records Office, London, CO 247/52.

201. **"confused and disgusting state"**   Barry to Glenelg, August 16, 1838, and subsequent correspondence, Public Records Office, London, CO 247/49.

204. **F. E. Knowles**   For the lengthy dispute between Barry and Knowles,

and subsequent correspondence and court-martial charges, see Public Records Office, London, CO 247/52.

210. **"The inhabitants"** Letter from CO to East India Company, April 28, 1837, Public Records Office, London, CO 247/44.

212. **"The writer of this article"** See Dickens, "A Mystery Still."

213. **"I have to regret"** Despatches, April 2, 1838, Public Records Office, London, CO 247/46.

214. **"In common with"** Letter, *Lancet* (October 14, 1895).

214. **"a very bold person"** See R. T. McCowan, *Whitehaven News,* September 7, 1865.

215. **"I had, in the last named"** Edward Bradford, letter, *Medical Times and Gazette* (September 9, 1865).

215. **"In many cases"** Barry, "Returns of Reports on Delirium Tremens in Reply to Circular of 9 March 1841," No. 12378, Barry Papers, RAMC, Wellcome Library, London.

216. **"Permit me here"** Barry to Glenelg, August 16, 1838, Public Records Office, London, CO 247/49.

217. **"The Board is willing"** *Proceedings of a Board of MOs, James Town, St Helena,* February 25, 1859, Despatches, CO 247/50.

218. **"Could such sum"** Barry to Sir George Grey, November 1, 1838, Public Records Office, London, CO 247/49.

219. **"always evinced a dislike of medical men"** William Chamberlayne, letter, *Lancet* (November 1895).

219. **"When ill"** Edward Bradford, *Medical Times and Gazette* (September 9, 1865).

220. **"short in stature"** Lieutenant Edward Rogers, letter to Jamaican newspaper, unidentified, Barry Papers, RAMC, Wellcome Library, London.

220. **"pale, sallow look"** Ibid.

220. **"his stature scarcely"** Edward Bradford, "The Reported Female Army Surgeon," *Medical Times and Gazette* (September 9, 1865).

220. **"Home, sick"** Statement of Home and Foreign Services of James Barry, Public Records Office, London, WO 25/3899, No. 614.

221. **"by which, in the space"** William Makepeace Thackeray, *Notes on a Journey from Cornhill to Grand Cairo* (London: 1845).

222. **"stretched on a handful of straw"** Barry to Major Pippin, Assistant Military Secretary, October 2, 1848, Public Records Office, London, CO 158/143.

222. **"invaluable researches"** This and the following quotes are from Barry to Captain Packenham, ADC, October 13, 1848, Public Records Office, London, CO 158/143.

CHAPTER 9: THE LAST POST

225. **"to show some civility"** See Rose Weigall, *The Spectator,* August 2, 1919.

225. **"When he arrived"** Ibid.

227. **"a lovely grey Arab"** See Rae, *The Strange Story of James Barry.*

228. **"The enraged officer"** See Edward Rogers, letter to Jamaican newspaper, unidentified, Barry Papers, RAMC, Wellcome Library, London.

228. **"punctuality itself"** R. F. Hutchinson, letter to Jamaican newspaper, Barry Papers, RAMC, Wellcome Library, London.

230. **"as useful as possible"** *The Humble Memorial of Dr James Barry, Inspector General of Hospitals,* Barry Papers, RAMC 373, Wellcome Library, London.

231. **"that he possessed"** General MacIntosh to Lord Raglan, May 7, 1855, Public Records Office, London, WO 25/3899.

231. **"I am sorry"** Raglan to MacIntosh, May 21, 1855, Public Records Office, London, WO 25/3899.

232. **"It is possible"** Sir John Hall, *Diary,* December 17, 1854, Barry Papers, RAMC, Wellcome Library, London. See also papers of Sir John Hall, 33rd Reg in WI, 1841–43, PMO in Crimea, 1855, Public Records Office, London, FC 019.

233. **"I never had"** Nightingale to Parthenope, Lady Verney, July 1865, Barry Papers, RAMC, Wellcome Library, London.

233. **"I myself proceeded"** *Memorandum of Services,* Barry Papers, RAMC, Wellcome Library, London.

233. **"I may as well"** Letter from A. Cumming, Scutari, to Sir John Hall, October 16, 1855. See papers of Sir John Hall, above.

235. **"I hear they"** Barry to John Hall, in June Rose, *The Perfect Gentleman.*

235. **"For my efforts"** *Memorandum of Services,* Barry Papers, RAMC, Wellcome Library, London.

235. **"while I was crossing"** Nightingale to Parthenope.

237. **"So I am to go"** Barry to J. Bell, August 3, 1857, Barry Papers, RAMC, Wellcome Library, London.

238. **"One of the sights"** See James Bannerman, "The Double Life of Dr. James Barry," *Macleans: Canada's National Magazine* (December 1, 1950).

239. **"nothing contributes more"**   Barry to Deputy Quarter Master General, April 7, 1858, Public Records Office, London, WO 25/3899.

241. **"being unable"**   Records of the St. James Club, Montreal, April 20, 1859. See also Rose, *The Perfect Gentleman.*

241. **"immediately on my arrival"**   *Memorandum of Services,* Barry Papers, RAMC, Wellcome Library, London.

243. **"his hair cut"**   J. C. McCrindle, *Glasgow Herald,* December 1949.

244. **"One piece he gave to my father"**   Ibid.

245. **"morning drives"**   *Whitehaven News,* August 24, 1865.

246. **"intimately acquainted"**   Major McKinnon to George Graham, Registrar General, August 24, 1865, Barry Papers, RAMC, Wellcome Library, London.

246. **death certificate**   No. 4883, July 26, 1865, General Register Office, Marylebone District. See Barry Papers, RAMC, Wellcome Library, London.

247. **"no comment"**   General Court Martial, November 24 to December 3, 1836, "The Trial of Dr Barry," Public Records Office, London, CO 247/52.

CHAPTER 10: BEYOND A DOUBT

249. **"and there the woman"**   Major McKinnon to George Graham, Registrar General, August 24, 1865, Barry Papers, RAMC, Wellcome Library, London.

249. **"I received also"**   *Memorandum of Services,* Barry Papers, RAMC, Wellcome Library, London.

252. **"It is high time"**   See Brian Hurwitz and Ruth Richardson, "Inspector General James Barry: Putting the Woman in Her Place," *British Medical Journal* (February 4, 1989).

255. **"The mystery was"**   Bannerman, "The Double Life of Dr James Barry."

256. **"undesirable in every"**   See J. Manton, *Elizabeth Garrett Anderson* (London: Methuen, 1965).

257. **"It has been stated"**   Graham to Major McKinnon, August 23, 1865, Barry Papers, RAMC, Wellcome Library, London.

260. **"During the choleras"**   *Statement of the Home and Foreign Services,* no. 614, Dr. James Barry, Public Records Office, London WO 25/3899; and Rose, *The Perfect Gentleman.*

263. **"Gentlemen, if I had not"**   For the most complete consolidation of Dr. Campbell's recollections, see James Ross MacMahon, *McGill Medical Journal* (February 1, 1968).

263. **"astonished as anybody"**   Janet Carphin, letter to *Lancet* 2 (October 14, 1895).

263. **"There was a Dr B——"**   Sarah Esther Horniman, *Memoirs 1844–1880,* excerpt concerning Barry in Barry Papers, RAMC, Wellcome Library, London.

264. **"The stories"**   Edward Bradford, General Correspondence, *Medical Times and Gazette* (September 9, 1865).

266. **"In the natural sciences"**   James Barry, "Report upon the *Arctopus echinatus.*"

266. **"The assistant surgeon"**   Edward Rogers, *Lancet* (October 26, 1865, and November 16, 1865).

267. **"I was not"**   T. de Montmorency to Edward Rogers, February 16, 1882, Barry Papers, RAMC, Wellcome Library, London.

267. *The Modern Sphinx*   Edward Rogers (London: J & R Maxwell, 1881).

267. **"Just put Flora"**   *The Journal of Mrs Fenton 1826–1830* (London: Edward Arnold, 1901).

268. **"I lived"**   Anonymous army medical surgeon, *Lancet* (October 16, 1865).

269. **"I had heard"**   Keppel, *Fifty Years of My Life.*

269. **"The ship had not long"**   Dillon, *A Narrative of My Professional Adventures.*

270. **"The poor Dr"**   Las Casas, *Mémorial de Saint Hélène.*

271. **Lieutenant Colonel R. C. Francis**   See *Guy's Hospital Gazette* (September 27, 1986).

272. **"No he wasant!"**   C. B. Mosse, letter to Jamaican newspaper, unidentified, Barry Papers, RAMC, Wellcome Library, London.

272. **"He was rather short"**   Annotation to Mosse letter, W. Portlock-Dadson.

273. **"I recollect him"**   J. M. Howell, *South African Advertiser and Mail,* November 18, 1865.

274. **"Nobody knows"**   Bannerman, "The Double Life of Dr. James Barry."

274. **"Motive alleged for"**   Racster and Grove, *The Journal of Dr James Barry.*

274. **"The explanation"**   See Weigall, *The Spectator,* August 2, 1919.

275. **"A woman"**   See Wheelwright, *Amazons and Military Maids.*

275. **"adopted and reared"**   See Rose, *The Perfect Gentleman.*

276. **"my late uncle"**   Barry to Miranda, *Archivo del General Miranda.*

277. **"a young lady"**   This and all subsequent correspondence from Mary Anne Bulkley and Margaret Bulkley are to be found in James Barry, R.A.,

Papers and Letters, Horace Walpole Collection, Yale University, Lewis Walpole Library, Farmington, Connecticut.

285. **"tho' he is much younger"** See Edward Bradford, *Medical Times and Gazette* (September 9, 1865).

286. **"Dean Swift's famous"** Lord Buchan, *Anonymous and Fugitive Essays* (1812).

288. **"When I was a boy"** General Court Martial, November 24 to December 3, 1836, "The Trial of Dr Barry," Public Records Office, London, CO 247/52.

CHAPTER 11: HABEAS CORPUS

289. **"I received a Diploma"** *Return of the Services and Professional Education of James Barry MD,* Public Records Office, London: WO 25/3910.

290. **"Few diseases are"** Astley Cooper, "The Anatomy and Surgical Treatment of Inguinal and Congenital Hernia" (London: 1804) Hunterian Library, Royal College of Surgeons, London.

291. **"Supposed hernias"** Alice Domurat Dreger, *Hermaphrodites and the Medical Invention of Sex* (Cambridge, Mass.: Harvard University Press, 1998).

291. **well-known cases** See Vernon A. Rosario, ed., *Science and Homosexualities* (London: Routledge, 1997).

292. **"blushed to her forehead"** and **"If the appearance"** See Dreger, *Hermaphrodites.*

292. **"not a tear"** See Rosario, *Science and Homosexualities.*

294. **"When I was sixteen"** See Brock, *The Life and Work of Astley Cooper.*

295. **"directed that special"** Ibid.

295. **Cooper and James Barry, R.A.** In a letter to Lord Buchan, Barry referred to Cooper as "My long esteemed and ingenious friend Mr Cooper." See Fryer, *The Works of James Barry* (London: 1809).

296. **"Hernia Cruralis"** *Edinburgh Medical and Physical Dictionary* (1807).

296. **"The parts of the human body"** Ibid. See also Henry Gray, *Gray's Anatomy* (New York: Gramercy, 1977).

297. **"This species occurs"** James Barry, "Disputatio medica inauguralis de merocele vel hernia crurali," M.D. dissertation (Edinburgh: C. Stewart, 1812).

303. **Today it is still possible** See Anne Fausto-Sterling, *Sexing the Body: Gender Politics and the Construction of Sexuality* (New York: Basic Books, 2000).

304. **long history**   See Michel Foucault, "Introduction," *Herculine Barbin: Being the Recently Discovered Memoirs of a Nineteenth-Century French Hermaphrodite* (New York: Pantheon Books, 1980).

305. **"it shall be published"**   *Minutes of the Council and General Court of Virginia,* "Case of Thomas Hall," No. 194, March 25, 1629.

305. **Chevalier D'Eon**   See Wollstonecraft, *Vindication,* and Garber, *Vested Interests.*

305. **inverted version**   See Thomas Lacquer, "Orgasm, Generation, and the Politics of Reproductive Biology," *Representations* 14 (1986), and *Making Sex: Body and Gender from the Greeks to Freud* (Cambridge, Mass.: Harvard University Press, 1990).

306. **uncrossable binary division**   See Anne McClintock, *Imperial Leather: Race, Sex and Gender in the Colonial Contest* (New York and London: Routledge, 1995).

307. **"the animal economy"**   John Hunter, *Observations on Certain Parts of the Animal Economy* (London: 1786).

EPILOGUE

314. **dynamic developmental system**   For this and an introduction to contemporary scientific, political, and cultural work on intersex diagnoses and identity, see *New Scientist: Gender Special* (May 12, 2001), No. 2290; Alice Dormurat Dreger, *Intersex in the Age of Ethics* (University Publishing Group, 1999); Anne Fausto-Sterling, *Sexing the Body;* and the publications of the UK Intersex Association and the Intersex Society of North America (ISNA).

INDEX

RACHEL HOLMES attended King's College, London, and received her doctorate from Queen Mary and Westfield College, London. She has held professorships at the University of London and the University of Sussex. She judged the 2000 Whitbread Novel Award and the 2001 Orange Prize for Fiction. She writes for many newspapers and journals, and is a frequent broadcaster. Rachel Holmes resides in London, where she is completing a biography of Saartjie Baartman, the Hottentot Venus.

ABOUT THE TYPE

This book was set in Bembo, a typeface based on an old-style Roman face that was used for Cardinal Bembo's tract *De Aetna* in 1495. Bembo was cut by Francisco Griffo in the early sixteenth century. The Lanston Monotype Company of Philadelphia brought the well-proportioned letterforms of Bembo to the United States in the 1930s.